Sailing on the Sea of Love

Sailing on the Sea of Love

THE MUSIC OF THE BAULS OF INDIA

Charles Capwell

Seagull Books
NEW YORK LONDON CALCUTTA

Seagull Books 2011

First edition published as *The Music of the Bauls of Bengal* (Kent, Ohio: Kent University Press, 1986)

This edition by Seagull Books (2011) includes 2 audio CDs digitally remastered by John Holbrook.

ISBN-13 978 0 8574 2 004 6

British Library Cataloguing-in-Publication Data
A catalogue record for this book is available from the British Library

Typeset by Seagull Books, Calcutta, India
Printed at Leelabati Printers, Calcutta, India

For the Madmen of Bengal—
and for their sane brethren, too

Contents

Preface to the Second Edition

This study of the Bauls and their music was based on the research I did from January 1969 to June 1971 for my doctoral dissertation in musicology from Harvard University—a long time ago now, and much has changed since then. Worries then that the traditions of the Bauls were likely to disappear have proved groundless; if anything, the Bauls are in many ways flourishing. The technological changes of the last forty years have had as profound an impact on the Bauls as on the rest of us, and the development of new media, increased mobility, the interest of the state in defining cultural identity, awareness of gender discrimination, continuing issues of communal relations—all these and many other elements of contemporary life have given the Bauls opportunity to be more engaged with their Bengali confreres and more visible to the world at large. Nowadays, it would seem that the typical depiction of a Baul with an ektara in one hand should have the other hand holding a cell phone!

Once confined to their homeland, the songs of the Bauls have been honored by the United Nations in 2005 with a proclamation declaring them a Masterpiece of the Oral and Intangible Heritage of Mankind, and Baul philosophy and life views have been the recent focus of several excellent academic and personal accounts, making Shashibhushan Das Gupta's inclusion of them in his *Obscure Religious Cults* of 1941 now seem paradoxical.[1]

Even when this book was first publlished, there were few recordings of Bauls songs that were widely available, one of the first being the 1967 release by Elektra, *The Bauls of Bengal*, which is still in ciruclation as a CD reissue. Now, of course, the Internet has changed things dramatically (you can download cuts from *The Bauls of Bengal*, for example) with sites like YouTube where one can find everything from TV music videos and documentary film excerpts to amateur videos of Baul performances. Most significantly, Sally Grossman, whose husband, the musical talent manager, Albert, had brought Purna and Luxman Das with their troupe to the U.S. for the first time in 1967, has sponsored the creation of a web-based archive for Baul related materials, the core of which is professionally shot videos of complete performances by over one hundred Bauls (www.baul-archive.com). And it is because of Sally's urging that Naveen Kishore of Seagull Books has generously agreed to reissue this book—my thanks to them both.

With the greater celebrity and ubiquity of the Bauls, many of the circumstances described in this book will naturally have changed—on p. 69, for example, when I say that in urban festivals and ceremonies, if a Baul singer is asked to perform it is most likely to be Purna Das, that might have been true thirty or forty years ago, but today, even though Purna continues in advanced age to be a major presence, there are newer and more numerous alternatives such as Paban Das with a celebrity of a different, if not necessarily, greater kind.

Most of the musical observations I made in this study seem to me still to be generally valid though they could certainly be amplified. Occasionally, an observation could be radically altered like the description of the *khol* which should now mention that not only is it more commonly used today but that one of its most brilliant performers is a woman, Uma Rani Das. In trying to deal with terminological problems, I think I sometimes tried too hard to bring order to something inherently disordered; choosing to use "*gopiyantro*" for the iconographical metonymn of the Bauls instead of "*ektara*," for example, seems to me now to have been too fussy as practically everyone knows the instrument by the latter name. In terms of the Bengali language, I would say that the former is too "*sadhu*" and the latter is more appropriately "*colti*."

One grievous lapse found its way into the book that I am aware of—though the reader may find more—and I am happy to have the opportunity of correcting it in this republication. At the time I was finishing the original manuscript, I had just purchased my first computer (for techonological antiquarians, it was a Commodore 64), and I used it to prepare the references list. Unfortunately, through clumsy inexperience, I inadvertently deleted the most important scholarly monograph on the Bauls from that list, Upendronāth Bhaṭṭācāryo's *bāṅlār bāul o bāul gān*, which the reader can now find cited in the references.

As I write this prefatory note, I have received the news of a dear friend's death. Pradip Sinha, Professor of History at Rabindra Bharati

University, was my guide to Calcutta and Bengal and made my stay there as a graduate student both more enlightening and more pleasurable. This reissue is dedicated to him.

Note

1. See e.g.: Jeanne Openshaw, *Seeking Bauls of Bengal* (Cambridge: Cambridge University Press, 2002) and *Wrting the Self: The Life and Philosophy of a Dissenting Baul Guru*; Mimlu Sen, *Baulsphere: My Travels with the Wandering Bards of Bengal* (Noida, UP: Random House India, 2009); *Fakir: la quête d'un bâul musulman* (Paris: Harmattan, 2000).

Preface to the First Edition

Having had to explain on many occasions over the last twenty years how I came to be interested in the music of India, I am here compelled by force of habit to preface this acknowledgment with one more such explanation.

Nearly twenty years ago I began to investigate the musical output of Rabindranath Tagore as a result of my having met his amanuensis Professor Amiya Chakravarty, then teaching comparative religions at Boston University. During the course of my research on Tagore I discovered the Bauls and learned of their influence on Gurudev, as Tagore is called by admiring Bengalis. Everything written about the Bauls, a kind of free-spirited religious sect, made them seem irresistible—they were the gadflies of hide-bound social and religious convention and their songs seemed to give musical expression to their dissatisfaction with smug prejudice and complacency. In those early days of my research, Professor Chakravarty's encouragement of my interest and his praise of my miserable Bengali (written in Devanagari script!) were very valuable to me.

One of the few books available twenty years ago that was in large part devoted to the Bauls had the not very encouraging title *Obscure Religious Cults;* it made me wonder whether the music of some more accessible group of Indians might not be a wiser choice for a dissertation topic. The Bauls' obscurity was not to last much longer. In fact, they were never really obscure in Bengal and they were already becoming world travelers, a fact unknown to me, at the time I began to learn of them. I heard of the first tour of the States by Bauls from a fellow graduate student who had been entranced by the performance he had heard given by Bauls as an intermission feature in a concert by the Paul Butterfield Blues Band in New York. They had performed, he told me, as the League of Spiritual Discovery Band (the LSD Band). I assured my friend that he must be mistaken, whereupon he handed me a business card, not his, but that of Pūrṇo Candro Dās, "Baul

Emperor," complete with Calcutta address and phone number. He also introduced me to the Elektra album the Bauls had made while in the States, and listening to that recording resolved me to meet them and write about them.

The conversation I have just reported took place at Wesleyan University (Middletown) where I had gone in the fall of 1967 as a special student, and it is there I must continue the list, begun with Professor Chakravarty's name, of people to be thanked for fostering my interest in India. My stay at Wesleyan was made possible by the first of four Traveling Fellowships from Harvard, for which I am indebted to Professor John M. Ward, my advisor. For the waiver of tuition at Wesleyan, I thank Professor Richard K. Winslow, then Chairman of the Music Department, and for their wholehearted acceptance of my participation in the World Music program I am grateful to Professors Robert E. Brown and David McAllester.

My profoundest thanks for my teachers at Wesleyan are reserved for my first Indian teacher, T. Ranganathan, and for the other members of his remarkable family. Their extraordinary musicianship and humanity taught me the real value of ethnomusicology.

The remainder of my Traveling Fellowships supported me for two and a half years in Calcutta, and there I incurred an unpayable debt to all the Bauls who tolerated my bothersome questions. The first Baul I met was Pūrṇo Candro Dās to whom I had been led by Professor Edward C. Dimock of the University of Chicago, whose sympathetic interest in my research has always been greatly appreciated. To his student, Professor Clinton Seely, I must say thanks for taking the trouble to track down articles for me in the Regenstein Library and for sending me portions of his dissertation.

I have incurred a particular debt of gratitude to Lakṣm̃aṇ Dās Baul of Mallarpur, but I trust that friendship will have redeemed it. To Professor Pradip Sinha of Rabindra Bharati University is owed thanks for his having introduced me to Jayadeva *melā* and for his countless informative conversations, which helped me understand Bengal a little better. Through Pradip Sinha, too, I became acquainted with the nephew of the renowned Baul Gō̩sai Gōpāl, G. Rakhal Raj Joarddar, and his patient help in translating many Baul texts was inestimable.

Among those who have shared with me their knowledge of the Bauls, I am particularly pleased to thank Carol Salomon for her generous help, and I shall conclude this acknowledgment with a word of thanks to Sally Ann Grossman whose generosity financed Subrata Kar's handsome collection of black and white photos which is scattered through the pages of this book.

Introduction

For the reader unfamiliar with the situation of Bengal, where the Bauls are located, within South Asia, these introductory pages are meant as a brief guide to the area and to the language spoken by its inhabitants, including the Bauls. The maps on pages 2 and 4, besides showing the political boundaries and geographic location of Bengal, also show the particular places where field work was done and may be helpful to the reader in chapters 3 and 4 where these places are referred to.

Bengali is the language of Bengal and is one of the most important in India, even within the small group of languages recognized by the government of India as media of instruction and of provincial government communication. It has its own script, which is related to that used for Hindi, the most widely known Indian language, but its pronunciation differs considerably from that of Hindi. For those particular about knowing how to pronounce the Bengali words used in this book a transliteration and pronunciation guide has been provided on pages 6–9.

The Geography

The geographic area of Bengal, in which the Bauls are located, because of the political history of its districts, is rather cumbersome to describe. The heart of the area is the riverine delta formed by the mouths of the Ganges River which form the northernmost shores of the Bay of Bengal on the east coast of peninsular India (see map 1). The main mouth of the Ganges, the Padma, exits into the bay through Bangladesh, passing near the capital Dacca. A smaller mouth, the Hooghly, exits to the southwest in the West Bengal province of India just after passing the provincial capital Calcutta. The area stretches some four hundred miles inland to the north and is bounded by the Himalayan foothills at Darjeeling with Nepal to the west, Sikkim and Bhutan to the north. Then descending in the east to the bay, the area is confined by Assam, Meghalaya, Tripura, and Mizoram, all part of India, and finally by Burma, which continues to form the northeastern shores of the bay begun by the Chittagong area of Bangladesh. Descending

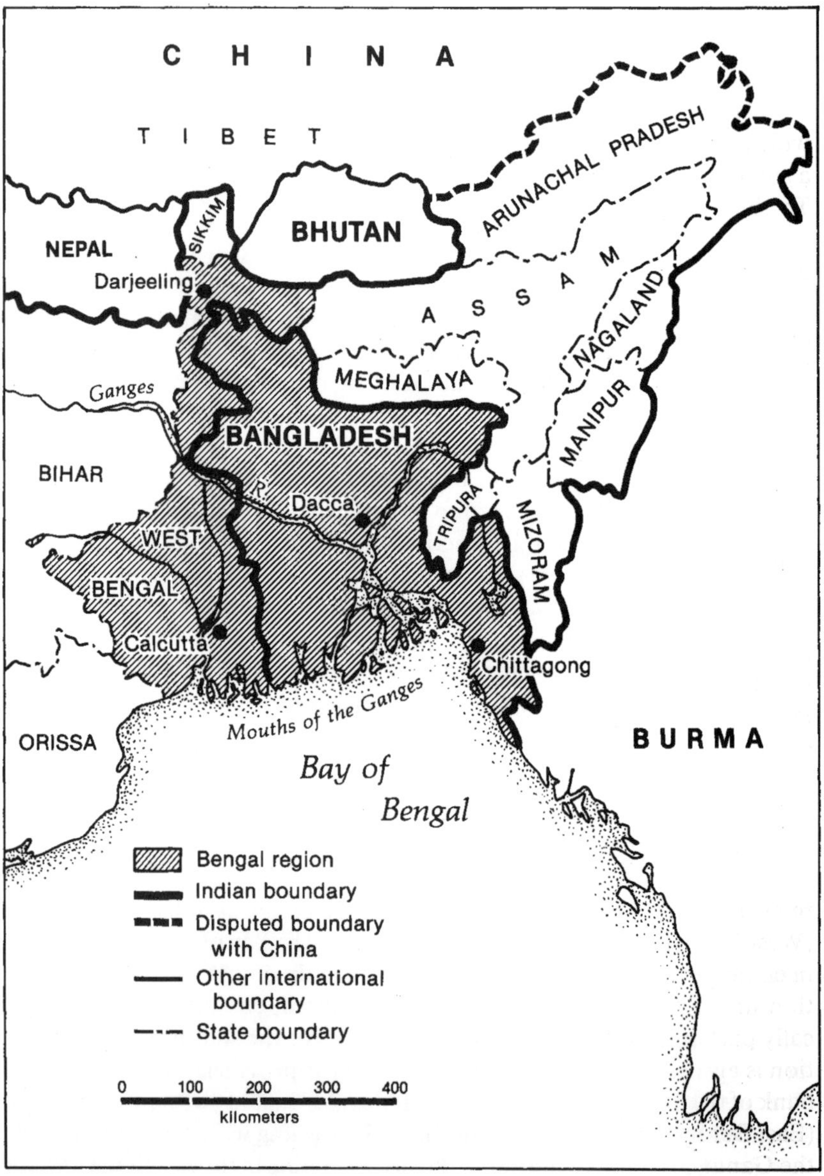
C H I N A
T I B E T
NEPAL
SIKKIM
BHUTAN
ARUNACHAL PRADESH
Darjeeling
A S S A M
NAGALAND
MEGHALAYA
Ganges
BANGLADESH
MANIPUR
BIHAR
R.
Dacca
TRIPURA
MIZORAM
WEST
BENGAL
Calcutta
Chittagong
Mouths of the Ganges
ORISSA
BURMA
Bay of
Bengal
Bengal region
Indian boundary
Disputed boundary
with China
Other international
boundary
State boundary
0
100
200
300
400
kilometers

Map 1

in the west from Darjeeling toward the bay, the area is bounded first by Nepal, then by the Indian province Bihar, and finally, to the extreme southwest, by the province Orissa. The 231,851 square kilometer area so circumscribed contains some of the most densely populated land in the world; the total population in 1982 was about 155,000,000.[1]

The name for this entire area, Bengal, is derived from Sanskrit *vaṅga,* which, it is postulated, may be related to a Tibetan word meaning "watery," a suitable adjective for the Ganges delta and its numerous fluvial arteries. To the inhabitants of the area it is known as *baṅgo* (*deś*), *deś* meaning "country." This is somewhat literary; the colloquial *bāṅlā* is more frequently used for both the name of the geographic area and its language. Another version of *bāṅlā, bāṅgālā,* is the closest version to English "Bengal" and is the progenitor of "bungalow." In Bengali, *bāṅ(g)āl* refers to an inhabitant of eastern Bengal, with the uncomplimentary connotation, in Calcutta, at least, of provinciality and bumpkinness. The neutral term for any Bengali, *bāṅ(g)āli,* is very close to English.

During the time Bengal was a province of British India an attempt was made, in 1905, to divide it, ostensibly for reasons of administrative efficiency. The attempt was abandoned when it aroused the already inflammable anti-British spirit among middle-class Bengalis, the so-called *bhadrolōk.*[2] With independence from the British in 1947, however, came successful partition, this time on the grounds of religious incompatibility between the Muslim and Hindu communities of British India. A similar partition divided Panjab in the opposite, northwestern corner of India, and the two amputated extremities formed the Islamic state Pakistan. As a result of civil war in Pakistan in 1971, the province East Bengal, with Dacca its capital, declared its independence and adopted the name Bangladesh. Bangladesh constitutes East Bengal only, while West Bengal, with Calcutta its principal city, remains a province of India.

The political divisions of the land do not quite correspond to the areas referred to when people use directional names in Bengali. *Paścim baṅgo* (West Bengal), for instance, commonly refers to the area which bellies out in endless plateaux from Calcutta, toward Bihar, but does not include the thin strip of land reaching up to and including Darjeeling, which is politically part of West Bengal. The reason for this exclusion is that an association is always made by Bengalis between the traditional name for the west bank of the Ganges, *rāṛh,* and the newer name, *paścim baṅgo. Pūrbo baṅgo* (East Bengal) is generally equated with the ancient "watery" *vaṅga,* east of the Ganges and centering round Dacca. The large, gently hilly area above it, from Rajshahi to Dinajpur, Rangpur, and Cooch Behar, is not included in the designation *pūrbo baṅgo,* and when thought of as a unit by itself is sometimes called *uttar baṅgo* (North Bengal), or the more traditional *bā-*

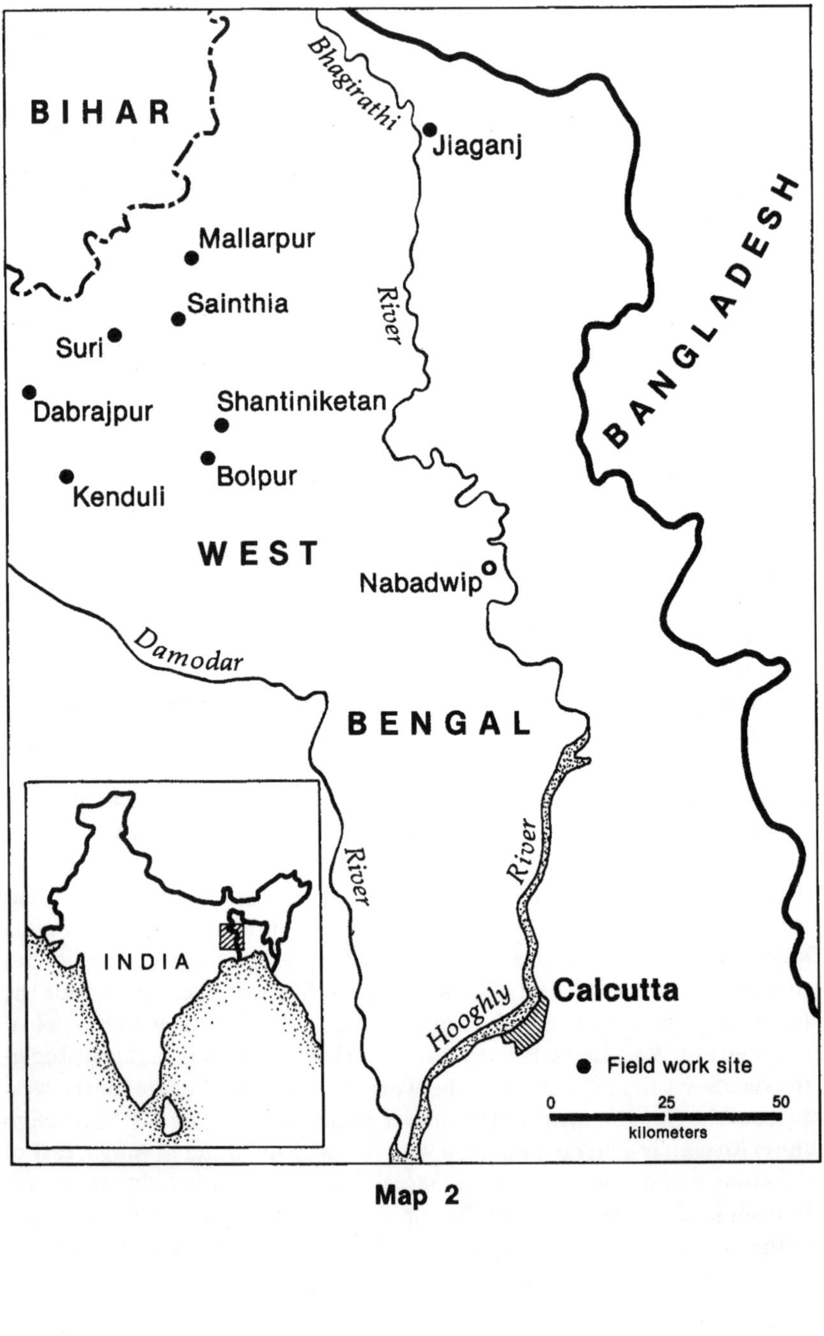
BIHAR
Bhagirathi
Jiaganj
BANGLADESH
Mallarpur
Sainthia
Suri
River
Dabrajpur
Shantiniketan
Bolpur
Kenduli
WEST
Nabadwip
Damodar
BENGAL
INDIA
River
River
Calcutta
Hooghly
Field work site
0
25
50
kilometers

Map 2

rendro. The remaining areas of East Bengal are generally evoked in Bengali by the names of their principal cities, Sylhet in the easternmost projection lying under Meghalaya, and Chittagong in the coastal hills along the Arakan littoral of Burma.

While research for this book was done exclusively in West Bengal (see map 2), the study includes interviews and recordings of East Bengal Bauls, who, like millions of other Hindu-Bengalis, had become refugees from East Bengal after the partition. All the Bauls met, including those from the predominantly Islamic area of East Bengal, had acquired a veneer of Vaisnavism; perhaps those who were more Islamicized in their ways felt no compulsion to leave when Pakistan was formed.

THE LANGUAGE

The language spoken throughout Bengal is an Indo-Aryan tongue, like all the major languages of Hindustan or Northern India, from which it became clearly differentiated at least a thousand years ago. About that time some song texts were composed, now extant in a manuscript of a somewhat later date; the texts bear a striking resemblance to those the Bauls sing today. The earlier songs are called *caryāpad*s, a name signifying poetry concerned with religious practice, and the principles of which they speak in cryptic and symbolic language espouse the use of sexual congress for the attainment of spiritual equilibrium, as well as of the importance of the guru and the insignificance of spiritual aids external to oneself.

As is to be expected in an area which has the geographical diversity of Bengal, there are many dialects of the language, some of which are mutually unintelligible. The standard refined language, *sādhu bhāṣā,* derives mainly from the dialect used in Nabodvip to the north of Calcutta, on the Hooghly River. It derived its influence from the fact that in the fifteenth century Nabodvip was a famous center of learning, particularly of the Navya Nyaya school of religious logic, and it was there that the saint Caitanya was born and later, in reaction to religious pedantry, founded a revivalist religious movement based on *bhakti* (devotion).

The standard colloquial language, usually spoken of as *colti bhāṣā,* is derived mainly from the speech of two towns, Krishnagor and Hooghly, to the south of Nabodvip and just north of Calcutta. One of the things which most easily distinguishes the *bāṅāl* from his supposedly more sophisticated Calcutta-bred and educated brethren is his speech, which has a number of phonological and lexical differences from the *colti bhāṣā.* Since the Bauls whose songs are transcribed in this study come from different areas, they naturally demonstrate some phonological variety. In the speech of Pūrṇo

Candro Dās Baul, for example, an initial consonant cluster of the type *Cr* is often pronounced *Cø* with an increase in tension of the first consonant in the cluster; this contrasts with *colti bhāṣā* pronunciation, in which the *r* would sound, but is typical of some speakers of Birbhum district dialect. In the speech of Ýotin Dās Baul, however, contrasts such as *z* for *j* and *s* for *ch* are typical of many dialects in Bangladesh, from where Ýotin emigrated to India.

The script used for Bengali is an ornamental relative of the Devanagari used for Hindi (the lingua franca of Hindustan) and Sanskrit. It orthographically represents the phonology of Sanskrit just as Devanagari does, but because Bengali is not pronounced like Sanskrit, the orthography is not phonetic as it is for Sanskrit. The disparity between the spelling and the pronunciation, however, is not so great or diverse as in English, and after a few basic principles have been learned it is possible to work out that *nȳāsa*, for example, pronounced as it looks in Sanskrit, in Bengali is pronounced like the English name Nash. There is no widely accepted system of transliteration which combines both spelling and pronunciation, but Professors Edward C. Dimock and Ronald Inden of the University of Chicago have recently proposed such a system, which is adapted here.[3]

TRANSLITERATION AND PRONUNCIATION GUIDE

Bengali sign		*Transliteration*	*Pronunciation*	*Example*
1.	অ	1. *a*	1. law (New England speech)	*apar*
		2. *o*	1. so (no diphthongal glide)	*śānto*
		3. *á*	1. fan (a little lower)	*bȳábsā*
		4. *Ø*	1. silent, omitted when not pronounced at ends of words	
2.	আ	1. *ā*	1. father	*pān*
		2. *ā́*	2. fan (a little lower)	*bȳā́pok*
3.	ই	1. *i*	1. sit	*kintu*
			2. chlorine	*nim*
4.	ঈ	1. *ī*	1. chlorine	*īśvor*
5.	উ	1. *u*	1. ruin	*ghum*
6.	ঊ	1. *ū*	1. ruin	*dhūp*
7.	ঋ	1. *ṛi*	1. rinse (with lightly flapped *r*)	*kṛiṣṇo*

Bengali sign	*Transliteration*	*Pronunciation*	*Example*
8. এ	1. *e*	1. set	*chele* (first e)
		2. sleigh (no diphthongal glide)	*chele* (second e)
	2. *ē*	1. like *a* in fan (a little lower)	*ēk*
9. ঐ	1. *oi*	1. showy (without intermediary *w*)	*boi*
10. ও	1. *ō*	1. so (no diphthongal glide)	*ýōg*
11. ঔ	1. *ow*	1. show (not cow)	*gowr*
12. ং	1. *ṅ*	1. si*ng*	*býāṅ*
13. ঁ	1. ̣	1. nasalization of vowel	*ạcol, ẹṭō, etc.*
14. ঃ	1. *ḥ*	1. happen (with more friction)	*bāḥ*
		2. geminates succeeding consonant	*duḥkho*
15. ক	1. *k*	1. skin (i.e., unaspirated)	*pākā*
16. খ	1. *kh*	1. kin	*pākhā*
17. গ	1. *g*	1. gust	*gā*
18. ঘ	1. *gh*	1. no equivalent, like 17, but aspirated	*ghā*
19. ঙ	1. *ṅ*	1. si*ng*	*diṅi*
20. চ	1. *c*	1. no equivalent, like *ch* in church but unaspirated	*cāl*
21. ছ	1. *ch*	1. like *ch* in church	*chāl*
22. জ	1. *j*	1. job	*jāl*
23. ঝ	1. *jh*	1. no equivalent, like 22, but aspirated	*jhāl*

Bengali sign		Transliteration	Pronunciation	Example
24.	ঞ	1. *ñ*	1. can	*bȳáñjon*
25.	ট	1. *ṭ*	1. stop (i.e., unaspirated; also more retroflexed)	*ṭak*
26.	ঠ	1. *ṭh*	1. top (but more retroflexed)	*ṭhak*
27.	ড	1. *ḍ*	1. down (but more retroflexed)	*ḍāk*
28.	ড়	1. *ṛ*	1. no equivalent, like 27, but flapped	*bāṛi*
29.	ঢ	1. *ḍh*	1. no equivalent, like 27, but aspirated	*ḍhāk*
30.	ঢ়	1. *ṛh*	1. no equivalent, like 28, but aspirated	*rāṛh*
31.	ণ	1. *ṇ*	1. more dental than English *n* 2. more retroflexed than English *n*	*puṇȳo* *daṇḍo*
32.	ত	1. *t*	1. no equivalent, more dental than English *t*, also unaspirated	*tān*
33.	থ	1. *th*	1. more dental than English *t*	*thān*
34.	দ	1. *d*	1. more dental than English *d*	*dān*
35.	ধ	1. *dh*	1. no equivalent, more dental than English *d*, also aspirated	*dhān*
36.	ন	1. *n*	1. more dental than English *n*	*nā*
37.	প	1. *p*	1. spot (i.e., unaspirated)	*pāg*
38.	ফ	1. *ph*	1. pot (but less closure)	*phāg*
39.	ব	1. *b*	1. ban	*bāg*
40.	ভ	1. *bh*	1. no equivalent, like 38, but aspirated	*bhāg*

Bengali sign		*Transliteration*	*Pronunciation*	*Example*
41.	ম	1. *m*	1. man	*mālā*
		2. *m̄*	1. geminates preceding consonant	*ātm̄iyo*
42.	য	1. *ý*	1. jam	*ýōgī*
43.	য়	1. *y*	1. no equivalent, semivowel similar to *a* in pane	*ýāy*
		2. *ȳ*	1. silent	*diȳe*
44.	র	1. *r*	1. no equivalent, single dental flap	*bāri*
45.	ল	1. *l*	1. list	*lāl*
46.	ব	1. *v*	1. geminates preceding consonant	*biśvo*
		2. *b*	2. ban; Bengali pronunciation of Sanskrit *v* in contexts other than that of 45.1	*biśvo*
47.	শ	1. *ś*	1. shun	*śilpī*
			2. misrule (with no hiatus, flapped *r*)	*śrī*
48.	ষ	1. *ṣ*	1. shun	*ṣāṭ*
			2. geminates and aspirates preceding *k* (silent)	*kṣetro*
49.	স	1. *s*	1. shun	*sāt*
			2. aster	*āste*
50.	হ	1. *h*	1. happen	*hori*
		2. *h̄*	1. geminates succeeding consonant (silent), or inverts order of consonants (*Ch-hC*)	*brāh̄mon*

As the Bauls are not ethnically a distinct group in Bengal, Bengali is their mother tongue and not an acquired language as it may be for some tribals like the Santals who live within Bengal. Although it is their mother tongue, the Bauls are rarely said to be literate in it; though they may not be learned, basic literacy seems common among them, and one of its chief uses for the Bauls is the preservation of song texts in notebooks which, after a few generations, are considered family treasures.

CHAPTER ONE

The Bauls: A Brief Description

The Name "Baul" and What It Applies To

The songs which are the subject matter of this book are sung by members of a Bengali religious sect called Baul (*bāul*). The members of the sect are themselves called Baul(s), and the songs they sing are named for them, Baul-*gān* (Baul song or songs). When the word *bāul* first came to be used to designate the sect and its members is unknown. It has been suggested that, etymologically, the word derives from Sanskrit *vātula,* "windy, affected by the wind disease, mad," or *vyākula,* "restless, disordered," and in medieval Bengali literature of the fifteenth to the seventeenth century, the term apparently meant "mad" and did not refer to a religious sect (Dimock and Levertov 1967, 250–51, 254). Today, Baul is used exclusively with reference to the religious sect, and although it still carries a connotation of "mad," it no longer means simply that.

The madness which the name Baul implies is one characterized by a disregard of social and religious conventions accepted by the great majority of Bengalis, and this disregard is perhaps best exemplified in the Bauls' rejection of caste, the foundation of Indian social organization, and of scripture-based creeds.

The attitude of the Bauls regarding caste has been nicely put by the most celebrated of their number, Lālon Phokir, who said, "What form does caste have? I've never seen it, brother, with these eyes of mine!" (*phokir lālon bale jātir ki rūp? āmi dekhlām nā bhāi e nayone.*) Many Baul songs recall the behavior of persons who are known for their transgression of caste limits: "There was a brahman boy who was so wicked that having fallen in love, he drank the water with which he had washed the feet of a washerman's daughter!" (*ēkjon brāh̃moner chele, se to emni khiṭkhele, pirit kore dhōbār meȳer pā dhuȳe khele.*)[4] Anti-caste sentiment, however, is not exclusively Baul; Gauriya Vaisnavism, which has deified its founder, the early sixteenth-century Bengali revivalist saint, Caitanya, is also characterized by some anti-caste feeling, at least on certain occasions. This is one reason the Bauls, too, venerate Caitanya and, more particularly, his chief disciple Nityananda, who is specially credited with a brotherly love that transcended caste: "Gour [Caitanya] and Nitai [Nityananda] were two brothers; such kindness I've never seen; my most kind Nitai makes no distinctions of caste prejudice." (*gowr nitāi tārā duṭi bhāi ēmon doyāl dekhi nāi / parom doyāl nitāi āmār jāter bicār nāy.*)

As with other social or religious movements that have rejected caste in India, the Bauls seem to have appealed mainly to those castes identification with which meant institutionalized backwardness, harassment, and exploitation, and today the Bauls continue to be basically rural, ill-educated, and poor.

The Bauls' refusal to accept the fundamental basis of social organization in India stems from their insistence on the necessity for judging men individually with love and not as members of a group with preordained virtues or faults. Combined with this characteristic is a belief that life is meant to be enjoyed; in particular, they reject outright the traditional Indian religious path of ascesis, calling it "dry" (*śukhno*). Nor do they accept the extreme of hedonism. Both ascesis and the extreme of hedonism are pursued without the concern for general physical well-being that is central to the Bauls' belief that the mind-body is the sole instrument through which men can achieve a better state of being. For this reason they reject the "dry" path for a "juicy" (*rosik*) one. The word *rosik* is difficult to translate; it derives from *rasa* (Skt.) which, basically, means "sap," and all its connotative meanings have reference to a kind of freshness and vitality, both physical and mental, which are the opposite of the connotations of *śukhno*.

Especially, it is the celibacy enjoined upon ascetics which the Bauls find repugnant and ridiculous. While agreeing that virtue, in its physical and psychical as well as its moral aspects, may suffer degradation through sexual incontinence, the Bauls assert that sexual intercourse is a sine qua non for the preservation and increase of such virtue. Not surprisingly such a belief, and its ritual expression, is considered a secret matter among Bauls, though it has not always been a well-kept one, and its significance for some song texts will be further discussed in chapter 5.

Despite the secrecy of their core belief, the Bauls have paradoxically spent much time and effort in drawing attention to themselves through the medium of public performance of their songs. This does not constitute an abuse because the songs are neither a constituent of nor an accompaniment to secret practices, but, on the contrary, are meant for casual rendition to audiences which only rarely consist exclusively of other Bauls.

The composite quality resulting from the Bauls' esoteric and exoteric activities has resulted in a comparable ambivalence on the part of Bengali society at large, which has accepted them as cultural emblems in their exoteric form while often ignoring or condemning the esoteric core of their belief. The development of the Bauls as emblems of Bengali culture and the ambivalence it entails is one of the more fascinating aspects of the Bauls' role in Bengali culture and will consequently be treated in some detail in the next chapter.

Public performance of songs is not required of the Bauls, and while open to all, it is mainly the men who perform. Their singing rarely brings them more than small amounts of money, and they usually supplement that income with what can be made through such other work as agricultural labor.

While maintaining separate households with their families, Bauls may often live in a small community of such households which owe allegiance to a guru living in the area or buried nearby.[5] As the Bauls do without the constraints of scriptural dogma or caste regulations, they also dispense with any formal hierarchical organization of their sect—the guru-disciple relationship is the only discipline—and there is no supreme Baul either in matters of social organization or beliefs and practices.

As is suggested by the fact that Bauls are householders and sometimes form small communities, many Bauls have inherited membership in the sect, but conversions are regularly made, particularly of young men who believe the Bauls hold the key to physical and spiritual enrichment or, more recently, to public acclaim and geographic mobility.

Just how large may be the number of Bauls, born or converted, is impossible to say. The only estimate of its size was made by the literary historian Upendronāth Bhaṭṭācārẏo, who says that, in 1942, there were about 250,000 Bengalis who considered Baul-*gān* their religious music (p. ṭ). This, of course, is not really an estimate of the sect's size, since many among that quarter million may not have been initiated into the sect, and many others may not have considered Baul-*gān* their only religious music. The census of the government of India is no help in this matter, because it is concerned solely with the size of the most broadly defined religious groups, such as Hindus, Muslims, Christians, Buddhists, and Sikhs. One census report, however, does give information about the sect without mentioning its size (O'Malley 1913, 239–41).

As is pointed out by their ready acceptance of many of the traditions of Vaisnava Hinduism and Islam with which they have lived so long in proximity—this despite their heterodoxy and fundamental agnosticism—the Bauls are remarkably adaptable, and they may survive the changes of urbanization and modernization without their numbers diminishing severely.

While the Bauls may have a somewhat chameleon-like quality in their exoteric character that allows them to adapt to a changing environment and yet maintain their core of beliefs and while their social organization may be loose, they nevertheless have a strong sectarian identity. Unlike the average religious man or woman who may at various moments, frequent or not, be reminded of his or her religious affiliation, the Bauls are always Bauls and view the activities of life from the viewpoint of being Bauls. Like religious, they adopt a peculiar style of dress and grooming which makes them readily recognizable to others and constantly reminds them of their own sectarian identity.

The Dress of the Bauls

The Baul costume consists most notably of a half-dhoti and an *ālkhāl-lā*. The former name implies that the garment is half the length of the common Hindu man's covering for the lower body known as *dhuti,* which is a seamless length of cloth approximately two meters by one meter. As the half-dhoti is short, it cannot be passed between the legs in the customary manner to form the usual flowing pantaloon. Instead, it is wrapped around the waist once to form a skirt in the manner of the Muslim lungi or the South Indian *veṣṭi.*

Covering the torso and reaching down to the knees, the *ālkhāllā* is a longer version, sometimes with half-sleeves only, of the North Indian man's shirt known as *kurtā* or, in Bengal, *pāñjābī* (*kurtā*), which is a pullover type of shirt with long sleeves and long flairing tails. Neither of the terms—dhoti or *ālkhāllā*—used to denote these garments is a peculiarly Baul word, though the latter is used infrequently in common speech, since the type of garment to which it refers is uncommon; even the Bauls may use a regular *pāñjābī.*

The half-dhoti is normally an ordinary white dhoti which is torn in half; the *ālkhāllā* is made of cloth often dyed an ochre-umber color called *geruẏā* in Bengali ("saffron," in English, when reference is made to the color of the robes of Buddhist monks).

In addition to the two articles of clothing described above, the particular manner of wearing the hair is another of the more noticeable identifying signs of the Baul. As the hair is not cut, a manner has been devised for coiling it neatly atop the head in a bun, at least by the Bauls of West Bengal. The bun, however, is not discernible as such since it is kept in place by pulling the hair straight up from the nape over the bun and then tucking the ends into the center (fig. 1). This manner of tying up the hair and the fact that the bun is usually worn at a fairly rakish angle make the style quite

Fig. 1. Baul hair style as worn by Tinkoṛi Dās.

different from that of the better-known Sikhs of the Punjab, who also do not cut the hair and wear it in a bun. The Sikhs, whose sect is not related to the Bauls, also do not cut facial hair, and though most Bauls now shave, past custom would seem to have required letting the beard and moustache grow. How and when the custom developed of leaving hair and beard uncut is unknown; it probably stems from the practice of the Muslim Fakirs, a practice which R. M. Martin (1838, 177) mentions as characteristic of the Fakirs then. The extinct *nēṛā* ("shaveling") caste / sect, with which the Bauls apparently had some connection (Dimock 1966, *"nēṛā,"* passim), derived their name from their custom of keeping the head and face free of all hair, a practice inherited from their Buddhist ancestors. The word *nēṛā* still occurs in Baul songs. With regard to the Neras, Martin (1838, 177) says:

> Those among the vile castes, who dedicate themselves to religion, are usually called Narha Vaishnavas, or shavelings. This class seems to be peculiar to some

> parts of Bengal. . . . They shave their heads, live entirely by begging and induce people to bestow charity by singing the praises of the three great luminaries of the Goswamis of Bengal. These songs were composed by Ramananda Ray, a Narha, who by some extraordinary circumstance could read and write, and by the Brahmans even is considered an elegant poet.

Accessory items a Baul may wear to complete his ordinary dress include items which appear merely decorative but are not. Most common is a kind of choker necklace made of beads formed from the stems of the basil plant (*tulsī*) (fig. 2); this plant is widely venerated by worshippers of the avatara Krishna (*kṛiṣṇo*), who, according to various theologies, is related in various ways to Vishnu (*viṣnu*), one of the gods of the Hindu trinity. Another of these gods, Shiva (*śiva*), is represented by the large red seeds known as *rudrākṣo*, which may be incorporated into necklaces (*mālā* is the

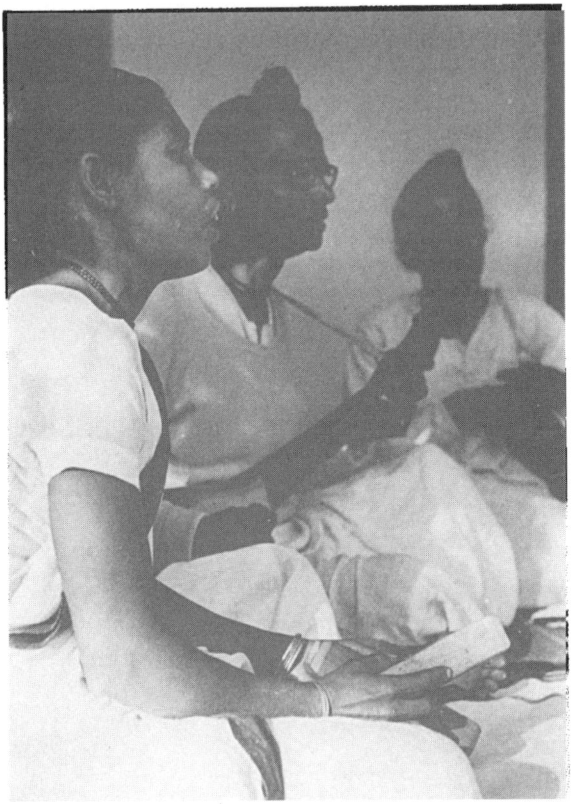

Fig. 2. *Tulsī mālā. Left to right:* Prem Dāsī, Ýotin Dās, Nārāyoṇ Candro Odhikāri.

Hindu term for these rosaries, *tosbi,* the Islamic). Other necklaces may be worn that include stones and metal or even money, and bracelets, particularly of copper, are favored (fig. 3). None of these items, however, is worn merely as decoration. Various plant and mineral substances are used because they represent, invoke, or please a deity. Stone and metals are chosen for their properties which alter the physical and mental states of those who wear them. Wearing them to take advantage of their properties is not a peculiarly Baul practice but one that is widespread in Bengal. Nearly everyone who can afford to do so, for example, will wear a stone not for its beauty—indeed, it may even be an inferior gem, crudely cut—but for the ameliorative effect it will have on the wearer's life. The choice of stone will have been made by an astrologer after consulting the wearer's horoscope in order to discover what bad influence needs counterbalancing or what good one needs reinforcement. Motives familiar to Westerners for the acquisition of jewels, such as wanting to invest money or to beautify the person, though present among Bengalis, would, in most instances, be subordinated to a concern about the jewels' potential for benefiting or harming the wearer.

Underneath his outer garments, the Baul wears a type of supporter, or cache-sexe, called (*doṛ*) *kowpīn.* It consists of a cord (*doṛ*) tied round the

Fig. 3. *Tosbi.*

waist and over which a yard-long piece of cloth (*kowpīn*) about six to eight inches wide is draped in front of the genitals and then pulled between the legs and buttocks and over the cord in back. The remainder is then secured by twisting it round the part passing between the buttocks. Traditionally, nothing is worn under the dhoti by ordinary men, though shorts are now considered decent by urbanized men, who are more apt to prefer pants or *pāẏjāmā*, the loose, thin, white-cotton, draw-string slacks. In the city, the dhoti is becoming a ceremonial garment for weddings and similar festivities. The man who wears a *kowpīn* is identified as one involved in religious pursuits, a *sādhu* (holy man). Bauls, then, are not the only ones to wear it. Those who practice physical yoga without any particular religious initiation also may wear it.

Other articles of dress the Bauls generally reserve for occasions when they perform. These include a pair of sashes, one tied round the waist and the other passing over a shoulder and diagonally across the back and chest and knotted at the waist; these are worn over the *ālkhāllā* or *pāñjābī* and are generally of *geruẏā* color, as is the turban (*pāgṛī*). A final item in the Bauls' wardrobe is a patchwork coat, known as *guduṛi*,[6] which is sometimes worn over the *ālkhāllā*. These articles can be seen in figures 4 and 5.

All these items of the Baul wardrobe and its accessories serve to make

Fig. 4. *Guduṛi* worn by Bauls at *Pouṣ melā*.

Fig. 5. *Ālkhāllā* worn by Lakṣm̃aṇ Dās.

the male Baul a distinctive figure; female Bauls do not customarily employ special dress or grooming. I observed only one female Baul who cultivated a strikingly different look from that of the average village Vaisnava (worshipper of Krishna-Vishnu) woman (fig. 6). Like the men, she wore her hair in a top-knot, and the color of her sari was *geruỹā*. She had a bold, independent manner of behavior in general, and while singing was more expressive and mobile than was usual among women singers. She was not in the company of any male and was treated with affectionate amusement by other Bauls who called her *buṛi-mā*, "old-lady mother."

Fig. 6. "Buṛi-mā."

CHAPTER TWO

The Evolution of the Bauls as Cultural Emblem

The Bauls in the Eyes of Nineteenth-Century Bengali Scholars

Having become familiar with the dress of the Bauls, the reader should have little difficulty in recognizing the charming imposter in figure 7 as a pseudo-Baul. This photograph was displayed in the window of a photography studio in 1970 in the fashionable Ballygunge area of South Calcutta. That a middle-class family should choose to immortalize the darling of the household by garbing him like a Baul reveals a certain indulgent affection not only for the boy but also for the character he impersonates. Despite the attitude of the boy's family when the picture was taken, if, some years thereafter, the boy were to don the dress of a Baul in earnest rather than in play, there would no doubt be an outcry in the family. However much respectable Bengalis may long for the freedom from conventions that they romantically associate with the Bauls, they are generally, and understandably, content with retaining their respectability while allowing the Bauls to express those longings for them. The imagery and the tunes with which the Bauls do this so successfully have acquired for them the status of representing something quintessentially Bengali, but this role is relatively recent and is the result of many decades of evolution.

When the Bauls first attracted the attention of the newly established Bengali urban middle class of Calcutta in the mid-nineteenth century, it was to be included as one among many of the various religious sects described by Akṣay Kumar Datto in his book *bhārotīyo upāsok-sampradāy* (*The Religious Sects of the Hindus*). Given the tenor of the times and the mores of his class, it is unlikely that Datto would have thought the Bauls admirable since he was aware of the emphasis they placed upon sex in their *sādhonā* (religious practice): "I have scarcely heard one or two Bauls who

Fig. 7. Boy dressed as Baul.

did not agree. By enjoyment of desire they eventually come to pure love in their sadhana. Then they perceive the full lila [divine play] of Radha and Krishna" (1277 [1870–71], 168). But Datto expresses neither approbation nor disapproval and maintains a scholarly objectivity in his description.

Some twenty-five years later in 1896, Jogendra Nath Bhattacarya expressed a more personal view of the Bauls in which he both praises the Bauls for not being idolaters and pleads for their rescue from moral degradation:

> The Bauls are low class men and make it a point to appear as dirty as possible. They have a regular costume, which consists of a cone-shaped skull cap and a long jacket of dirty rags patched together extending from the shoulders to the lower part of the legs. Not only their dress, but their musical instruments, their dancing, and their songs are all characterised by a kind of queerness which makes them very amusing. The quaint allegories and the rustic philosophy of their songs are highly appreciated by the low classes. Their exhibitions are

upon the whole so enjoyable that, in most of the important towns of Bengal, amateur parties of Bauls have been organised who cause great merriment on festive occasions by their mimicry.

The Bauls are spoken of as Vaisnavas; but properly speaking they are a godless sect. They do not worship any idols, and on that account, their religion may be regarded as a very advanced one. But according to their tenets, sexual indulgence is the most approved of form of religious exercise, and it is said that they have been known to drink a solution made from human excretions. The moral condition of these and some other sects . . . is deplorable indeed, and the more so as there is no sign of any effort in any quarter to rescue them. Aristocratic Brahminism can only punish them by keeping them excluded from the pale of humanity. The modern religions can afford to give them better treatment. But they seem to be considered as too low or incorrigible by even the proselytising religions. If the Chaitanite Gossains [elders of the Bengali Vaisnava sect founded by Caitanya], Christian missionaries, or Mahomedan Mullas could reclaim these they would be entitled to the everlasting gratitude of mankind. (1896 [1968], 381)

In the above quotation, Bhattacarya mentions a second aspect of the physical *sādhonā* of the Bauls, namely, the ingestion of human excretions.[7] This practice was already known to A. K. Datto, who described its occurrence in other sects like Aul, Sai, Darbes, and Kartabhaja (1277 [1870–71], 175) which seem to share some tantrik elements with the Bauls and are therefore sometimes referred to as Baul subsects. Although contemporary Bauls have confirmed for the author that they do have a ritual involving human excretions, which are called the "four moons," requests for further information were deflected with the statement that it could be gotten only from the guru—that is, one would have to become a Baul first. That the Bauls do continue to have a ritual of the "four moons," indirectly confirms the antiquity of some of their beliefs and practices, for the "four moons" are discussed in one of the oldest tantrik treatises, the *Hevajra*.[8] In this treatise they are mentioned as camphor, musk, frankincense, and a potion of four ingredients, and elsewhere in the treatise these are defined as *sandhābhāṣa* (Skt., code language) for urine, feces, semen, and menses, the excretions known to the Bauls as the "four moons" (Snellgrove 1959, 99).

That there is a lengthy tradition behind matters connected with the sexual ritual may be confirmed in like manner. As coitus reservatus is performed during the ritual, it is necessary for the male to gain control over sphincter muscles in order to prevent ejaculation. The manner in which this feat is to be learned, as described to the author, could have been lifted directly from the *śiva-samhitā,* a treatise on tantrik yoga (Banerjee 1894, 55).

Whoever, according to the teachings of his adept teacher, daily attracts and stops the ejectment of urine during the time of micturition with the help of

> Vayu [yogic breath control] and allows the urine to flow out again in very small quantities, again drawing the urine upwards, attains without doubt, the Bindu-Siddhi [semen-control] which brings every variety of Siddhi under his command.

However deplorable the condition of the Bauls may have seemed to Bhattacarya because of their sexual and scatological peculiarities, he noted that they nonetheless appeared to be highly entertaining—at least to the lower classes. The lower classes, he also noted, appreciated the "rustic philosophy and quaint allegories" that would soon become acceptable in more sophisticated circles when reinterpreted by the great Bengali poet Rabindranath Tagore. But at the time Bhattacarya was writing, the city dwellers still looked upon the Bauls as a source of merriment and an object of mockery, or, as Bhattacarya himself looked upon them, as sheep who had strayed from the fold.

The Baul Image Rehabilitated by Rabindranath Tagore and Kshitimohan Sen

The rehabilitation of the Bauls' image was already under way when Bhattacarya published his report, for in 1883 the twenty-two-year-old Tagore had published a review of a collection of Baul poems which he praised as models for Bengali writers. In so doing Tagore had in mind the reform of Bengali literature; in the process, the image of the Bauls benefited fortuitously because attention was directed towards Baul songs as an indigenous source of inspiration for a native literature and away from the esoteric beliefs and practices. In his review, Tagore chastised those Bengali writers who sought to translate into their language the themes and idioms of English literature as well as those writers who tried to counteract foreign influences by "purifying" Bengali with stilted Sanskritisms. As an inspiration to those who wanted to learn a congenial and forceful vehicle for genuine expression in their own language, he pointed out how the Baul songs dealt with themes as weighty as those authors were seeking in foreign literature and how direct and natural to the language was their use of Bengali (Ṭhākur 1966b, 269):

> How natural the Bengali, and how straightforward the affect . . . without giving it a thought, we let them enter the innermost part of our souls—
>
> I have seen on the lake of love the Man of my heart (*moner mānuṣ*),
> purest gold.
> Thinking to catch him, I went to catch him but did not get him.

> . . . "Universal Love" and other such great ideas sound well to us from the mouths of foreigners, but how is it that the beggars who go about singing of these things in front of our very doors do not reach our ears?

Elsewhere, Tagore explained his understanding of the term "Man of the Heart" (*moner mānuṣ*) in the song *āmi kothāy pābo tāre* (Tagore 1922, 76).

> This phrase, "the Man of the Heart," is not peculiar to this song, but is usual with the Baul sect. It means that, for me, the supreme truth of all existence is in the revelation of the Infinite within my own humanity.
>
> "The Man of the Heart," to the Baul, is like a divine instrument perfectly tuned. He gives impression to infinite truth in the music of life.

In explaining that the Bauls referred to "the supreme truth of all existence" with such terms as "Man of the Heart," Tagore certainly did much for the reputation of the Bauls, but at the cost of neglecting their own interpretation of those terms. For the Bauls, the term *moner mānuṣ*, or as it is called at other times, *adhar mānuṣ* (uncatchable man), alludes to the eternal substance of the universe which takes a volatile, physical form in human beings as semen and menses. It is *adhar* (uncatchable) because its normal flow is downward and outward, leading to physical and psychical degeneration, to death and rebirth. In the sexual *sādhonā*, performed when the woman is menstruating, the flow is reversed, upward and inward, the *adhar mānuṣ* is caught and retained, enabling the individual to escape from phenomenal existence, the cycle of death and rebirth, and to be reunited with the immobile, immutable, and immaterial form of the universal substance. Although Tagore was aware of a secret *sādhonā* among the Bauls, he did not define it specifically (Tagore 1922, 83, 85):

> These Bauls have a philosophy which they call the philosophy of the body (*kāyā-sādhonā*); but they keep it secret, it is only for the initiated. Evidently the underlying idea is that the individual's body is the Temple in whose inner mystic shrine the Divine appears before the soul, and the key to it has to be found from those who know. . . . I had neither the training nor the opportunity to study this mendicant religious sect in Bengal from an ethnological standpoint.

It is doubtful that he had the interest to do so, either, since it was the spirit of the Bauls that attracted his own spirit; he never had any use for mere scholarly observation of fact or theological definition of dogma (Tagore 1922, 86). "On the inaccessible mountain peaks of theology the snows of creed remain eternally rigid, cold, and pure. But God's manifest shower falls directly on the plains of humble hearts, flowing there in various channels, even getting mixed with some mud in its course, as it soaks into the underground currents, invisible, but ever moving." In Tagore's poetic conception, the mud is a regrettable but understandably human defilement of God's pure distilled truth. As Bauls themselves conceive it, truth is perpetually degraded in men and must be filtered through the mud of their own bodies for them to retain its pristine being. For the Bauls, the body *sādhonā* is only a means to an end, but it is the *only* means.

Tagore, who was city-bred, first took notice of the Bauls when as a young man he went to manage his family's estates in Silaidaho near the present border with Bangladesh. There he encountered followers of the famous Baul, Lālon Phokir, and, according to the report of Bauls met there later by U. Bhaṭṭācārẏo (1364 [1957–58], 533), he took away with him the original notebook of Lālon's songs, for which reason he was able to achieve such great fame as a poet!

The profound influence the Bauls had on Tagore's creative imagination prompted the Bengali literary and religious historian S. Das Gupta to call him "the greatest of the Bauls" (1969, 87), and Edward Dimock (1959), the American scholar of Bengali literature and religions, found the epithet appropriate enough to use as the title of an article in which he examined Tagore's poetical and philosophical debt to the Bauls.

The adoption of Baul thought, diction, and music by a man of Tagore's position and talent brought the sect as much attention from the urban upper classes as it had had from the rural lower classes among which it had long been familiar. Further, Tagore's representation of Baul character and personality in his dramatic works presented a man admirable for his perceptive wit and humorous wisdom. From the point of view of drama, the Baul role has sometimes an interesting similarity to that fulfilled by the chorus in classical Western drama. Dhanañjay, in *Prāyościtto* (*The Atonement*), for example, is only circumstantially involved in the action of the play, but it is clear from the advice he gives characters and from his aphoristic comments that his non-attached life-view is the central point of the play.[9] He is listed in the personae of the play as a *boirāgẏo*, a general name for Vaisnava mendicants, among whom Bauls are sometimes included. That Tagore was thinking of a Baul when he created Dhanañjay is evident from the character's behavior as well as from the numerous songs he is given to sing, some of which are accompanied by dance in the typical Baul manner. At least one of these songs, *āmāre pāṛāy pāṛāy khepiẏe bēṛāy*, has become well known as a Tagore Baul song (*robi-bāul-gān*); another one perfectly summarizes the belief which Tagore felt and inspired in others, that the Bauls' worth lay in their sense of inner strength derived from the discovery of a spiritual guide within themselves. The discovery of this interior friend, Dhanañjay says elsewhere in the play (Ṭhākur 1963, 34), is made through repeated heartbreak, but is well worth the suffering endured.

Who has told you, friend,
    to endure so much sorrow?
Why have you come, friend,
    freely to bear my burden?
Friend of my soul, bosom friend,
Friend of my happiness, friend of my sorrow,
I shall give you no sorrow, and shall receive no sorrow;
    I shall look upon your gratified face;
In happiness, in sorrow, friend,
    I shall remain in everlasting bliss—
    shall speak to you
    my soul's secrets wordlessly.

Tagore's *Phālgunī* (*Maytime*) is an extended allegory of the mystery of eternal renewal and rejuvenation; in this play, a blind Baul appears as the one character who understands the mystery and is not disturbed by the continual renunciation of the old and familiar it necessitates. The blind Baul's wisdom, like Dhanañjay's, is also derived from self-searching rather than from reliance on externals, as is revealed in his answer to one of the young characters who asks if it is because he is blind that he does not react with the fear shown by others when the "Old Man" is mentioned (Ṭhākur 1966a, 71): "No, my dear, let me tell you why I am not afraid. Once, I could see. When I became blind, I was afraid; I thought, 'I have lost my sight.' But while the sight of those with eyes was setting, there arose the sight of the blind. When the sun had gone, then I saw light within the bosom of darkness. From that time on I no longer feared the dark." Immediately after this speech, when requested to lead the way to the Old Man, the Baul replies, "Let me go along while singing, you follow behind. If I don't sing, I can't find the path." The Baul sings, according to Tagore, in order to aid his personal search.

Not only does the Baul in *Phālgunī* represent Tagore's image of the Baul but so too does the character called the Poet-Laureate, who explains the nature of the Baul's non-attachment (Ṭhākur 1966a, 17–18). The Baul addresses the Maharaja:

P: The mundane is merely a coming and going. That man who, while dancing to the sound of the *ēktārā* [a Baul instrument], merely comes and goes, *he* is *boirāgī* [non-attached], *he* is a pilgrim, *he* is the poet-Baul's disciple.

M: If that is so, how shall I find peace?

P: We have no attachment to peace, that's how non-attached we are.

M: But I want to obtain possessions and riches!

P: We have not even a little greed for possessions and riches, that's how non-attached we are.

M: What do you mean? You'll cause trouble, I can see.

Shortly, after this exchange, the Poet-Laureate sings a phrase of a song couched in the obscure language of the Bauls, to which the Maharaja replies (Ṭhākur 1966a, 19), "I don't understand a word of what you say, though your tune pierces my heart." Tagore's experience was that song is the essential expressive medium of the Bauls, whether the text be significant or not.[10] Although the Bauls might agree that the tune contains the real *ras* (vivifying sap), it is doubtful they would overlook the importance of the *tattvo* (doctrine) of the text.

For Tagore it was not the doctrinal side of the Bauls that was of interest but the spontaneous emotional way they could react to and understand the human situation. Such emotion could never be expressed fully in words, so they resorted to song. In the play *Phālgunī*, there is another poet of sorts, the character Śrutibhūṣaṇ, who is never at a loss for an appropriate quote and a cunning exegesis. Dry pedant that he is, his predicament upon listening to the Poet-Laureate's song, of which the Maharaja could appreciate only the tune, is to understand the words without in the least being affected by the tune.

The Band of Youths who represent eternal renewal in *Phālgunī*, also demonstrate an appreciation for the importance of song as communication that is now widely thought of as typically Baul. In response to the query of a constable, they sing a song, after which the constable asks (Ṭhākur 1966a, 54–55):

C: I gather that to answer a question you sing a song?

Y: Yes! If we don't, the answer doesn't come out right. If we speak in plain words, it is terribly unclear, can't be understood.

C: Do you believe your songs are so clear?

Y: Yes—don't they have tunes?

As represented by Tagore, the Baul's philosophy allows him to enjoy the beauty and to endure the suffering of life with an equanimity that enables him to objectify his experiences in the form of a personal spiritual guide. The Baul is portrayed as being free from the common necessity for formalistic conventions because he confronts life directly, without the mediation of social, religious, or personal ritual. To do so requires of him an emotional sensitivity that cannot be fully expressed in speech and therefore must have recourse to song.

In molding this image of the Baul, Tagore was greatly aided by his long-time associate, Kshitimohan Sen. Sen's *bānlār bāul* (*The Bengali Bauls*) was the first sizeable published essay about the sect, and was originally presented as a lecture series in 1949. Much earlier, both Sen and Tagore had published shorter lectures. In this lecture-essay Sen gives an interesting account of heterodoxy within the Indian religious traditions. Beginning with the ideas expressed in the Vedas and Upanishads, he traces the tendency of religious thinkers to get away from all confines of external religion and social structure in order to concentrate on inner wisdom. Discussing modern exponents of this thinking, he paraphrases A. K. Datto's descriptions of such Bengali sects as Nera, Kartabhaja, Sahebdani, etc., all of whom, he says, are Bauls. And when it comes to mentioning the *prokṛiti sādhonā* (worship of the female principle), Sen uses elliptical language that leaves the reader with no idea of what the ritual is, but implies that "pure Bauls" have nothing to do with it. What Datto claims, Sen inverts. For him only a few Bauls, or "unBauls," as he names them, accept the sexual and scatological rituals; the real Bauls follow nothing but their own "inner truth" (Sen 1954, 50).

At the end of his essay, Sen's summary of the attitude of the Bauls so strongly recalls themes of Tagore's *Phālgunī* that I quote it here, for comparison (1954, 64).

> They [the Bauls] say, all these scriptures are nothing but leftovers from ancient celebrations. What are we, dogs?—that should lick these leftovers? If there is need, we shall make new celebrations. By the grace of God, ever new sustenance will come. The truth of truths is their faith; however long the Word is needed, for so long will the Word arrive ever renewed—there will never be want. Having lost their faith, men, like dogs, collect together the left-over leaves [*pāt*, meaning leaf of banana or other plant used as a plate, and leaf of palm used for pages of a book]. Even dogs one day abandon the leaves. Men are still more despicable. Their pride is showing which among the leaves is oldest!

In a letter to a friend, Tagore explicitly states the theme of *Phālgunī* to be that of learning to celebrate living truth and to leave behind what has ossified and decayed (Ṭhākur 1966a, 102).

> As far as "Facts" are concerned, we see decrepitude and death; as for "Truth," we see incorruptible life and youth. . . . It is in the nature of the universe that the ever-new is born in the ever-old of every Spring; it is in the nature of men, too, that this lila of oldness moves. . . . The Band of Youths came to understand that again and again they had to lose life and youth, otherwise they would not be able to have a celebration of Return.

Sen stresses the constant search for new truth on the part of the Bauls because he wishes to prevent scholars inferring from any written texts what fixed beliefs and practices the Bauls might have. Even though he paraphrases much of Datto, for example, he neglects to reiterate Datto's (1277 [1870–71], 170) statement that, "They have many books," and dismisses M. M. Bose's discussion of Sahajiya Vaisnava literature as having no importance for understanding the Bauls.

Whether or not the Bauls retain and use exegetical or instructive treatises is, however, irrelevant because none of the tantrik-oriented sects can be said to rely mainly on the written word for transmission of their beliefs and practices.[11] The essense of these sects is the *demonstration* of a method by a teacher and the student's experimentation with it. The treatises may not always be respected or used by the Bauls, but they may be informative to outsiders, particularly when the information contained can be confirmed orally by what the Bauls are willing to say or sing about their beliefs.

As for what and why the Bauls communicate in song, Sen's explanation (1954, 64) is remarkably similar to that of one member of the Band of Youths in *Phālgunī* (cf. Ṭhākur 1966a, 19): "If one asks a question of the Bauls, they do not give much of an answer in words. They answer in song. And what a storehouse of songs they have! And how appropriately they come to their minds! If one asks them why they sing, why they do not speak in words, they say, 'We are a bird-like species. We don't know the tendency to plod along, ours is a soaring spirit.' " In the few songs that Sen published, one does find a lofty sentiment and a felicitous expression, but as U. Bhaṭṭācārẏo (1364 [1957–58], 70 ff.) has pointed out, these few songs seem to have an air of modern, sophisticated expression about them, and he goes so far—no doubt too far—as to suggest, on the grounds of stylistic analysis and exegetical criticism, that Sen's Baul songs have at least been tampered with if not created by Sen himself.

According to Sen, Bauls object to a popular interest in their songs because they are for *sādhonā*, not for literary enjoyment. He quotes a Baul (Sen 1954, 60–61) as having said that to ask for his songs for religious purposes is like asking for the hand of his daughter in marriage—everyone concerned is blessed; but to ask for them merely for literary satisfaction is like asking for the temporary use of his daughter for sexual pleasure—it is a shame to everyone concerned. Curiously, though, the Baul songs Sen published are quite literarily conceived, and there is little in them, as interpreted by Sen, that requires an understanding of *sādhonā*. However deep and moving the emotional affect, they do not require *practice* of religious discipline. The Baul's objection is more appropriate and understandable in reference to the songs published by U. Bhaṭṭācārẏo which do deal with yoga and doctrine.

In Tagore's opinion, songs worthy of *sādhonā* or as literature are few in number (Monsur Uddīn 1942, x): "Folk literature is like all literature; there is a difference of good and bad. . . . For this reason, all those Baul songs gotten from here and there are not worth much whether from the *sādhonā* or the literary point of view." For Tagore, the tunes of Baul songs were more affecting than were the texts. In recalling his first hearing of the now famous Baul song, *āmār moner mānuṣ ýe re*, he said (Monsur Uddīn 1942, x): "The words are very plain, but in conjunction with the tune, their meaning flashes up in an unprecedented brilliance . . . like the sobbing air of a child who cannot find its mother in the dark."

When Tagore criticized most Baul songs for being worthless as literature or philosophy, he was also circumstantially rebuking those who collect them without exercising discrimination. Aware that such a rebuke was somewhat beside the point in a scholarly edition, he admitted that the songs had "historical worth." Specifically, he noted that they suggested the possibility of Hindu-Muslim reconciliation, since the Bauls have accepted elements of both religions in varying degrees.

Sen was attracted to the Bauls for a similar reason; having written a book on the fruits of Hindu-Muslim cooperation in the past (1949), he was anxious to show that the Bauls were modern apostles of this cooperation and that though some might call on Allah in their songs and others on Krishna, they were united in seeking the Man of the Heart. This antisectarianism had a particularly strong appeal for liberal-minded men in the decades of increasing communal feeling in India before the partition and Independence from Great Britain. Of course, Hindu-Muslim cooperation in India had always been based on a willingness to relinquish much that defined one as either Hindu or Muslim. The great emperor Akbar, for example, is often mentioned as having shown how the two beliefs could coexist harmoniously, but he really sought to synthesize a new religion from the many represented at his court. The Bauls, though they may outwardly give evidence of being on the one hand more Vaisnava, on the other more Islamic, are in reality basically agnostic. They are more interested in a state of being, like the Buddhists, than in worship of a personal God, like the Vaisnava or Muslim.

The Bauls' symbolic representation of Hindu-Muslim unity is the final aspect in the image of the Bauls fashioned by Rabindranath Tagore and Kshitimohan Sen. The essential difference between the image the Bauls have of themselves and that fashioned by Tagore and Sen is that each expresses different views on the relationship of the individual to some greater general principle. Tagore was continually aware of a rift, a gap between himself and some undefined deity, and the Baul, for him, represented the spiritually quickened state of eternal longing akin to the Sufi's longing for the impossible union with a transcendent God, or Radha's pining for

Krishna. The Bauls, who adopted many Sufi and Vaisnava mannerisms, having themselves experienced this longing, believe that its resolution and satisfaction can be and must be attained through prescribed means involving the use of the body, a means to be learned from a teacher. Few obtain the goal of *siddhi* (success in *sādhonā*); most remain in the novice's state of emotional upheaval which Tagore, as an artist, prized above all.

Although there may be a fundamental dichotomy between Tagore's Bauls and the Bauls of reality, the poet's conception of them has helped him to convey his artistic intuition of beauty and truth; the same may be said of Sen, but in his case, there is a qualification. He was not an artist, but a scholar, and his romantic idealization of the Bauls, though it increases admiration for them, does them a disservice by misrepresenting them. Sen had a profound personal interest in the Bauls as well as an equal concern for their privacy, a fact which caused him to be accused in print of being "very stingy" with information about them (Monsur Uddīn 1942, xxxvi). The general human incapacity to accept the mixture of vices and virtues each man encompasses was the impediment preventing Sen from objectively confronting the Bauls in whom the vices and virtues appear to the outsider to be so exaggerated. Thus the prejudicial image he constructed, reinforced by the artistic power of Tagore, has had widespread influence on the way Bengalis view the Bauls.

Another admirer of the Bauls, one who did not feel the means to spiritual ends chosen by the Bauls invalidated those ends, has sought to clarify the ambiguities arising from contradictory opinions about the sect. Upendronāth Bhaṭṭācārŷo, in his *bāṅlār bāul ō bāul gān*, has given a detailed account of the Bauls, based on more than twenty years' personal contact with them. This account convincingly establishes their connection with early tantrik sects and the importance of sexual ritual in their belief. Bhaṭṭācārŷo presents his research for the proper interpretation of Baul song texts, over five hundred of which form the second part of his book. His interpretation is that the philosophical attitude of the Bauls derives from a psycho-physical, rather than an emotional, intuition.

Despite the thoroughness of his work, Bhaṭṭācārŷo did not entirely succeed in separating the myth from the reality of the Bauls. Six years after publication of his work, a book entitled *bāṅlār bāul: kābŷo ō darśon* (*The Bengali Bauls: Poetry and Philosophy*) was published by Sōmendronāth Bandŷōpādhŷāy, who, without referring to any of the earlier literature on the Bauls and related sects, dismisses the notion that the Bauls practice any *sādhonā,* revere their gurus, or have any resemblances to any other tantrik related sects. Instead, his main contention is that the Bauls are to be identified by their belief in action without attachment to goals—in other words, they practice the philosophy of the *Bhagavad Gita*, a portion of the ancient epic *Mahabharata*, in which Krishna convinces the warrior Arjuna of the necessity for detachment in performing the duties of one's life and the requirements of one's caste.

It is doubtful whether even Kshitimohan Sen would have approved so imaginative an assessment of the Bauls, since he at least acknowledged the work of other scholars. But Sen's reluctance to apply scholarly method to an investigation of the Bauls when it involved distasteful material, and his accusation that scholars violated the privacy of the Bauls by "waving their pencils like pistols" while recording interviews with them, certainly encouraged the replacement of objective research on the Bauls with romanticizing myth-making. The result is that the Bauls have assumed a dual existence in the minds of Bengalis, and in both these existences, their musical performances are what most attract attention and admiration.

CHAPTER THREE

The Place of Baul-*gān*

THE CONTEXTS OF BAUL-*GĀN*

Baul-*gān* is one of the few widely known and appreciated types of folk song in Bengal, a province with a large variety of types. To show how Baul-*gān* fits into the larger Bengali musical context, I will discuss some of the ways in which Baul-*gān* is similar to or contrasts with other Bengali music. The *caryāpad*s mentioned in the introduction in connection with the development of the Bengali language are of interest regarding the origins of Baul-*gān*. That thousand-year-old *caryāpad*s were meant to be sung is evident from the refrains required after each couplet. This indication of structure and the similarity in textual style and mystical meaning to the texts of Baul-*gān* suggest that *caryāpad*s are predecessors of Baul-*gān*. A significant difference setting them apart, however, is that in the manuscript the *caryāpad* texts are preceded by the name of a *rāg*, a rubric which connects them with the art-music practice of their time. Today's Bauls do not mention *rāg*s in connection with their songs, and though it is reasonable to point out similarities between melodic phrases and scales of Baul-*gān* and those of some *rāg*s, no Baul-*gān* consistently follow the prescriptions for any particular *rāg*.

Other types of spiritual song, which do not consistently follow the practice of art music and which are of more recent origin than the *caryāpad*s, are current on many social levels and are known to have been the artistic creations of particular persons. *Śyāmā-songīt* (music for the Dark Mother), for example, contains a category of songs known as *rāmprosādī*, named for the eighteenth-century devotee, Rām Prosād Sen, who wrote the texts and created the tunes. The latter he apparently based on pre-existent folk tunes as well as on some features of *rāg* music (Ray 1973, 53).

Even if its connection with the *caryāpad*s is uncertain, Baul-*gān* may certainly be considered indigenous because the Bauls, as speakers of Bengali, have long been linguistically separated from speakers of neighboring languages, and though they travel extensively, their travels are almost exclusively within Bengali speaking areas. When they perform occasionally outside Bengal, it is most likely at the invitation of a Bengali community or for a special multi-regional folk music conference. The Bauls are a provincial phenomenon unlike, for example, the Hijras who, though common enough in Bengal, originate in Western India and are widespread throughout the North (and perhaps the South). The Hijras are a community of males who suffer physiological and/or psychological sexual disabilities and who dress as females. Traditionally, they sing at homes where a birth has recently taken place, though they may also entertain at tea stalls.[12] Although information about them is scanty, they are clearly regarded by Bengalis as alien to their society, unlike the Bauls; but Hijra musical performances are accepted as part of the musical life of Bengal.

Unlike many types of song in Bengal, including those of the Hijras, Baul-*gān* is not hampered by considerations of appropriateness or validation but may be sung anywhere at any time without a gain or diminution in significance. The Bauls may show some hesitancy when asked to sing texts dealing with secret beliefs. Particular events such as the gathering of people at a village fair increase the likelihood of Baul-*gān* being sung, but do not make it more proper to do so, nor are the performances necessary to the event. In contrast to the loose connection between Baul-*gān* and its contexts, the tradition of Hijra singing for a new birth, and that of young female relatives of the bride singing to welcome the bridegroom, are examples of singing that is called forth by a special event. Such occasional songs and calendric ones, like those used for the advent and departure (*āgāmonī-bijayā*) of the Goddess Durga in the fall, have validating contexts, and whether associated with rites of passage or cyclical religious festivals, the context is necessary for the songs and probably vice versa.

Though no particular context is necessary for Baul-*gān*, something of an ideal context is created in the popular depiction of the Baul singing rhapsodically, alone, in the broad fields of West Bengal; according to this depiction, the genuine Baul performance takes place when the performer and the fortunate eavesdropper are the only audience.

Two other types of folk song in Bengal, *bhāōyāiyā* and *bhāṭiyāli,* which are closely related to Baul-*gān* in musical style, are ideally performed, like Baul-*gān,* in isolated settings. *Bhāōyāiyā,* according to the folklorist Cittorañjan Deb (1966, 197ff.), is the type of song performed by a group of people in North Bengal known as *bāudiyā,*[13] who lead lives similar to those of the Bauls, but without their religious orientation. Within the *bhāōyāiyā* category, Deb includes the songs of North Bengal herdsmen, called *moiṣāl* (from *mohiṣ,* buffalo), and of that region's ox-cart drivers, called *gāṛōȳāl* (from *gāṛi*, cart). *Bhāṭiȳāli* are the songs sung by East Bengal boatmen on rivers so broad that one loses sight of the shore. When sung in less isolated surroundings, *bhāṭiȳāli* changes its musical character by adding accompaniment and meter (Cakrobortī 1962, 676).

Among these three B's of Bengali folk music—Baul-*gān*, *bhāōȳāiȳā*, and *bhāṭiȳāli*—Baul-*gān* is distinguished from the others textually as *dharmosoṅgīt*, religious music. The texts of *bhāṭiȳāli* and *bhāōȳāiȳā*, though they may concern Radha and Krishna, are usually about the problems of love in separation or unrequited love; Radha and Krishna are merely among the more familiar pairs of lovers. In Baul-*gān*, however, though songs of a similar nature occur, they are thought of as allegories on the state of separation existing between the souls of men and the spiritual ground. Other texts may deal with such matters as the necessity of relying upon the guru or the yogic view of the body, and because all of them may have religious interpretations or a sectarian viewpoint, they are called *dharmosoṅgīt*, in contrast to the otherwise similar *bhāōȳāiȳā* and *bhāṭiȳāli*. The religious music classification, however, does not mean or imply that Baul-*gān* are associated with some ceremony or ritual; they have neither the prescribed uses nor the supernatural power of Vedic chant, for example, nor the capacity to unite people in regular congregational devotions, as group *bhajan* does or the Christian-influenced *brāh̄mo-soṅgit*.

As pointed out, *bhāōȳāiȳā* and *bhāṭiȳāli* are ideally associated with the exercise of particular occupations: in the former, the pasturing of kine or their use in transporting goods overland, in the latter, the transporting of goods over water. The songs function as time fillers for their performers "to help them forget the difficulties of their long journeys" (Deb 1966, 224).

In other work situations songs have a more intimate connection with the occupation they accompany than do *bhāōȳāiȳā* and *bhāṭiȳāli*. Well drilling and roof beating, for example, are done to the accompaniment of songs which help to coordinate the laborers' movements when the drill bit is turned into the ground or when wooden bats are swung onto the gravel mixture used for roofing brick houses. Baul-*gān*, too, may be used to accompany physically coordinated movement, namely, dance, but there is no special functional relationship between them as there is in work songs.[14] If Baul-*gān* can be considered functional, it is in the looser sense of providing entertainment and religious instruction for the auditor, and money and esteem for the performers.

The dance which Baul-*gān* accompanies is always the dance of the singer. There is never an occasion when one Baul provides the vocal accompaniment for the dance of another. The dance exists as an intermittent ornament to the musical performance and is not a continuous, defined, or choreographed performance in itself, although its movements are stereotyped. Further, it appears that only some types of song are suitable for dancing while others are not, and those that are suitable are not necessarily danced.

Baul-*gān* performance is essentially a one-man show of song, instrumental accompaniment, and dance. In an environment where other Bauls are gathered, however, the soloist may acquire a group of supporters: a chorus, which may repeat phrases, percussion and melodic accompanists, and a chorister who may occasionally dance. But the participation is never so general as to obliterate the performer / auditor distinction, as happens in popular devotional music, like group *bhajan* or some *nām-kīrton,* in which everyone may join.

The types of accompaniment in Bengali folk music are varied, and most of the widely known genres of folk music use some kind of accompaniment. Rural *bhāṭiẏāli,* the boatman's song, is an exception, but it too has acquired accompaniment in its urbanized form. Accompaniment may be simply percussive, like the slaps of roof-beaters' bats or the cacophonous punctuation of cymbals and clappers in group *bhajan;* it may mix the percussive and the melodic, as when a harmonium is added to the group *bhajan,* or a *sārindā* (bowed lute) is added to the *khōl* (double-headed barrel drum) of *kīrton;* purely melodic accompaniment is theoretically possible, but unlikely. *Bhāōẏāiẏā,* for example, could be considered a type of folk song which may have only melodic accompaniment because it is usually accompanied by *dōtārā* (plucked, fretless lute) alone; solo *dōtārā* accompaniment, however, has a lot of percussive, rhythmic quality about it even when it is used to play a melodic line. Bauls who accompany themselves with *dōtārā* always include percussion in the form of ankle bells (*ghuṅur*). Because Baul-*gān* is essentially solo music, the performer always provides some kind of self-accompaniment—perhaps only that of a *khañjoni* (small frame drum)—even if he has several willing accompanists to support him. Its solo nature allows Baul-*gān* to be elaborate in range, structure, and ornament in comparison with song types requiring large group participation.

Despite the comparative sophistication of their songs, however, the Bauls do not practice their singing in order to improve their technique or style; there is no clear distinction between practicing and performing. They do not think of themselves, nor are they viewed by others, as musicians, but as Bauls, whose natural inclination is to sing. Consequently they are not hired to perform, for example, in the way a *sānāi* (oboe) party is for a wedding; the Bauls' pay is not exactly a fee, but *bokśiś,* a gratuity. The Bauls are not considered professionals who fulfill a musical function and for whose services one is expected to pay a certain agreed upon amount, but more as mendicants who receive charity. For those Bauls who may still go door to door, like countless other musical mendicants in India, their songs may be little more than a cry for alms; in the context of performance, the songs have greater entertainment and instructional value than in the mendicant context, so that the begging signal is less conspicuous.

Most folk songs are sung by persons with no specifically musical identity in society, who acquire their songs from a common heritage, and perform them without expecting recompense or recognition. The Bauls who sing, however, spend a good part of their lives performing and expect both recompense and recognition. They seek to increase their repertoires and there is some competition among singers for recognition. By comparison with the average villager who sings, the Bauls are specialists because they perform a particular repertoire identified with them and semi-professional because they do so on request rather than for occasional reasons. A few among them now do receive contracted fees from time to time at All India Radio in Calcutta, so that they, at least temporarily, achieve a kind of professional musician status; one Baul, Pūrṇō Dās, has succeeded in achieving his goal of becoming a professional entertainer who performs exclusively by contract.

The Classification of Baul-*Gān*

Baul-*gān,* like the Bauls themselves, seems capable of evolving to suit its surroundings. Thus, for example, a particular Baul-*gān* as sung by Nirmalendu Chowdhury and by Tinkoṛi Dās Baul, though it be the same tune and text, has two different sets of qualities involving such differences as place of performance, audience to whom the performances are directed, the type of accompaniment, and the type of vocal production. Chowdhury is a professional, trained singer of Bengali folk songs who has performed throughout the world and has a teaching post in an important university; Tinkoṛi is a Baul who lives in a village and sings only for such gatherings as village fairs. Besides the objectively determinable differences in this hypothetical pair of performances, there is also the subjective matter of *quo animo.* It is necessary to assume that the intention with which the Baul sings his song carries with it a desire to perpetuate a tradition and to stir up interest in religious matters, a desire which is absent from the professional's performance.

The distinctions between the performance of a Baul-*gān* by a professional singer and by a Baul are manifest, but they become confused in the performances of Pūrṇo Candro Dās Baul, for he, like Nirmalendu Chowdhury, is a Calcutta-based professional singer, but he sings Baul-*gān* exclusively, performs only by contract, and has toured the world, perhaps even more extensively than Mr. Chowdhury. Like Tinkoṛi Dās, however, Pūrṇo Candro Dās was born into a Baul family and learned his songs from his father and other Bauls rather than from books of notation, and as a youngster, he sang in the villages for gratuities.

Baul-*gān* may even be used by instrumentalists, rather than by singers, as the foundation around which an improvisation may be spun in *dhun* style, a "light classical" genre. Such a performance would normally come near the end or conclude a recital of *rāg*-based music in the *ālāp-gat / tōṛā* genre. Nikhil Banerjee, one of today's premier sitarists, and a Bengali, has recorded such a Baul-*gān* based item on the disc EASD-1318 of the Gramophone Company of India.

Bengali Musical Classification Terms

Indian musical theorists have evolved a classificatory terminology capable of dealing with Baul-*gān* and similar types of song and their various performance styles. In Bengali, Baul-*gān* is included in a large, indistinct category known as *deśīsoṅgīt,* which comprises all music not covered by the term *mārgsoṅgīt.* This general division of music into two types has survived from the practice of ancient and medieval theorists who wrote of music as being divine and secular; that of divine origin was preserved in the Vedic melodies of religious sacrifice for which reason it was known as *mārgsoṅgīt,* music of the Way, while every other kind of music, but particularly art music, was called *deśīsoṅgīt,* provincial music. In contemporary musicological parlance, *mārgsoṅgīt* has come to mean the major art music systems of Hindustani and Carnatic music, while *deśīsoṅgīt* has taken on the meaning of regional music. There are, however, regional forms of art music of a lighter sort, Bengali *ṭappā* or *rāgprodhān,* for example, which, despite their regional origin, would not ordinarily be included in the *deśīsoṅgīt* category because that term's general connotation, "popular and folkish," does not fit the refined quality of that music.

In more common use than *mārgsoṅgīt,* is the word *uccāṅgosoṅgīt,* literally "high-class music"—*śastriyosoṅgīt,* "canonical music," is an equivalent term—under which heading the pan-provincial art forms like *kheyāl* and *dhrupad* can be grouped with regional ones like Bengali *ṭappā.* Contrasting with this category is that of *lōksoṅgīt,* the direct equivalent, semantically if not musicologically, of "folk music." Whether this term arose in spontaneous pairing with *uccāṅgosoṅgīt* or as a translation of the Western term is not known, but it is used to refer to a wider variety of types, including urban music, than is normally the case with the English term "folk music." Like the *mārgsoṅgīt-deśīsoṅgīt* pair of terms, *uccāṅgosoṅgīt-lōksoṅgīt* tends to be used to cover all kinds of music.

Within each category, of course, there are numerous subdivisions. Within *uccāṅgosoṅgīt,* the divisions are according to specific types of music, each having relatively fixed procedures and manners of performance, loosely called forms, like *dhrupad, kheyāl, gat-tōṛā, ṭhuṅri, ṭappā, tārānā, hori-dhāmār, bhajan.* Within *lōksoṅgīt,* the divisions are according to more restrictive class names, and on the inclusion of some names agreement would not be general among Bengali musicologists. Just as such regional light classical types as Bengali *ṭappa* or *rāgprodhān* might be considered too provincial to be *mārgsoṅgīt,* or too refined to be *deśīsoṅgīt,* the classification of a type of music as *lōksoṅgīt* or *uccāṅgosoṅgīt* may also be controversial. The music of the poet-composers—*robīndrosoṅgīt,* the songs of Tagore, or *najrulgīti,* the songs of Qazi Nazrul Islam, among others—can be considered too sophisticated musically, despite its emphasis on text, to be anything but *uccāṅgosoṅgīt,* or it can be excluded from *uccāṅgosoṅgīt* because of the limited freedom or lack of it, to improvise, the significance of the text, and the personal, idiosyncratic styles of such music. Regarding *ādhunik-gān,* modern song, which one might translate in a phrase of the popular music industry as "lyric ballad," there would be no disagreement about the unsuitability of its inclusion in *uccāṅgosoṅgīt,* but to call it *lōksoṅgīt* might also be inappropriate because of its commercial production for an urban audience. A similar problem exists with the classification of *philmi-gīt,* the pop music of the film industry. Such a narrowing of the meaning of *lōksoṅgīt* tends to assimilate it to *pallīgīti,* village music, but these two terms are not coextensive, and *lōksoṅgīt* is meant to be a much looser and broader classification.

By *pallīgīti,* Bengali writers on music mean the unsophisticated, noncommercial music produced by untrained musicians who perform for their own and each other's benefit. Baul-*gān* is one of the many types of music included in the class *pallīgīti,* although some writers, like Maniklal Sinha (1971, 50), may object to this inclusion because the texts of Baul-*gān* are too narrowly sectarian to be a commonly shared tradition among Bengalis; as Baul-*gān* is obviously well loved by a large portion of Bengalis, however, this objection is usually mentioned only to be criticized as being itself too narrow (S. K. Bose 1960, 47). Those who maintain the objection would probably be content to classify Baul-*gān* as *dharmosoṅgīt,* religious music, but though such a classification says something about the nature of the texts, it is neutral about the music. *Pallīgīti* at least implies something about the how and why of the music.

Bengali musicologists and folklorists, when writing in English about their music, often use the English classificatory terms "classical," "folk," and "tribal" rather than transliterate the Bengali terms. The writer Sudhibhusan Bhattacarya has acknowledged that far too many diverse types of music are ordinarily lumped together under the heading folk music and has attempted to refine the term by giving it a pair of subcategories.

> Indian music may be classified into two types, cultivated and uncultivated. The former type is chiefly represented by the Indian Classical music both of the northern and the southern varieties. A number of books analysing and describing this music for the purposes of teaching it, have been written from ancient times. The professional musicians of India are devoted mostly to this type of music, the standard of which is very high, and far above the reach of the uninitiated. It is usually associated with the high cultures of India. These high cultures have created also a new variety of folk-music which is much more refined and well-defined than the traditional folk-music current among the unsophisticated rural people of this subcontinent. The kirtan of east India, bhajan of north India, Tagore music of Bengal, all of which are mainly based on the Indian classical music, are a few examples of this variety of folk-music. It has found a place in the University curricula for music, and also in the Radio programmes and the commercial Gramophone discs. The variety of folk-music should also be counted as "cultivated." (1968, 15)

It is necessary to point out here that *kīrton* and *bhajan* are names for a wide variety of musical styles ranging from the simple amateur performance of anonymous village groups to the elaborate solo performances of such specialists as the *kīrtonīyā* (performer of *kīrton*)Rathin Ghosh of Calcutta or the *kheyālīyā* Bhimsen Joshi of Maharashtra, who is known throughout India for his *bhajan* performance. Bhattacarya refers to these latter types of *bhajan* and *kirton* in his references to "cultivated" folk music. The inclusion of Tagore music in this cultivated folk music category and the facts that these types are included in the university curricula and find a place on radio programs and gramophone discs clearly put them in a category which is very "cultivated" indeed. That Bhattacarya credits the "high cultures" with having created these new varieties also puts them in a category of folk music different from that in which he would place Baul-*gān*: "Pure folk-music, i.e., the traditional uncultivated folk-music, is predominantly representative of the rural people and rural cultures. Tagore music of Bengal occupies an intermediate position between folk-music and classical music, for it has the openness of the former and the urbanity of the latter." Therefore, he names Tagore music as an example of cultivated folk music.

Sukumar Ray, in his *Music of Eastern India,* has paid special attention to the development and nature of urban popular music in Bengal and has tried to establish as worthy of serious attention the new types of music which have arisen since the 1930s. He chooses 1930 as significant in the history of popular music in Bengal because the circulation of gramophone records began to increase then as did the number of radio broadcasts of popular music and film music; as a result, the music heard through these media had an influence in shaping the musical tastes of urban audiences. He notes in particular how the new media reshaped traditional music types:

> We would therefore focus our attention on the songs, which were composed in the past, but have been newly produced after the 1930's, e.g. selections from old form of *Kirtan, Syamasangeet* as, nowadays, sung in Radio and produced in commercial recordings. . . . New productions of old folk music have been accepted as a Form by sophisticated people in the country and are presented abroad before international audience also. It is not that the original colour of these items are going to be lost now, but some new features have been added to these during the period. (1973, 3)

Among these "new productions of old folk music," Ray gives prominence to *bhāṭiyāli, bhāōyāiyā,* and Baul:

> *Bhatiali, Bhaoaia,* and *Baul* are classed as the standard music of the popular type, these items being cultivated widely now in some institutions also. Songs have been collected and popularized. Notations are also made available and the tunes have infiltrated in common music, film-tunes, lyrical songs of poet-composers. *Bhatiali* is a standard folk music of urban type popularized greatly within a period of half-a-century. Its subject matter with specific themes, based on definite form of tune and mode of performance, is familiar to a section of composers and artistes of urban areas. As a result they have begun to compose songs in a like manner and they name these as *Bhatiali.* (1973, 110)

Ray is the first writer to make the pointed distinction between traditional performance of folk music and popular performance involving musical arrangements, notation, studio broadcast, and recording. Other writers do mention such popularized performances, but only to criticize them as corruptions unworthy of notice; Ray considers them a new phenomenon requiring the same attention from musicologists that the more traditional music has received: "On the whole, the principal features of the music of the period starting from the third decade of this century in Bengal have since reached a phase which needs an appropriate unconventional approach for an objective assessment" (1973, 3). Ray's comments on the popular versions of folk song are particularly pertinent with reference to *bhāṭiyāli* and *bhāōyāiyā.* As popular entertainment, they have been taken up by professional singers, composers, and arrangers; though this is also true of Baul-*gān,* the Bauls themselves are everywhere the chief performers and interpreters of their own musical heritage. In the case of *bhāṭiyāli* and *bhāōyāiyā,* the only versions most people are likely to hear are those performed by professional singers, while even the most inveterate city dwellers may, with a little effort, hear a live performance of Baul-*gān* by an untrained carrier of the tradition. The professional performances of Baul-*gān* predominate on radio and records and before international, as well as Indian, paying audiences. The Bauls, themselves, have gained some footholds in these less traditional contexts for Baul-*gān* performance; this circumstance, no doubt, facilitates the change of their folk heritage, but perhaps it may also help to retain the tradition among the Bauls by giving them a new source of patronage.

To conclude this consideration of the various ways in which songs are classified by Bengali writers on music and of how Baul-*gān* fits into those song classes, I will mention Sureś Cakrobortī's bipartite classification of folk song (1962, 675). This writer has pointed out that there are essentially two kinds of folk song—that sung in groups in the house or courtyard and that sung solo in the open, in the fields, and on the rivers. The distinction between the groups is categorical and does not cover all the possibilities one can think of, but it strikes at something significant in the folk music of India, which Cakrobortī may have been the first to state as a general principle. In contrast to Cakrobortī, Sukumar Ray prefers a tripartite division of folk music. "Folksongs may be firstly classed into three sections: (1) emotional and secular, (2) religious and sectarian, e.g., Baul, Vaisnava songs and Sakta songs, (3) occasional, ceremonial and occupational, viz. festival songs—parvageeta, marriage songs, etc" (1973, 103).

The American anthropologist Edward O. Henry (1976a, 49–66, 1976b) has proposed classifying the music he finds to be common in North Indian villages into two categories similar to those of Cakrobortī. Henry's categories, the "participatory" and the "non-participatory," are best represented, respectively, by the general participation of all present in group *bhajan,* and the exclusive performance of a professional *kāōyāli* party performing popular songs for a village audience. Henry's first category, participatory music, and Cakrobortī's, group songs of the home and courtyard, are pretty much coextensive. Both have in mind the familial, communal kinds of music used for devotions and occasional ceremonies and festivities. The other pair of categories, non-participatory music and solo song in the open, do not overlap so well. Cakrobortī has in mind especially the music typified by the three B's, *bhāṭiỳāli, bhāōỳāiỳā,* and Baul, whose ideal performances include only eavesdropping audiences. When other Bauls join in a performance by accompanying and intermittently responding to the soloist, the performance verges upon Henry's non-participatory category—the participation is limited since there is a distinct audience of non-participants, just as there would be in the *kāỳōāli* performance.

Finally, I would suggest the classification term "professional folk music" for Baul-*gān* and some other types of Indian music sharing some of its characteristics.[15] Baul-*gān*'s claim to the term "folk music" is based on the fact that it is ubiquitous in rural Bengal and is understood and appreciated by all; it is orally transmitted, although texts may be collected in notebooks, akin to the "ballet" books of Anglo-American ballad singers; it is performed by naive musicians—although a boy may be apprenticed to a Baul and learn his songs, instruction is unsystematic; it is not commercial music—although Bauls may be paid for performing, the pay is not contractual and is, at least abstractly, alms rather than a fee. But because the songs are elaborate enough and the texts abundant enough to require devotion and talent for learning them, if not training and skill, because many Bauls earn their living singing, and because their songs, if not their property, are at least recognized by all as the particular repertoire of an exclusive group, the qualification "professional" may precede the term "folk music" in reference to Baul-*gān*. The qualification is equally appropriate for other types of commonly appreciated folk music that form the special repertoire of a particular caste, sect, or other group. The drumming the Dom caste provides for village festivals and sacrifices would be specialist folk music as would the singing of the *gōpi-cạ̄d* ballads by the Yugi caste. The Bauls, the Doms, and the Yugis all have primary identities derived from something other than musical performance—the Bauls are a religious sect, the Doms a caste which burns the dead and works leather, the Yugis weavers. They all are thought of as groups that also specialize in a particular kind of music, and this differentiates them from professional musicians, whose first identity for the auditor is most apt to be "musician," and from ordinary villagers who are not responsible for providing a specific kind of music for the rest of the community.

CHAPTER FOUR

Backgrounds of Some Singers

To give the reader an idea of the way present-day Bauls relate to the tradition they carry and of the milieu in which they exist, those several Bauls with whom I had the most contact in my two-and-a-half year stay in West Bengal are described in this chapter. Besides descriptions of living situations, the Bauls' explanations of religious concepts, their thoughts about music, their self-image, and their accounts of familial or spiritual lineages are also covered. Particularly with Lakṣm̃aṇ Dās, the conversations in which this information was elicited were based on friendly intimacy, and our awareness of "doing research" was often in the background; with other Bauls, though conversation was friendly, I was more evidently a curious foreigner.

While the information given in this chapter concerns the few individuals I knew well, my observation of and encounters with other Bauls suggest that the data are representative of the Bauls as a group. Those other Bauls, though not mentioned in this chapter, the reader may find named elsewhere in the book, but I wish to list them here as well by way of acknowledging their help in my attempts to understand the sect and its musical activities: Bimal Dās, Dinobandhu Dās, Gaṅgādhar Dās, Gōṣtho Gōpāl Dās, Kṛiṣnā Dāsī, Lakṣm̃aṇ Dās (of Burdwan), Monorām Dās, Nārāyoṇ Candro Odhikāri, Nonigōpāl Dās, Sadānando Dās, Śambhu Dās, Śaśāṅko Dās Mohant, Subol Candro Dās, Śyām Sundor Dās, Tinkoṛi Dās, Biśvonāth Rāy.

The Bauls who figure in the following account, except Sonāton Dās Ṭhākur, visited me in Calcutta and received me in their own homes. Sonāton was interviewed at length in the home of a professor of Viswabharati University during *Pouṣ melā* in January 1971. Most of the other Bauls mentioned hereafter divide into two families: a) Ýotin (sometimes Ýotendronāth) Dās and his wife, Prem, and b) the family of the late Nabonī Dās Khēpā Baul, namely, his wife, Brajobālā, and their grown children, Rādhārānī, Pūrṇo Candro, Lakṣm̃aṇ, and Cakrodhar.

THE FAMILY OF NABONĪ DĀS KHĒPĀ BAUL

Pūrṇo Candro Dās is the most widely known Baul today. Since 1969, when he led a troupe of Bauls on a tour of the United States as the intermission feature with the Paul Butterfield Blues Band and recorded his first American disc for Elektra (*The Bauls of Bengal,* EKS-7325), Pūrṇo has continued to bring Baul music to an ever wider audience both in India and abroad. In 1969 his home was in a moderately well-to-do area of South Calcutta, where he lived with his second wife, Mañju, their three young sons, and a servant. His previous address had also been in the city, but his change of residence had brought him into a more prosperous neighborhood. Recently, he has built a new home in yet a better area of South Calcutta. In his success, Pūrṇo Dās is atypical of the Bauls, but not in his upbringing or in his attitudes about the significance of being a Baul.

Like Pūrṇo, Pūrṇo's father, the late Nabonī Dās Khēpā,[16] was the best-known Baul of his generation. From his early childhood, Pūrṇo traveled widely with his father, learning his songs and performing with him. At age seven, as Pūrṇo records in the short autobiograpical sketch he includes in his publicity booklet, he won a gold medal for his singing at a music conference in Jaipur, then a princely state in the west of India (Das Baul n.d., 27–30).[17] Even as a child, then, Pūrṇo had a different view from that of other Bauls of what recognition could be gained from singing Baul songs; a later experience, making the sound track for a film with his father, taught him that recognition for his talent might not always be so readily granted since he and his father were omitted from the film credits. As Pūrṇo states it, "Similar shocks were not rare in the life that followed. . . . I have been observing that people belonging to the elite not unoften tape recorded my songs and later exploited it without acknowledging my credit" (n.d., 29).

Although appreciation of Pūrṇo's performances by members of literary and cultural organizations was not uncommon in his youth, he had a harder time competing with popular music artists for recognition by the general public.

> I remember on one occasion when I was invited to participate in an Engineering College in Calcutta and as my programme was announced immediately after popular modern singers left the dias and I took up my songs, maddening claps practically forces me to abandon. But there was a healthy trend too that was taking shape side by side due to programmes which organisations such as Banga Sanskriti Sammelan, Juba Utsava and similar progressive cultural associations organised every year. In fact, Baul started becoming a "must" in musical soirees during the late fifties and became quite popular from early sixties. By popularity, I mean in metropolitan cities, of course. (n.d., 28–29)

Having established his popularity with urban audiences, Pūrṇo has never looked back to the rural audiences for whom most of his brethren perform. He now performs almost exclusively in musical "functions"; this is the term used in India for concerts by professionals whose payment is raised by general ticket sales, club dues, or local subscriptions. He has made several foreign tours with his own group of performers and with other "folk" artistes, and, in addition to these public appearances, he occasionally records songs for broadcast on All India Radio Calcutta and for release on commercial discs of Hindustan Records in India and Nonesuch in the United States.

Because recordings of his performances may have been exploited by others, Pūrṇo has learned to be wary, and a lawyer or agent is apt to be consulted now before any agreement is made regarding performances, recordings, or even teaching. The fee agreed upon through a mediator for my own instruction in Baul songs, for example, was 100 rupees per month for three or four lessons. This fee was double that asked by a highly respected sarod player and teacher for private one-hour lessons once a week. During the time of my instruction, Pūrṇo Dās did not have many pupils because his repertoire was not varied like that of a professional instructor of popular folk music, and he could not acquaint a student with the wide variety of folk song styles needed for a successful career.

In order to make his programs more varied, he now performs with his present wife, Mañju, who sings other types of folk songs and traditional popular songs. Having had some general education, as well as training as a singer, she has brought Pūrṇo a degree of social status consonant with his having abandoned the life of a village mendicant to take up residence in an urban middle-class neighborhood. His first wife, obtained in a marriage arranged by his father, remains at her father's home in the countryside of Murshidabad District. The term "wife" is used here as a convenience; in fact, as Pūrṇo explained it, Bauls do not marry but take one another as partners in *sādhonā*, the pursuit of spiritual perfection.

Although Pūrṇo Dās has become widely popular as an entertainer, he is criticized both by his peers and by some of the urban elite for his new lifestyle and for having transplanted Baul-*gān* to new performance contexts. The Bauls agree with the assessment of Monōhor Khēpā, a popular Bengali holy man, who says that though Pūrṇo may sing Baul songs, he is not, therefore, a Baul; Monōhor believes Pūrṇo has forsaken the spiritual values of the sect for material well-being. Among the urban elite, Pūrṇo is criticized for no longer singing like a Baul; they say his performances are too polished and have lost the crude, rustic style of the village.

Pūrṇo is aware of the criticisms but has not let them undermine his resolve to become a well-paid and well-respected singer. Having learned that affectionate condescension and charity are not substitutes for social position and financial security, Pūrṇo proposes an objective for all Bauls: "No more begging!" Although his lifestyle has changed and he has left the intimacy of the Baul community without finding a substitute, Pūrṇo does not admit to having abandoned the Baul values, beliefs, and practices learned from Nabonī Dās and which he now teaches to his own sons. He is a jealous guardian of the songs that are part of the heritage of the Baul sect and insists that any description or exegesis of the doctrine contained in their texts is the privilege or obligation only of the Bauls themselves. Just as the songs have been exploited by those who have nothing to do with the sect, so, in Pūrṇo's opinion, has much information about doctrinal matters been made public by those who have no right to that information and who do not understand it. The question, whether a Baul can remain loyal to his heritage while seeking to attract and satisfy the same audiences as the popular singer, the folklorist, religious historian, or popular essayist, does not occur to Pūrṇo. As he sees it, others are acquiring money and position by the use of what is rightfully Baul property, and this he feels to be an intolerable wrong.

While he intends that his sons should receive the traditions of their grandfather, Pūrṇo also intends that they should be well educated, so he sends them to a good, expensive private school. His prosperity was sufficient in 1970 to enable him to undertake building a new private residence in Calcutta and to keep his private car and chauffeur for his personal use rather than make them available to the public as taxi and driver.

Pūrṇo Dās's less prosperous brother, Lakṣm̃aṇ, was in his early to middle thirties in 1970, a few years younger than Pūrṇo. Unlike his brother, whom he had accompanied on an American tour, Lakṣm̃aṇ is not fond of the city and his visits to it are for extraordinary reasons such as to meet an American friend, to make a recording for the radio, or to perform at the home of some admirer of Baul-*gān*. Most of the time he spends traveling around Bengal visiting friends and holy men, singing here and there, or in residence with his wife and children at his mother's house in a small village near the city of Sainthia. At other times, he and his family live with his elder sister at a home belonging to Pūrṇo just outside the city Suri.

In 1970, Lakṣm̃aṇ had a daughter about eight and a son about five. Since his father had told him to have two sons, he has tried adding another to his family, but has succeeded in getting only two more daughters. Pūrṇo, too, claims to have regulated his family according to the instructions of his father. Both sons idolize their father, but Pūrṇo, the elder, seems to have been the father's favorite, because he most often accompanied Nabonī on his wanderings while Lakṣm̃aṇ stayed at home. Yet it is for Lakṣm̃aṇ that Nabonī is an ever present ideal; the intimacy with his father which La-

Fig. 8. Lakṣm̃aṇ at his father's *somādhi.*

kṣm̃aṇ missed as a child, he seems to strive for now by trying to imitate Nabonī's way of life and by venerating the site of his grave (fig. 8).

Like Pūrṇo, Lakṣm̃aṇ has fond memories of America and is proud of having been asked to go there. On his mailbox, in the manner of Indian gentlemen of the last century who had been to the U.K. to study, he has written: "Lakṣm̃aṇ Dās Baul, U.S. Returned." Lakṣm̃aṇ's impressions of America can be summed up in his statement that the gods and great beings who once inhabited India have been reincarnated in America. Fervently hoping to see America again some day, he is content in the meantime with having seen it once and with continuing now to wander about the villages and towns of Bengal.

The Bauls who went to America in 1967 must have heard a good deal of American pop music, of a certain kind at least, as they were on tour with the Paul Butterfield Blues Band and visited Bob Dylan and the Band at Big Pink, but it would seem not to have made a lasting impression. By chance, Lakṣm̃aṇ once heard a recording of Janis Joplin when he was visiting an American friend at her hotel in Calcutta. Listening with surprising intentness, he occasionally murmured a word of approval. After the song was over, he inquired about the meaning of the text, and when he learned that the text concerned a woman's desire that her lover buy her a Mercedes Benz automobile, he asked, slightly puzzled, if there were not mention of yoga or some other spiritual-physical discipline; he was incredulous to think that such emotional energy as Joplin put into her performance could be expended on such a trivial matter as the desire for a car.

For Lakṣm̃aṇ and Pūrṇo, singing is a *sādhonā;* Pūrṇo likened it to yoga, for it requires control of the breath. The affect Lakṣm̃aṇ felt in Joplin's song he could conceive of as stemming only from some deep emotional and spiritual longing since that was the familiar reason given for the great energy behind many Baul performances.

Since his youth, Lakṣm̃aṇ had been engaged in spiritual experimentation. He was a Baul by virtue of his birth and training from his father, but he sought other spiritual paths as well. He had, for example, recently been given a Shiva lingam, a commonly worshipped phallic idol, by a sadhu who was instructing him in its worship. As a youth, Lakṣm̃aṇ had wandered in the Himalayan foothills, the traditional home for sadhus of exceptional power and discipline. He was asked to join a pair of them at their cave retreat and did so for a while until he found their routine of continually meditating while standing on their heads and their diet of nothing but a particular kind of leaf to be too arduous for him. At another time he and his brother received *dikṣā* (ceremonial bestowal of a mantra) from a widely renowned Bengali tantrik sadhu who was reported to raise the dead. Lakṣm̃aṇ considered becoming his disciple but finally concurred with his father's opinion that total asceticism was an unnatural path to enlightenment compared to the more human Baul way.

With Lakṣm̃aṇ, one is able to discuss some elements of the Bauls' beliefs and to learn that sexual congress is considered necessary, but that it should not result in ejaculation. Semen is venerated because, as Pūrṇo had explained, Krishna resides in it; to destroy it heedlessly is to destroy one's own capacity for the enjoyment of divine bliss. Ejaculation is excusable in order to sire children, as Nabonī had directed both his sons to do, but otherwise, the retention of semen is necessary to achieve the perfected state.

Lakṣm̃aṇ often said that he no longer needed a woman, that he himself combined male and female and could perform the Baul *sādhonā* interiorly. To those who had not received instruction in Baul matters, he explained that masturbation or sleeping with a woman is *mohāpāp* (great sin) when it produces ejaculation, and in order to allay sexual desire he prescribed chewing the leaves of an herb until a viscous, milky white fluid was produced.

Lakṣm̃aṇ's claim that he had passed the stage of needing a female partner in *sādhonā* recalls one of the songs he sings, *sājo prokṛiti,* in which the mind is exhorted to take up the role of a partner in *sādhonā*. The reason a partner is needed at all is that semen must be activated, not merely retained, in order to force it along the reverse path up the spinal column from the mystical plexus near the genitals, to which it has descended, to the plexus in the brain where it can unite with its female counterpart—in the words of the song:[18]

Turn up-side down
    that which is in the six-petals.
If that goes to the two petals,
    the light will burst forth.

In order to get into a good frame of mind for singing such songs, Lakṣm̃aṇ often smokes a mixture of tobacco and *gą̄jā,* (marijuana), not that smoking is restricted to that purpose only. *Gą̄jā,* as the smokable form of marijuana is called, is one of the most widely used intoxicants in India. Although it is theoretically controlled by sale in government shops, it is easily available elsewhere and is used by many village men. It has distinct class connotations, however, and normally is used only by such lower classes as peasants or rickshaw pullers; holy men may use it, too, as an aid in meditation, but they are outside society. Only in its ingestible form, as *bhāṅ,* is marijuana considered an acceptable drug among the upper classes. Brahman households might be considered remiss in hospitality, or too modernized, if *bhāṅ* were not offered guests at the time of the Spring Saturnalia, Holi, and some men may enjoy a daily glass as routinely as it is offered in worship of the household image of Krishna.

For those who use it, *bhāṅ* is most acceptable when prepared at home in a milkshake, less so when incorporated into ices and cookies peddled by vendors. Its respectability in comparison to *gą̄jā* may have to do with the fact that a *bhāṅ* milkshake is generally so mild as to make little subjective or objective change in the person who consumes it, although it can be made overwhelmingly potent.

Like many of his friends, Baul and non-Baul, Lakṣm̃aṇ enjoyed his tobacco and *gą̄jā*, but his special fondness for it is one of the things which strains his relationship with his brother. Pūrṇo does not smoke *gą̄jā,* and he and his wife feel that Lakṣm̃aṇ's incapacity to make a surer life for himself and his lack of ambition are linked to his attachment to smoke. They find it vexing that he should continue a habit that will only bring him the condescension rather than the respect of his social betters.

Although Pūrṇo does not smoke *gą̄jā*, he does drink occasionally, and displays with pleasure the cognac he brought back with him from a foreign tour. In the traditional scheme of things, alcohol is even less acceptable than *gą̄jā*; country rice or palm liquor is drunk only by the lowest classes and by tribals (and by Calcutta's intellectual Bohemians), usually with the aim of getting drunk. It may also be used by holy men and offered to deities, including Krishna himself. "Social drinking" has an ambiguous place in the life of urban middle classes, being both scandalous and chic. Even those who disapprove of such drinking would not do so with the same condescension as they show in disapproval of *gāj̣ā* smoking, since the former is associated with position, education, and wealth, while the latter is identified with their lack. Pūrṇo is a sober man and is not much concerned with *gāj̣ā* or drink, but he is aware of their social connotations. Though he does not necessarily commend society's judgment, he recognizes that *gāj̣ā* is one of the things that have kept Bauls beggars, while good alcohol is one of the things that facilitate intercourse with the "better" classes.

Pūrṇo is the eldest male sibling in his family, but his sister Rādhārānī is elder to him. In 1970 she lived in the family home outside Suri city, keeping house for their younger brother, Cakrodhar, whose first wife had recently died in childbirth. At that time, Cakrodhar did not appear to follow Baul ways, at least in externals. He did not sing, he cut his hair, and he wore a bush shirt and trousers, the uniform of the modern Bengali young man.[19]

Rādhārānī is married to Gōpāl Dās Baul, who spends much of his time traveling about like Lakṣm̃aṇ. Perhaps Rādhārānī would accompany him if she were not caring for her infant nephew. She and Gōpāl have no children of their own, because, as Lakṣm̃aṇ explains, they are yogis, that is, they are adept at Baul *sādhonā*, an effective means of birth control.

Rādhārānī likes to sing and does so well; nevertheless, she does not get as much opportunity to sing as she would like because most of the attention is given to the men. Her husband, who appears to be in his mid-to-late fifties, ten to fifteen years older than Rādhārānī, says he has given up singing because his voice is no longer good.

The house where Rādhārānī, Cakrodhar, his infant son, and new wife reside is built upon a dirt road leading to Suri and is just a few yards from a large tank, an artificial pond of the type that dot the Bengal landscape. Having a well and an outhouse within the compound, the house, not so substantial as some of its neighbors, nevertheless aspires to the quality of brick and tin rather than mud and thatch. Because the house is relatively close to the city, shops of various sorts and a doctor's surgery are not far off. The neighbors to one side are a Brahman family, the son of which was studying mathematics at Jadavpur University in Calcutta, but on the other side of the pond lives a community of very low status, a fact revealed by their habit of dredging the pond for edible snails.

Lakṣm̃aṇ, with his wife and children, generally resides at a home which has been in his mother's family for several generations and which now belongs to her. It is part of a small village composed mainly of farming families removed some distance from the town Mallarpur near the large city Sainthia. The hut is a typical village bungalow, as are the others in its vicinity, and does not have the more up-to-date pretension of the Suri house where Rādhārānī lives. It is of wattle and daub construction with a thatched roof that extends out over a platform of daub in front of the house, a kind of porch called *dāōȳā* where one may sit to converse or to eat from leaves placed on the platform. This type of dwelling most commonly has a single room entered via a door at the middle of the *dāōȳā*, but this house also has a cramped second floor under the thatch with a separate entrance and stair at one end of the *dāōȳā*.

A wattle and daub and partly brick wall encloses the compound in the usual way and borders the footpath that passes in front of the house. Two parts of the front wall, flanking the entrance from the footpath, are incorporated as sides into two smaller huts, one used as a cow shed, the other as a kitchen; between them runs another thatch covered *dāōȳā* onto which one steps when entering the door from the footpath.

Extending from the interior wall of the cow shed toward one side of the house is an area of ground which distinguishes this dwelling from those of the other villagers, for it is a cemetery (fig. 9). Although the usual custom of secular Hindus is to burn the dead, the Bauls and some other classes of Vaisnavas, bury theirs. The Bauls are considered not to die but to pass into eternal *somādhi*, a state of perpetual removal from phenomenal existence and the cycle of rebirth. They are buried in the *padmāsana*, the cross-legged position for meditation, and in this state are thought to have achieved permanent reunification with the ground of being.

Because so many of the family have been buried within its compound, the dwelling is not called simply a *bāṛi*, house, but an *āśrom*, a religious retreat. It could also be called an *ākhṛā*, particularly as the term is defined in Melville Kennedy's book on the followers of Caitanya.

> Sometimes it is an institution capable of sheltering a score or two, but more often it is the simple village hut, where one or two vairagis (Vaisnava mendicants) make their abode, joined now and then by a few of their fellow mendicants. Strictly speaking an akhra is to be looked for in connection with a temple or shrine; but as commonly used in Bengal the term includes any place where a few vairagis congregate, whether with a temple or not. (1925, 166)

Presumably, Brajobālā Dāsī, Lakṣmaṇ's mother, will also be buried within the walls of her family *āśrom* one day. It was to attend the death anniversary celebration for one of her brothers that I first visited the *āśrom;* Brajobālā had had two brothers, Ẏoti and Patol, and a sister Nitȳo. Their father, Hori Dās, carried the title *mohant,* usually given the head of an *ākhṛā*.

Brajobālā was married to the most famous Baul of his time, Nabonī Dās Khēpā. His family had at one time been well-to-do and had settled in a

Fig. 9. *Somādhis* in *aśrom* of Brajobālā Dāsī.

village near Visnupur in Birbhum District, but in the generation of his father, Okrur, the family fortunes dwindled and Okrur, with his son Nabonī, took to a life of wandering minstrelsy (Cākī n.d., 14). This way of life Nabonī continued to pursue with his own son Pūrṇo.

During Tagore's lifetime, and long after, Nabonī Dās was the favorite of such literary men as Tarasankar Bandyopadhyay and Annada Sankar Ray as well as of such cultivated folk and art song singers as Santidev Ghosh; it was through continual contact with such persons and with eminent foreigners like Allen Ginsberg that Pūrṇo, no doubt, learned the value placed upon Baul song by the men who made judgments about what was significant in Bengali culture.

Nabonī Dās's popularity naturally aided in establishing the lasting popularity of some of the songs he frequently sang. Perhaps most well known of any Baul song today is his own *gōlemāle, gōlemāle pirit koro nā,* which Pūrṇo and Lakṣm̐aṇ continue to sing. They also regularly sing *tōrā āi ke ẏābi re,* a song by Nabonī's father Okrur, who used the name Ananto. Just as well, if not better known, is a song by Nabonī's elder brother Rasorāj—*ẏēmon beni temni rabe.*[20]

Lakṣm̐aṇ shares the respect for Nabonī which men of position have shown, but his admiration is for his father's spiritual prowess as well as for his capacity as a singer. Lakṣm̐aṇ recalls with pride and perhaps some envy that his father would sometimes levitate while in meditation or, seeking absolute solitude for meditation, would resort to lying at the bottom of a pond and remaining in *somādhi* for great lengths of time. Just as significant and indicative of his exceptional powers was Nabonī's capacity for intoxication—ordinary tobacco and *gā̧jā* were too innocuous for him, so he would mix them with ingredients of greater potency, such as jimson weed soaked in cobra venom.

The forcefulness of Nabonī's personality has been captured in some arresting photographs accompanying Deben Bhattacarya's *Mirror of the Sky,* an English translation of Baul poems, including some that Bhattacarya recorded from Nabonī. According to Nabonī's wife, Brajobālā, it was Nabonī's father who helped make the *khamak* as popular as it is today; Nabonī is shown playing this instrument in plate 3 of *The Mirror of the Sky*. Today, Pūrṇo and Lakṣm̃aṇ display an unmatched virtuosity and sensitivity in their use of the instrument to accompany themselves.

According to Pūrṇo and Lakṣm̃aṇ, their family has been Baul for seven generations, but it is difficult to get more specific information from them about those generations than what has been recorded here and confirmed by their mother. Whatever the number of generations, the family feels securely rooted in the Birbhum district of West Bengal, which is considered by Bengalis to be the particular area of Baul culture.

Ýotin Dās Baul

Bauls come from other districts as well, however, and the most famous of them all, Lālon Phokir (1774–1890), came from an area now within Bangladesh. Many whose original homes are in Bangladesh became refugees when Bengal was divided at the time of independence in 1947, and they now reside in West Bengal. One such, who has neither the international nor local repute of Pūrṇo and Lakṣm̃aṇ, is Ýotin Dās Baul, whose family hails from the Dinajpur area of North Bengal; he now resides in a village near Murshidabad where the court of the Nawab was maintained by the British, but he spends much of his time on the road, performing at various village festivals. Because his manner of performance is more sedate and his singing more mellifluous than that of most Bauls, Calcutta residents who patronize Baul singers find him lacking in color, so he is not as frequently invited to the city as he deserves on the basis of his repertoire and musical competence.

Ýotin lives with his wife, mother-in-law, and two children in a one-room wattle and daub hut within a fenced compound. There is a separate kitchen hut but no cow shed (fig. 10). Among Ýotin's neighbors is another Baul, and a couple of steps down the footpath lives a potter whose entire

Fig. 10. Porch (*dāōyā*) of Ýotin Dās Baul's house.

family participate in the cottage industry of manufacturing the unglazed, disposable teacups used at nearly every tea stall in India. The potter family, which is of low caste, is situated quite near the large pond that provides water for the small community on its banks.

A moderately trafficked dirt road is separated from the community by a small field on which is housed the large cart of Jagannāth (Juggernaut) belonging to the Auliya monastery next door. The monks reside in an impressive stucco building facing the road; they run a girls' school on the premises and cultivate the mango and jackfruit grove that is part of the property granted them, according to Ýotin, by Sirajuddaula, the Nawab of Black-Hole infamy.

In response to questioning, Ýotin said that this group of celibate monks were Auls, one of the four groups into which the Baul sect is divided by some writers who rarely say more about the matter. The word *āul* may have a Sanskritic etymology similar to that of Baul; Shashibhusan Das Gupta (1969, 161), however, points out that the "Arabic word awliya (plural of *wali,* a word originally meaning 'near,' which is used for 'friend' or 'devotee') refers to a class of perfect men." Auliya is the form used by the monks in Murshidabad who, though Hindu, claim spiritual descent from a

Muslim saint. They have nothing to do with the Aul-Sahaj Kartabhaja sect, and Ýotin's mention of them as somehow related to the Bauls was probably nothing more than a courtesy recognizing their common interest in spiritual matters and their similar sounding names.

As did Pūrṇo Dās, Ýotin claimed to be descended from several generations of Bauls. In the sketchy genealogy he is able to provide (see below), it is noteworthy that Ýotin includes Cīrūp (Śrīrūp?) the husband of his paternal grandmother's sister. The probable reason is that he had earned the title Khēpā, which singles him out as having achieved distinction among Bauls; his guru, Balāi, whom Ýotin also mentioned, carried the same title. Both men were well educated; Ýotin says that Cīrūp had earned a master's degree and that Balāi had two master's degrees.

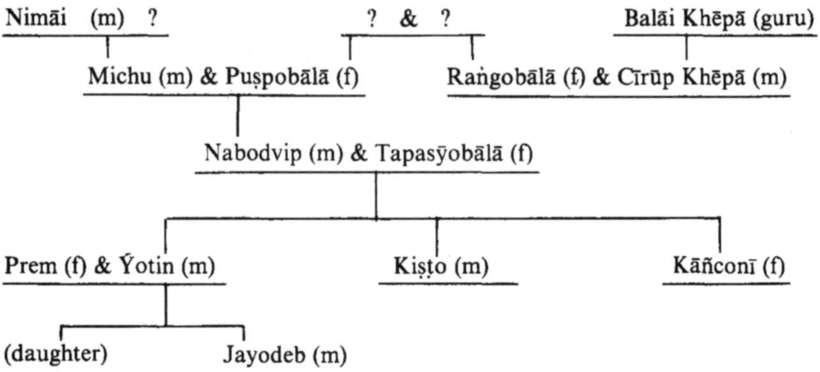

Balāi's reputation is also enhanced by the fact that he had seven *prokṛitis* (female partner in sexual ritual) without any biological descendants, a testimony to the exceptional strength of his virtue. Such was his repute that even persons in high office, such as the magistrate of Pabna District where Balāi lived, sought to become his disciples.

Ýotin's own *śikṣā*-guru (the guru who gives practical instruction as opposed to the *dikṣā*-guru who gives a mantra), Rādhā Śýām Dās of Dinajpur, was dead by 1970, but his wife, Lolitābālā Dās Boiṣṇobī, was still alive. The title Boiṣṇobī, which ordinarily means simply a female worshipper of Vishnu, when attached to a woman's name, according to Ýotin, indicates that she has acquired the *śokti* of Vishnu; that is, in her dwells the unadulterated active female principle. She is the equivalent of the Khēpā Baul. The title Khēpā, Ýotin explained, is conferred—by whom he did not say—on worthy Bauls only after they have sung in Brindabon (*vṛindāvan*), the traditional site of Krishna's sport with Radha and the milkmaids in western

Uttar Pradesh and one of the towns associated with the Bengali Vaisnava revival initiated by Caitanya in the sixteenth century. Both Rādhā Śȳām and Lolitābālā wrote songs, and Ŷotin includes some of them in his repertoire.

From Rādhā Śȳām, Ŷotin learned a modicum of musical terminology, which was more than most Bauls gave evidence of knowing. This terminology appears to be derived from *kīrton,* but Ŷotin's use of it, particularly of *rāg* names, was very inconsistent. Part of his concept of *rāg* structure seemed to involve a theory of transposition and/or modulation. He illustrated this on the *dōtārā*, referring to *sthāyi* and *asthāyi sur* (fixed and movable pitch?) as tonics. The explanation was not clear, however, even to a musically educated Bengali whom I had asked to interpret.

Besides music, of course, Ŷotin also learned elements of Baul *sādhonā* from Rādhā Śȳām and Lolitābālā. For him one of the chief benefits of the *sādhonā*, and signs of its worth, was that he felt he had preserved his youth; he pointed out the superiority of his physical condition in contrast to that of one of his neighbors, a prematurely aged man with many children. Unlike Pūrṇo and Lakṣm̃aṇ, Ŷotin had received no instruction about the number of children he should have from either his father or his guru. His two children, toward whom he showed a usual fatherly affection, he referred to, somewhat ruefully, in English as the result of "accidents."

In truth, Ŷotin's condition was not remarkable, but his friend Nolinī Ghōṣ, who had taken up Baul ways in later youth, was a beautifully fit senescent man with youthful manners and was justifiably proud of his physical condition. He pointed out that his only child had been fathered before he met his guru, and that he had had no children since. He commended me and a friend for having remained bachelors, but warned that we should marry before the age of forty if we were to benefit at all from sex; he took it for granted that we would not be so foolish as to ignore the advice of the Bauls we knew. Not to marry at all would be equally foolish—like the Auliya monks next door who were "afraid of women." The Bauls had nothing to fear from contact with women, he explained, and could lead a life of natural enjoyment while benefiting, rather than impairing, their physical and spiritual health.

Not all women are of equal virtue, however, according to Ŷotin, who said some are *sādhāroṇī,* in whom there is little *śokti* (divine energy), some are *sāmoñjosȳo,* in whom there is a greater amount, and others are *somārtho*, in whom there is great power. These terms, Upendronāth Bhaṭṭācārȳo (1364 [1957–58], 107) has pointed out, are derived from Gauriya Vaisnava theology and describe the three types of love for God manifested by different women in the life of Krishna. The *somārtho* is personified in the Gopis whose sole concern was satisfying Krishna with no thought of self; the three types of women represent stages in the progress from *kām,* lust, to *prem,* love. The three terms, as the Bauls use them, also apply to the three days of the menstrual cycle during which *sādhonā* takes place. During this time, Ýotin explained, the *adhor mānuṣ,* which he described as *nitȳo bostu* (eternal substance), appears in menses "like a flower without a stem floating on water." The menstrual cycle demonstrates the presence of excess *śokti* in women from which men can benefit by absorbing it through their penes.[21] Ýotin's song *bṛindabone tin rañer tin phul phōṭe* (In Vrindavan, three flowers of three colors bloom) concerns the appearance of the *nitȳo bostu* during three days of menstruation.

Sonāton Dās Ṭhākur Baul

Like Ýotin, Sonāton Dās Ṭhākur Baul[22] was born in East Bengal, in Khulna, which lies in the heart of ancient Vanga; but unlike Ýotin, who is rather introverted in performance, Sonāton displays the panache which is sure to gain a Baul a good reputation as a performer. His family, in which Sonāton believes the Baul tradition is at least four or five generations old, left Khulna when he was a child. Despite being from Khulna, however, Sonāton now refers to his *bāṛi* (ancestral home) as being in Hooghly, just north of Calcutta on the river of the same name, and he resides in an *āśrom* in Bankura, the neighboring district to Birbhum in extreme West Bengal.

Sonāton is particularly appreciated for his attractive dancing, which, like his singing, has more conscious artistry about it than that of most Bauls. One of the few Bauls who is occasionally asked to perform on All India Radio Calcutta, Sonāton has also been invited to appear in music conferences in the city.

The conscious artistry of Sonāton's approach to Baul performance is palpably evident in his experiments. While he was being recorded in 1971, for example, at the annual festival held in January on the grounds of Tagore's university at Santiniketan, he sang a Baul text to a tune that adhered closely to the structure of *rāg pūrbi.* Some Baul tunes resemble certain other *rāgs*, and perhaps there may even be an organic connection between them since the *rāgs* are often considered to have folk origins, but even the pitch content of *rāg pūrbi* is alien to that of any Bengali folk tune, and Sonāton's performance was clearly an attempt to be innovative. However fascinated some auditors may have been by the rendition, Sonāton's peers were less charmed—one among them could not resist a few heavily ironic "*bāh bāh,*" ordinarily exclamations of approbation.

Apparently Sonāton has remained undaunted, because in a letter I received from Calcutta in 1975, a friend mentioned that Sonāton had "started composing Baul songs on Indian Ragas." He has also devised a type of chante fable which incorporates a number of Baul songs into the recitation of a traditional story. Carol Salomon, a scholar of medieval Bengali literature, recorded a performance of this story and in her report on it mentions that Sonāton had once been a *ýātrā* actor—*ýātrā* is a generic term for the rustic musical theatricals performed by traveling companies (1979). His experience as an actor, no doubt, accounts for the more artful and experimental approach he takes with Baul performance.

Although Sonāton may reveal a taste for innovation in his performances, in matters of Baul religious belief he appears strictly conservative. As he interpreted the esoteric meaning of the story Carol Salomon recorded, he showed that he views the plot as an allegory on the sexo-yogic ritual of the Bauls. As Salomon has illustrated in her paper, the Sahajiya literature, complete with its esoteric interpretation, is still in living oral tradition among the Bauls and is not merely embalmed in manuscripts and books.

The backgrounds of the several Bauls discussed in this chapter illustrate that the Bauls are increasingly subjected to influences usually thought to undermine the validity of a folk tradition. Traveling abroad, making commercial recordings, singing for films, recording for radio and television, broadcasting, and performing at urban music festivals are all outside the hypothetical realm of "folk." Even with the few Bauls who have had these new experiences and, as a result, have made idiosyncratic changes in the musical tradition they have inherited, there remains a firm belief in Baul religious tenets. Such a belief is the raison d'être and validation of their folk tradition, and without it, it is doubtful the Bauls would see much reason for continuing to sing.

CHAPTER FIVE

Performance Contexts

There are no proscriptions or prescriptions about where or when singing is permissible for a Baul; circumscribing the activity would be a contradiction of the very spontaneity he symbolizes. What prompts a Baul to sing may be his own pleasure at engaging in a familiar and enjoyable activity or the pleasure of others from whom he may expect appreciation and profit. The kind of song a Baul chooses to sing may be one which deals with the possibility of human perfection as envisioned by the Bauls or with the familiar stories and homilies of Vaisnava lore; perhaps in this choice there is some element of inhibition, because there may be some reluctance to sing of esoteric matters before an uninitiated audience. On the whole, there is no strong evidence of this inhibition; the texts are usually ambiguous, anyway, and just as a Baul is apt to speak frankly about the need for a properly regulated sex life to a young man, he may sing with a similarly evangelizing intention.

Pūrṇo Dās does seem to avoid performing songs that are about *sādhonā,* perhaps because he feels they should be reserved for initiates and not because he has made a professional judgment about what will please an audience. Sonāton Dās Ṭhākur, on the other hand, is more typical in that, though his songs, such as *mon āmār ēkbār hori balo,*[23] express conventional Vaisnava sentiments, he readily sings about Baul *sādhonā* in the song *mon mayrā* even for the radio audience.

Though free to sing whenever he chooses, there are times when it would be odd if a Baul failed to sing—at a *melā*, for example. A *melā* is a large fair that occurs annually, usually in the colder part of the year when people are less occupied with agricultural chores, and in connection with some auspicious occasion. It is a large-scale affair involving much of the community and, if well established, will attract tradesmen and shopkeepers from neighboring communities.

JAYADEVA *MELĀ*

One of the most popular *melās* in Bengal takes place in Kenduli on the banks of the Ajay River in Birbhum District on the several days leading to *pōuṣ soṅkrānti* when the sun passes from Capricorn into Aquarius. On this last day of *pōuṣ* (mid-January) the Ganges, so it is said, flows into the Ajay, making it the most auspicious time to bathe there. Near the site chosen for the ceremonial bath is Kenduli temple dedicated to the poet Jayadeva (Jayodeb in Bengali) and his wife Padmavati (Padmābotī), for it was on Jayadeva's account that the Ganges first flowed into the Ajay (fig. 11).

Jayadeva was a late twelfth-century poet whose famous work, the *Gītagōvinda* (Sanskrit), a series of songs on the love of Radha and Krishna, belongs to the great Vaisnava devotional literature still used in many temples. One day, the story goes, while Jayadeva was working on the *Gītagōvinda*, he was stricken with doubt about what he had written and decided to leave off working a while and go to take his bath in the Ganges some distance away. Noticing the trouble Jayadeva took to get to the river, the goddess of the Ganges decided to alter her flow for his benefit and told him she would pass through the Ajay River, which was closer to Jayadeva's house. When Jayadeva returned home with this good news, he discovered, much to his shock, that his wife Padmavati was eating her meal before she had fed him.[24] Now Padmavati was equally surprised by Jayadeva's consternation because, as she explained to him, he had thought better of taking his bath at the Ganges and had returned home quickly to finish the couplet he had been working on and then to have his meal before retiring for a nap. What she had seen, however, was really Krishna impersonating Jayadeva as a means of helping the poet resolve his doubts about the passage on which he was working, and when Jayadeva was confronted by the completed line in his manuscript he understood the *līlā* of Krishna.

This incident is recounted in poetry and prose in the many little booklets hawked at Jayadeva *melā*, some by the authors themselves, wandering throughout the milling crowds, and others by vendors at their stalls. At such a stall one might also find a colored picture illustrating the story (fig. 12). These popular pictures, often attached to calendars, form one of the main decorative items in village homes. At other stalls, one can purchase farming implements, kitchen utensils, foodstuffs, articles of clothing, and other necessaries. One of the chief attractions of the fair, however, is the variety of prepared food available in the tents set up by the proprietors of well-known shops from nearby towns, and among these the most eye-catching are the stalls where sweets are heaped up in monstrous mounds (fig. 13). Because the fair attracts large crowds, there are many alms seekers

Fig. 11. Temple of Jayadeva/Padmavati in Kenduli.

—common beggars, lepers, and holy men with a variety of spiritual talents —lining the paths in particular areas waiting for the charitable to pass by and leave a few grains of rice or a few pennies on the handkerchiefs spread out in front of them (figs. 14 and 15). Along the crowded paths an occasional procession of devotees may pass singing *kīrton*, or, as in figure 16, a pair of young boys, costumed as Radha and Krishna, may be propelled along by a small band of musicians singing the praises of the god and his consort.

Fig. 12. Jayadeva and Padmavati.

The large crowds at such fairs as Jayadeva *melā* make good audiences for the Bauls who provide for many a rare opportunity for entertainment. In certain areas within the fairgrounds some religious institutions erect shelters of bamboo and cloth or fence in an open area. One such compound is erected at Jayadeva *melā* by the followers of Monōhor Khēpā, a Vaisnava Sahajiya guru greatly venerated by the Bauls and an increasing number of Bengalis of all classes (fig. 17). The land on which the compound is situated belongs to one of Monōhor Khēpā's devotees, a Brahman whose family has resided in Birbhum for generations. When I visited the *melā* in 1970 and 1971, three areas had been arranged on the land belonging to the devotee. One enclosure was a cloth-covered bamboo framework for shelter and sleeping, another larger enclosed area accommodated the audience for

Fig. 13. Sweet-stall at Jayadeva *melā*.

the Baul singers, and a third area was an open space for cooking and serving free meals to all comers.

On a typical day among those I observed, the Bauls congregated towards late afternoon in the middle of the performance area where a microphone was suspended, and the onlookers, mostly villagers with a very few Calcuttans and a foreign student or two from Santiniketan, surrounded them, sitting on the ground. From time to time a coconut shell bowl belonging to one of the Bauls would be filled with liquor and passed around among them, and occasionally a pipe of *gā̦jā* would be lit in such a way as to avoid public notice.

Singing went on all through the night and more or less continually through the next day with customary breaks for meals and siesta. While singing, the soloist would stand, move about, and dance, a supporting singer sometimes joining him. The presence of the microphone, to be found now even at the most unpretentious village events, probably tended to limit the amount of movement. Most dancing took place during the refrain when the words did not require attention; during the stanzas, the singer was more apt to direct his song at the audience while standing and, perhaps, gesturing. This style of alternately dancing and standing seemed to fit naturally with the alternation of refrains and new text, and the use of a microphone

Fig. 14. Sexual icons constructed of mud that represent the union of the god Shiva with his consort. They are erected at Jayadeva *melā* to solicit alms from passersby.

Fig. 15. A holy man lying on a bed of thorns dispenses his blessings at Jayadeva *melā*.

Fig. 16. Boys impersonating Radha and Krishna at Jayadeva *melā.*

has probably only reinforced this style rather than initiated it. At the 1970 *melā,* a special award was made to one Baul, Subol Candro Dās, for his exceptional endurance and enthusiasm before the microphone; although he often needed prompting from his wife on how the texts went, he sang song after song until he was panting and hoarse.

Pōuṣ Melā

Near to Jayadeva *melā,* in time and geography, occurs *pōuṣ melā* at Santiniketan, the site of the rural university founded by Tagore in Bolpur, district Birbhum. The occasion for this *melā,* according to *Fairs and Festivals of West Bengal* (Mitra 1953, 6), is the anniversary of the *dikṣā* of Maharshi Debendranath Tagore, father of Rabindranath Tagore. The *melā* lasts three days, and in 1953 attendance was estimated at 5,000. Being within easy access by rail, the *melā* is attended by many Calcuttans seeking a rural outing. The nature of the *melā* is more likely to draw attendance from the educated and middle classes than Jayadeva *melā* because besides being more easily accessible it is more secular, has unusual attractions, like book displays aimed at a literate audience, and sideshows which appeal to everyone, but cost money.

Fig. 17. Monōhor Khēpā.

This *pōuṣ melā* differs from others like Jayadeva *melā,* too, in that its folkloristic elements are consciously fostered by the university sponsors who originated the event. The rural populace attends the *melā,* however, and is, in part, one of its attractions. The local Santals, a tribe of Austroasiatic-speaking aborigines, are invited to the *melā* and form a spectacle for the average Calcuttan comparable to that of an Amerindian pageant for the native of New York. The women of the tribe are very handsome, and their brightly black skins are set off by their colorful cotton clothing and by the flowers in their glistening hair. Appreciation of their beauty by the non-Santali Calcutta male is invariably accompanied by the fantasies, pleasant or fevered, of the sexually repressed contemplating the sexually free. One of the chief events at the *melā* is arranged for the Santali men who strive against one another in an archery contest.

The Bauls, like the Santals, are carriers of the folk heritage of Bengal that the sponsors of the *melā* wish to support, and for them, too, a scheduled concert was arranged. They did not sing through the night and much of the day, as at Jayadeva *melā,* where the tone of the gathering centers on the religious as much as on the entertainment aspect of the performance. Most of the time they spent by themselves in a temporary shelter talking and singing to one another, and they sang to the public only at their appointed time. During the performance they sat on a platform which raised and separated them from the audience. These physical circumstances and the occasional announcements and introductions made by officials made the performance of the Bauls into a concert or "function." Because the microphones were arranged as they would be for any formal, staged concert at which the performers would sit on the floor, the Bauls were constrained to sit in a group, the soloist being unable to dance or gesture (fig. 18).

During the concert, a couple of non-Bauls also performed Baul songs. One of these, a middle-aged man who had learned songs from Sonāton Dās Ṭhākur, was truly incompetent and could not carry a tune. The audience received his song with remarkable tolerance, however, recognizing the devotion of the singer and the humanistic message of his text. The other singer was put forth as a prodigy in the manner of show-biz hype. About seven or eight years old, the lad appeared exceedingly ill at ease and sang and danced like a crippled automaton.

Fig. 18. Bauls on stage at Santiniketan *pōuṣ melā.*

Pūjās and *Utsabs*

Besides the *melās* like those in Santiniketan and Kenduli, there are other types of annual celebrations. Some like the *pūjās* (worship ceremonies) are universally observed throughout the province or country and are not tied to a particular geographical or local historical event as the *melās* generally are. For the expense of celebrating a *pūjā,* subscriptions are solicited (or even extorted!) from neighborhood residents, and from the funds collected, a musical entertainment may be arranged as part of the festivities. A Baul may be asked to join such a program, but in the city at least, the film singers and other popular singers are a much greater attraction, so if any Baul is invited to perform, it is most likely to be Pūrṇo Dās because of his celebrity.

A Family *Utsab* in Calcutta

Smaller than the *pūjās*, which are the cause of general holidays, and even smaller than the *melās*, *utsavas* (festival, celebration) are arranged by a family or religious group. At an *utsab* (the Bengali pronunciation) the festivities are mostly confined to a single family or institutional compound where the participants enjoy food and listen to and participate in the music-making. One such *utsab* occurred annually at the suburban home of a man who had given up employment with the Customs in order to devote full time to being a *kīrtonīyā* (singer of *kīrton*); with a couple of friends he spent his time traveling about the country joining with others in ceremonies dedicated to singing the name of Krishna. He led the *nāmkīrton* (name-praise) at his household *utsab*, and his effectiveness as a leader of the devotions was attested by the ecstasy of several of the guests who were friends, relatives, and neighbors of the host. "One felt ashamed to have been merely an interested spectator amongst so much sincerity" (Fox-Strangways [1914] 1967, 485).

The *kīrtonīyā*'s brother, who was famous for his virtuosity on the *khōl,* a type of clay-bodied barrel drum used in Vaisnava music, sang a few songs after the end of the *nāmkirton* and accompanied himself on the drum. Among the songs he included a couple of widely known Baul songs.

Utsab for the *Somādhi* Anniversary of Ýotin Dās Mohant

At another *utsab,* which takes place in a rural area of Birbhum, many Bauls attend to celebrate the anniversary of the *somādhi* of Ýotin Dās Mohant, maternal uncle of Lakṣman̄ Dās Baul. This annual commemoration is held at Lakṣmaṇ's mother's home in a village near Sainthia, Birbhum. Within the compound walls of this home where the singing takes place, Lakṣmaṇ's uncle had been buried with other members of his family (see fig. 9). As the Bauls gather on the eve of the *utsab,* they sing among themselves, and sometimes heated discussion may arise over the interpretation of a song text. On one occasion, Lakṣmaṇ, the host, buttressed his explanation with quotes from the *Mahabharata* and the *Ramayana,* the two epics whose events and characters are familiar to all ranks of Indian society. A guest, also called Lakṣmaṇ, dismissed this learnedness by saying he could speak only what he understood, not what he read elsewhere. Finally, Lakṣmaṇ's brother-in-law, Gōpāl, who was senior to the others present, put an end to argument by saying a school ought to be opened to explain the meaning of *dehotattvo* (theory of the body) so that those who sing would know what they were singing about. He lamented that nowadays if a singer is asked the meaning of a song he is apt, from ignorance, to say, "The guru will explain," and that many boys are interested only in making names as performers and in singing down the weighty Bauls. Such comments recall a statement made by Ýotin Dās Baul about a well-known guru, who, he said, was like a *kalosi* (clay water jug)—the emptier it gets, the bigger sound it makes.

While the singing went on, it was evident that it was the source of much enjoyment to all, both as performers and listeners. At one point—perhaps the presence of a tape recorder had something to do with it—one Baul made the assertive statement, though in a somewhat embarrassed tone, "Well, I want to sing now," apparently fearing that another Baul, who had already sung several songs, would continue to monopolize attention. No sooner had he finished his song, however, than he announced, "I'll sing another."

Another incident involving the same pair of Bauls also suggests a certain rivalry but underlines its rather subdued, gentlemanly quality. One of them had sung at great length because memory lapses caused him to repeat verses or insert numerous melismas—*gājā* inspires the soul but may clog the memory. Occasionally, his rival, at first helpfully and then impatiently, would prompt him. Seeking to make a better impression, the first Baul started another song in which his memory failed him as badly. Feeling embarrassed when he had finished, he made something of an apology for his faulty performance, but his rival magnanimously dismissed it as unnecessary and complimented him on the beautiful *āp-ḍāun* (up-down) of his performance, a well-intended reference to the many ornamental melismas he had used to gloss over the memory lapses.

On the next day, much activity was devoted to preparation of the *paṅkti bhōjan* (line-meal), a communal meal in which all the guests, sitting

Fig. 19. *Pankti bhōjan* provided by Monōhor Khēpā at Jayadeva *melā*.

in rows, are invited to participate. On a much larger scale, this kind of meal is served at the pavilion erected in honor of Monōhor Khēpā at Jayadeva *melā* (fig. 19). The communal meals are a characteristic feature of the liberal Bengali Vaisnava sects, and one of the reasons that the more orthodox consider them degenerate, since the meals encourage a promiscuous mingling of castes.

After the meal and the customary post-prandial nap, preparations slowly got under way for an evening of song; among the preparations was the hooking-up of an amplification system, which hardly seemed necessary in the crowded confines of the *āśrom* compound; the amplification, however, was not for those within the compound walls but without, as the speakers were aimed to carry the festivities to the adjacent village. Presumably the amplification required a generator because the village was not electrified and illumination was from *hārikens* (hurricane lanterns) and pressurized kerosene lamps.

As the *utsab* was in memory of Lakṣmaṇ's *māmā* (maternal uncle), Lakṣmaṇ took the role of master of ceremonies; now and again taking the microphone in hand, he would announce the name of the singer or call for order when the crowd of neighbors became a little too noisy. When a Baul seemed to be giving a particularly good performance, Lakṣm̃aṇ would pin a few rupees to the performer's clothing. He had covered the expenses for the affair by soliciting subscriptions from friends and relatives.

Utsab for the *Somādhi* Anniversary of Otul Khēpā

Another example of the *utsab* type of celebration is that which takes place at an *āśrom* where a tiny Baul community had grown up outside the town Dubrajpur, also in Birbhum District. The *āśrom* had been founded by, and has been maintained in memory of, Otul Khēpā, who lived at an indeterminate and respectably distant time. Over the *somādhi* of Otul is a small *mandir* (temple) and in front of it a *maṇḍap* (roofed, but open-sided terrace attached to the temple). Adjacent to it, shaded by a copse, are the substantial *somādhi*s of several more Bauls.

Gaṅgādhar Dās Baul, a young man who appeared, in 1970, to be the leader of the *āśrom* community, though he was not called *mohant,* explained that the spiritual descendants of Otul Khēpā called themselves *darbeś* Baul, *darbeś* being one of the four sects into which the Bauls are sometimes divided. Though *darbeś* (dervish) is a Persian word and would imply a more Islamic than Vaisnava orientation, no evidence in their dress, speech, manners, or types of songs suggested that they differed from other Vaisnavised Bauls; indeed, as Lakṣm̃aṇ arrived at the *āśrom,* he used the customary Vaisnava salutation, "*Hori bōl*" (Say "Hari"), and was greeted with it in return, and Gaṅgādhar was a disciple of and sang songs of Monō-hor Khēpā, the Vaisnava guru mentioned in connection with Jayadeva *melā.* Perhaps the Vaisnava influence is relatively recent, as Gaṅgādhar claims his family have been *darbeś* Baul for seven generations.

When a few other Bauls had arrived, along with a number of pilgrims from neighboring villages and towns, everyone gathered in the *maṇḍap* to chat, and a *chilam* (pipe) was prepared. Nearly everyone accepted the *gā̦jā,* but Gaṅgādhar, who said he did not enjoy smoking and betrayed a slight embarrassment, such as a teetotaler might when offered a drink at a party. When it was discovered that the American woman in our party smoked—and could do so in a manner commanding respect—she became the focus of attention while everyone watched to see how brightly she could make the ash in the pipe glow by the force of her inhalation. Shortly, someone went to the kitchen area to fetch one of the women who was also a passionate smoker of *gā̦jā* so that she could meet and compete with her American counterpart. It is, of course, even more eccentric for a woman to be a habitual smoker of *gā̦jā* than for a man, but such eccentricities are prized among the Bauls.

When refreshment had been taken, Biśvonāth Rāy Baul[25] offered to show the meditation place of Otul Khēpā, which was situated a short distance from the *āśrom,* to any one who was interested. In the relatively flat, tan landscape, the great, gray rocks on which the meditation cave was located were an imposing freak of nature and did seem a suitable site for a spiritual retreat. According to Lakṣm̃aṇ, however, they were not a phenomenon of nature but an accident of divine hubris, for a god had had to leave them there in a clutter when he had been unable to finish an overly ambitious complex of temples in Banaras.

Near the top of the cluster of rocks stood a small brick hut which enclosed a gap in the rocks and through which one passed in order to enter the small cave where Otul had meditated (figs. 20 and 21). Just outside the brick structure, a fine cleft ran up the rock to widen at one point into a small oval depression resembling a *ýōni* (vulva) (fig. 22). It was brilliant scarlet

Fig. 20. Meditation cave of Otul Khēpā, entrance.

Fig. 21. Meditation cave of Otul Khēpā, exterior view.

from the vermilion powder (*sindur*) that had been rubbed into it and contained a single flower offering. Lakṣm̃aṇ explained that since Otul had been an exceptional yogi, the hardness of his erections was too much for a mortal woman to bear; this circumstance left him in a fix when he wished to perform the sexual *sādhonā*. Moved by his predicament, Mother Nature offered herself to him by cleaving the rock outside his place of meditation and menstruating three days monthly through the vulva, which now is adored by sundry pilgrims. Lakṣm̃aṇ asserted that even today there were yogis with such control over their sexual organs that they could lift stones by the strength of their erections, and Biśvonāth remarked that any Baul could keep an erection for as long as he liked. Such information was meant to be indicative of how well an adept Baul could contradict nature and achieve his personal removal from the cycle of birth, death, and rebirth, but it did seem an expression of masculine pride in sexual performance as well.

In the evening, after the *paṅkti bhōjan* had been served and people had taken their afternoon rest, the singing started in the *maṇḍap,* for once with no microphone. Among the singers was Sadānando Dās Baul; a friend of Pūrṇo and Lakṣm̃aṇ, he had been to the States with them and suspected that the recording they had made for Elektra was making a large profit of which they had not received a fair share. Consequently, he forbade any tape recording during the *utsab* for fear that he and his brethren would again be cheated.

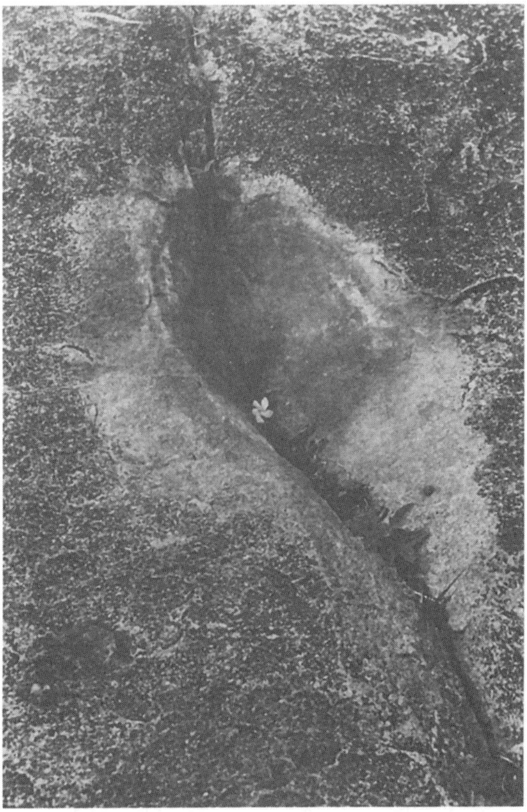

Fig. 22. *Ýōni* at Otul Khēpā's cave.

On the following day, Lakṣm̄aṇ somehow smoothed things over and Sadānando grudgingly agreed to sing for taping. Accompanying himself skillfully on the harmonium, he sang a popular religious song in a polished style resembling that of professional singers of folk songs; even Pūrṇo Dās, who sings almost exclusively for the audiences for whom this style is most familiar, leaves such songs for other members of his troupe. After Sadānando had sung, Gaṅgādhar sang a couple of songs by Monōhor Khēpā and these he would probably have allowed to be recorded the night before if Sadānando had not objected.

At the *melās* and *utsabs* described above, the Bauls congregate in groups; opportunities for solo performance take a number of other forms. Middle-class Bengalis, for example, may invite one or two Bauls to their homes to perform on occasion. Even in Calcutta this is done, and it helps those Bauls who now and then go there to make a radio recording for which their pay is hardly sufficient to cover their expenses.

At a Tea Stall Cum Bus Stop

If one lived in the countryside for a long enough time, perhaps one might encounter Bauls who sing door-to-door soliciting alms. Though such mendicant singers are common enough in Calcutta, too, they rarely appear to be Bauls. It is more likely that one would encounter a Baul singing for a ready-made audience of men relaxing at a tea stall; one such performance, arranged rather than spontaneous, took place at the suggestion of Lakṣm̃aṇ Dās. While waiting at a rural, open-air tea stall/bus stop situated at the base of a tree, he decided to fetch his friend Phokir Dās, who was working in a nearby field, so that he might record a couple of songs. Phokir Dās was a young man who had only recently undertaken to become the disciple of a Baul guru, but he already wore his hair in a bun in the Baul fashion and wore the half-dhoti and most likely the *kowpīn* as well. His songs were listened to attentively by the bystanders, who clearly thought such an occurrence unexceptional.

As Pūrṇo Dās is a unique example of a Baul who is able to earn a comfortable living by performance alone, Phokir Dās is typical of the opposite, of which there are more examples. He is primarily a peasant, as Pūrṇo is now a professional entertainer, and these identities seem to vie for precedence with their identities as Bauls. Both men appear to straddle two modes of being, or, perhaps, to be in transition from one to the other: Phokir Dās is becoming more a Baul while Pūrṇo is perhaps becoming less a Baul. In contrast, the other Bauls mentioned in this chapter, even if they travel abroad or experiment with new musical ideas, seem to be identified by themselves, and by others simply as Bauls.

CHAPTER SIX

Texts

TEXT CLASSIFICATION AND SUBJECT MATTER

Most Bengali writers on folk song use a few classificatory terms, probably borrowed from Vaisnava terminology, when referring to the texts of Baul-*gān* and other types of relatively sophisticated spiritual folk song. The Bauls themselves know and use these terms, and the list given here was elicited from Lakṣm̃aṇ Dās. The great majority of these terms ends with the word *tattvo,* which is awkward to translate. It means, in varying degree, such things as "principle," "theory," or "system of ideas." Lakṣm̃aṇ's list of terms included the following compounds ending in *tattvo: dehotattvo, premtattvo, gurutattvo, l̃ilātattvo, guh̃ýtattvo, bhajantattvo, parotattvo,* and *bhaktitattvo.* These refer respectively to the body (*deho*), spiritual love (*prem*), the spiritual preceptor (*guru*), the dalliance of Radha and Krishna (*l̃ilā*), esoterica (*guh̃ýo*), worship (*bhajan*), the highest, best (*paro*), and devotion (*bhakti*). In addition to these terms, Lakṣm̃aṇ also mentioned two others not including the term *tattvo;* these were *bhajanāroti* and *monośikṣā.* The former combines *bhajan* (worship), used previously in compound with *tattvo,* with a word meaning at least two unrelated things: one names the ritual of adoration, which involves the waving of lamps before an image or respected person; the other means "cessation." *Monośikṣā* means "mind-teaching."

Besides these terms, two others are commonly encountered both in writing and among the Bauls. These terms are *heẏāli* and *dhạdhạ,* both of which mean "puzzle, riddle"; they refer to songs in which doctrinal matters are stated in paradox and nonsense requiring hermeneutic exegesis.

Among the terms mentioned here, those most frequently encountered in the discussion of Baul-*gān* texts are *dehotattvo, premtattvo, gurutattvo, l̃ilātattvo,* and *monośikṣā,* and the first of them is of greatest significance in Baul songs. In the *dehotattvo* texts, the Baul obsession with the proper use of the body or the results of its misuse are stated in common allegories and metaphors. Because of their allegorical and metaphorical nature, some of the texts are capable of multiple interpretations, any one of which may be valid for a particular group or individual. For the Bauls, the validity of an interpretation depends on its relationship to an understanding of their particular tantrik physical *sādhonā;* for others, including writers like Kshitimohan Sen or Sōmendronāth Bandyōpādhyāy, who have sought to interpret and praise the Bauls, explanations of a more broadly humanistic and philosophical nature are appealing since the writers associate tantrik *sādhonā* with depravity.

The song printed here, transcribed from the performance of Ŷotin Dās Baul, is a *dehotattvo,* and may have two acceptable, though quite different interpretations.

> O, mind-boatman, brother, take up your oar;
> I cannot row any longer.
> I have rowed the loaded boat my whole life,
> and haven't reached the river bank.
>
> I came rowing my boat of desires,
> and have become exhausted from rowing.
> At every bend of the river, whirlpools form;
> the boat is caught in the ebb and doesn't go up-stream
> any more.
>
> Odin Sarat says, "The boat I rowed,
> that boat I didn't take care of;
> Salt-rot has attacked my boat,
> and it won't go any farther in this land."

Odin Sarat, the poet mentioned in the last stanza, is one of the better-known Bauls of the last century. The sentiment attributed to Sarat has broad appeal if interpreted to mean that the poet is lamenting a life ill-spent in the pursuit of personal goals (I came rowing my boat of desires) rather than in devotion. Sarat performs a last-minute act of contrition, asking for divine aid (O, mind-boatman, brother, take up your oar) to reach the other shore, presumably the life hereafter. Such an interpretation would be widely acceptable among Bengalis, or for that matter, among Americans who appreciate the sentiment of "Swing low, sweet chariot."

As the Bauls who sang the song interpreted it, however, the essential point is in the confession of Sarat who says, "The boat I rowed, that boat I didn't take care of." In the conventional understanding, the boat is merely a vehicle in which one is passively transferred across the river of life by reliance on divine grace, just as one must rely on the skill of a ferryman to get safely across a swollen and turbulent river; but in the Bauls' view, the boat is an allegorical symbol of the body, which is the very means of active self-realization. Since in the Bauls' view the song is an admonition about the proper use and care of the body, it is a *dehotattvo* song.

The manner in which the text is printed on page 78—without repetitions—suggests that it consists of three independent stanzas, but as it is sung, there are extensive repetitions because Baul songs employ a refrain structure. As a rule, the entire first stanza is repeated at the end of the song while, internally, only the first line recurs at the ends of stanzas. This recurrence of the last line happens at the end of the refrain stanza as well, both at the beginning and end of the song. To avoid redundancy, the first line of the refrain occurring after the last stanza is elided with the first line of the initial stanza when the latter returns at the end of the song. Thus, as sung, the text would have the following form:

O, mind-boatman, brother, take up your oar;
    I cannot row any longer.
I have rowed the loaded boat my whole life,
    and haven't reached the river bank.
O, mind-boatman, brother, take up your oar;
    I cannot row any longer.

I came rowing my boat of desires,
    and have become exhausted from rowing.
At every bend of the river, whirlpools form;
    the boat is caught in the ebb and doesn't go up-stream
    any more.
O, mind-boatman, brother, take up your oar;
    I cannot row any longer.

Odin Sarat says, "The boat I rowed,
    that boat I didn't take care of;
Salt-rot has attacked my boat,
    and it won't go any further in this land."
O, mind-boatman, brother, take up your oar;
    I cannot row any longer.
I have rowed the loaded boat my whole life,
    and haven't reached the river bank.
O, mind-boatman, brother, take up your oar;
    I cannot row any longer.

The image of the boat and boatman is one of the commonest in Bengali songs and is not uncommon in the rest of India. This second example of such a song text, recorded by Ŷotin and Prem Dāsi, may be classified as *gurutattvo,* since in it the boatman is an allegorical figure representing the guru.

Worship the guru, Golden Moon,
If a storm arises on the mind-river, who will give you
    refuge?

Worship the guru, know the guru, depend on the guru;
Except for the guru, there is no other friend in this
world.

You must come and you must go; who will take you across?

As in the previous text, the devotee may be thought of as depending on the boatman utterly for salvation. Many Hindus actually do "worship" their gurus as incarnations and seek the goal of their spiritual quest by annihilating their own personalities and wills in his service. At Jayadeva *melā,* one such devotee, made ecstatic by the presence of his guru Monōhor Khēpā, declared with a broken voice and with tears in his eyes that as Jesus Christ was to a Christian, so was Monōhor Khēpā to him. It is probably such automatic devotion that some scholars have in mind when they say the real Baul songs do not praise the guru. Kshitimohan Sen, for example, points out that it is interiorized emotion which leads the Bauls on to spiritual ends, not anything external, including a guru, and the folk song collector Sūrendro Candro Cakroborttī once commented on a song that it was not a Baul song "because there is no mention of the guru in true Baul."

Abject devotion of the kind which Monōhor Khēpā's disciple displayed is certainly inconceivable among the Bauls; they have too much awareness and love of their individuality. But gurus are praised because they can help the novice by instructing him in the techniques necessary for achieving the desired spiritual ends. To worship the guru because he has accomplished those ends is pointless for the Baul since he wants actively to attain *siddhi* and not merely to worship it passively.

This attitude of respecting the guru for his usefulness and not merely adoring him for his virtues is evident in the next song recorded by Sonāton Dās Ṭhākur. The text also includes elements of *dehotattvo.*

O, mind-confectioner, why haven't you learned sweet-making?
Having gotten the company of a good guru, why haven't you
known the secret of the art?

The strength of your mind-fire is not good; your devotion-
fan was waving, but that too has lessened.
The devoutness-pot has gotten holes; nothing has been
accomplished.

Though there was sugar in the house, you aren't acquainted
with sugar; being blind, you had molasses brought in.
If you cook molasses, will you get rock candy from it?

If you had done confectioning in a detached mood; if
you had taken it down from the fire with the strength
of the guru's given instructions,

Then perhaps there would have been good trade in
rasogōllās in name-syrup.

Thinking this, quoth Madan Nag, "Before knowing the guru,
why have you gone to do confectioning without knowing
sweet-making?
"The only result was the destruction of everything
and grief of mind; you lost one hundred per cent."

This text states unequivocally that the value of a guru is his ability to instruct one in the techniques needed to ensure success in a tricky business. The process of sweet-making, as the reader doubtless can guess by now, is a metaphor for sexual yoga.[26] As sugar, the valuable ingredient for the sweet-maker, lies unrecognized in the house, so does the substantial worth of semen remain unrecognized by the novice in the house of his body. By engaging in the sweet business of sex without the proper devotion to the instructions of the guru, the novice has lost one hundred per cent.

Again, it is not necessary to refer to the sexual *sādhonā* in an exegesis of this song—though such an exegesis would hardly satisfy the Baul who sang it, Sonāton Dās Ṭhākur.[27] Sweet-making might be understood to refer to any number of more conventional Vaisnava practices—*japā,* the telling of the rosary, for example—since the phrase "rasogōllās in name-syrup" is a direct reference to the practice of reciting the names of Vishnu in the formula *hare kṛiṣṇo hare kṛiṣṇo kṛiṣṇo kṛiṣṇo hare hare; hare rāmo hare rāmo rāmo rāmo hare hare.*

In some other songs, however, as in this one recorded by Ýotin Dās, it is difficult if not impossible to overlook the basic meaning of the text for the Bauls because the imagery is more directly based on Baul ideology.

In Vrindavan bloom three flowers of three colors:
blue, yellow, white.
In which flower is Sri Krishna, in which Sri Radha?

The flowers bloom after twelve years; month after month
those flowers drop.
To whom shall I speak of the flowers; except to the
rosik it is forbidden to talk of it.

My *Gosąi* Gurucąd says, "The flowers bloom on that
qualityless branch;
"If word of the flowers should enter your ears, Rādhāśýām,
you will be puzzled."

In this song reference is obviously made to the phenomenon of menstruation, which is of central importance to the Baul *sādhonā;* in Bengali, *phul* (flower) may also mean "menses," and the *phul,* which first blooms after twelve years and monthly thereafter, is clearly the *phul* of the human body. The flowers of three different colors are symbolic of the different qualities and virtues of menses during its three-day advent. With such a text as this it is difficult to find a convincing interpretation that would omit physiological references and be acceptable to more conventional Vaisnavas or romanticizing intellectuals. An element of Vaisnavization has crept in, obviously, since the hidden and manifest forms of the substantial element in men are referred to as Radha and Krishna; but these are merely symbolic and do not change what is referred to, which has been called Allah and Khoda in Baul songs as well as the more unsectarian and agnostic Man of the Heart and Elusive Man.

In the final couplet, the phrase about the "qualityless branch" refers to a physical manifestation of the attributeless substance; it is said that the mystical horticulture of the song will leave one puzzled (*dhạdhạ*), for which reason this song may be classified as a puzzle or riddle type (*hẹȳāli, dhạdhạ*) as well as a *dehotattvo*—because it deals with mystical physiology—and *guhȳotattro*—because it deals with secret truths. The final couplet also mentions two names; one is that of the poet Rādhāśȳām, guru of the singer, and the other is that of the poet's own guru, Gọ̄sāi (a Vaisnava religious title) Gurucạd. In other songs one will find the poet has quoted his guru as saying something or other as a comment on the song proper but without mentioning his own name; this habit may lead to confusion about the identity of the author. Most frequently, it is the poet himself who speaks a commentary at the end, and such has been the device for "signing" oral poems in India for hundreds of years. This type of signature is not universally employed, however, and it appears that only those texts which lay claim to some religious or literary significance make use of it; the majority of folk song is anonymous as are many of the song texts recorded for this book. Since the poetically archaic word for "says" or "speaks" is *bhaṇe,* the signature line is named the *bhoṇitā,* even though the poet more often *bale, kahe,* or *kay* ("he says" in *colti bhāṣā*) than *bhaṇe.* The next poem, by Monōhor Khēpā, is of the *hẹȳāli/dhạdhạ* type in which the word *bhaṇe* is used in the *bhoṇitā* (Gọ̄sāi Pūrṇānando is presumably Monōhor Khēpā's guru). This is as sung by Gaṅgādhar Dās.

Love-artisan, *rosik* gentlemen, has created a phenomenon
of love,
Before the father was born, there came three grandsons.

The husband was in heaven; the mother saw him in a dream.
How did the child come about? This is a very surprising
event!

Gọsāi Pūrṇānando *bhaṇe,* "You will get to see him through
divine knowledge.
"His is neither birth nor death—Khēpā has been blind
since birth."

The various elements of Baul poetry discussed so far—the signature, sexual yoga, praise of the guru, and riddles—can all be found in sectarian song-poems elsewhere in India, which suggests that the Bauls are merely one branch of a fairly ancient tradition. Written record of the tradition in Bengal goes back as far as the earliest known examples of the Bengali language, a collection of sectarian song texts called *caryāpad.* Composed during more than a hundred years beginning in the mid-tenth century, they have come down to present times in a recension compiled most likely during the twelfth century, that is, approximately within a century after their composition.[28]

A few examples from among the fifty *caryāpad* texts will suffice to show their closeness in all respects to the Baul songs. The first example is a fairly explicit discussion of sexual yoga in which the necessity for a yogic control of the breath is mentioned as a means of forcing the semen up from the seat of physical pleasure (Manimula) to that of spiritual union (Odiana) (S. Sen 1965, 98):

Pressing close the lap, O Yogini, give me an embrace;
In a play of the Lotus and the Bolt bring the day to a close.

O Yogini! without thee I live not for a moment:
By kissing thy lips I quaff a draught of lotus honey.

Through a splash, O Yogini, (it) is smeared through:
From Manimula running up (it) reaches Odiana.

To the House of Breath the key is turned in the padlock:
The Moon and the Sun, the two wings, are unfurled.

Says Gundari, We (are) stout in love sport:
Among men and women the banner is held aloft.

The first couplet of these songs is designated *dhruva* (refrain) in the manuscript and is to be repeated after each couplet. As usual in the *caryāpads* and in the Baul songs where it occurs, the *bhoṇitā* is in the last couplet —Says Gundari (*bhaṇai guṇḍāri*).

The riddle type song may also be found in the *caryāpad* collection, and as is still customary, the poet, in the *bhoṇitā,* comments on the difficulty of understanding the text (S. Sen 1965, 98).

A she-tortoise, having been milked, a pail overflows:
The tamarind (up) in the tree is eaten by a crocodile.

The courtyard belongs to the house; listen, O marriageable
girl!
The soiled rag is taken away by a thief at midnight.

The mother-in-law is asleep, the daughter-in-law keeps
awake:
The soiled rag is stolen by a thief: going where can it
be sought for?

In daytime the daughter-in-law is afraid of a crow:
Night falling (she) goes out to Kamarupa.

Such a mystic song is sung by the Reverend Kukkuri;
Among ten millions it has reached a single heart.

Finally, we may see in the next poem both the respect for the guru's teaching and the body-as-boat imagery which are common in Baul and other songs (S. Sen 1965, 110).

The Body is a small boat, the Mind is the oar;
Hold the helm by the instruction of the True Guru.

Pacifying the Heart take out the boat;
In no other way may one cross over.

A boatman tows his boat by a rope;
Coming together with the Innate again and again, one
may not go any other way.

On the way there is danger; pirates are strong;
In the tornado of Existence the possessions are lost.

Along the bank it pushes up stream against strong currents;
Saraha says, It comes to port in the Sky.

In the manuscripts of the *caryāpads*, each of the songs is accompanied by a scholium giving an interpretation of the texts in terms of tantrik yoga. Although they are in an early form of Bengali, the texts of the poems reveal a strong influence of Sauraseni Apabrahmsa, the cosmopolitan and literary lingua franca of upper India of the time.[29] The poems provide an early indication of an interest in popular vernaculars for literary use. The prosody is basically moraic (S. K. Chatterji 1970, 117) but reveals a tendency toward the greater freedom of later Bengali vernacular prosody in which syllable durations may be stretched or compressed as demanded by the context (S. Sen 1965, 125). It is clear that the *caryāpads* originated with and were used by members of an educated class, a fact which differentiates them from most Baul texts today.

Besides the literary gap between the *caryāpads* and Baul-*gān*, there is also a similar musical gap, for each of the *caryāpads* is preceded in the manuscript by the name of a *rāg* indicating that the music associated with it was more a part of art-music practice than are the tunes associated with contemporary Baul-*gān*.

Since neither the advent of Islam nor the Vaisnava revival had yet occurred in Bengal during the period of the *caryāpads*, it is not surprising to find no evidence of either in them. In Baul songs both Islam and Vaisnavism have contributed much terminology, imagery, and many story episodes. In the songs collected for this study, the Islamic influence is minimal, though it would certainly be greater in a collection of songs from Bangladesh, where Islam predominates. Vaisnava influences are all important in the class of *līlātattvo* songs which concern the love-sport of Radha and Krishna. Such songs as the one quoted here can be considered Baul songs only in the sense that Bauls may sing them, for they are concerned with Vaisnava theology; in this case, as sung by Pūrṇo Dās, the superiority of Radha's devotion to Krishna is illustrated by her sacrificing her good name and position in her husband's family in order to satisfy an adulterous attachment to her god-lover. This episode epitomizes the proper devotional attitude for the Gauriya Vaisnava who must show equal disregard for the conventions of society in his singular devotion to Krishna.

> "Don't play the flute like that any more Syam [Krishna],
> I am dying of shame sitting here among my in-laws."
>
> You don't know selfless love, Dark Gold,
> don't you know any name other than Radha?
> You intoxicate the women of Vraja, O Vraja's treasure.
>
> Mukuṇḍo Dās says, "Hari, don't ruin the women of
> good family;
> Have pity and give a place to this sinner at your feet."

Monōśikṣā songs are homilies that remind the listener of the necessity for paying attention to the goals and values of his life. The point is often made in an indirect manner by dwelling on the fruitlessness of death at the end of a thoughtlessly lived life. Such an admonition is evident in the song quoted next, as sung by Pūrṇo Dās, and it also illustrates the close ties of the Bauls with Gauriya Vaisnavism since the characters and places mentioned in the song are associated with Caitanya, the sixteenth-century founder of this revivalist Hindu sect, which stresses the fundamental worth of all men regardless of caste.

> Go study well in school; if you don't you'll suffer
> at the end.

In the chief school of Nodia District, kindly Nitai
is the Headmaster, having tested the students, he
distributes his love.
He even made the worthless students Jogai and Madhai pass.

Whom shall I call educated in this school?
The students Rup, Sonatan, and Ramanandoray,
having been made to pass at Nabodvip, went to Vrindavan.

There are six naughty students in that school whom I
chastise again and again, but they don't listen.
If you come under their influence, you'll forget your
first lessons.

My lord Khēpā Cạ̄d says, "Wearing the kohl of knowledge,
study in the school of the sadhus.
"Ajamil went to heaven just by saying 'Narayon' once."

Songs such as this one, which stress humanitarian disregard of caste, the legends and saints of Gauriya Vaisnavism, and the necessity for a moral life—i.e., avoidance of the "six naughty students" (*chay ripu,* "six enemies": *kām*-lust, *krōdh*-anger, *lōbh*-greed, *mōho*-infatuation, *mad*-pride, *mātsarŷo*-envy)—are among the most popular songs sung by the Bauls; indeed, the song just quoted was one of the first available on a commercial disc made by Pūrṇo Dās. The sentiments and particulars of such songs are widely understood, which, with the familiarity of the tunes, partially accounts for their popularity, but for the Bauls themselves, it is the more esoteric songs, such as the one about the three flowers, which have the most significance.

Aspects of Prosody

The prosodic qualities of the texts the Bauls sing are characterized by great flexibility in small matters and a general uniformity in large ones. There is little regularity, for example, in the construction of feet or the lengths of lines, not only from song to song but internally as well. All songs, however, have a refrain which alternates with succeeding stanzas. These stanzas are cast in couplets of varying construction, of which one type would seem to fit the meter type called "village *charā*" by Amūlŷodhon Mukhōpādhŷāy in his book on Bengali prosody (1962, 20).

Such texts consist of end-rhyming couplets of four divisions (*parbo*) of four morae (*mātrā*) each, the last being catalectic (4-4-4-2 or 1). The text quoted next fits this definition as closely as any collected for this study. (*Parbo* divisions are indicated with virgules.)

guru bhajo re ō re sōnār cą̄d,
dil doriāy / uṭhle tuphān / ke dibe ā / sān /

guru bhajo / guru ceno / guru karo / sār /
guru bine / e duniāy / bandhu nei re / ār

āite habe / ẏāite habe / pār koribe / ke /
deiȳā tui / dāruṇ jvālā / mone koriȳā / ne /

ei ẏe deher / maddhe / ke koreche / khēlā /
pichu pāne / caiȳā dēkho / ḍube gēlo / bēlā /

bhāi balo / bandhu balo / keu tō kāreri / nāi /
diner pithe / dēkhā śōnā / pather pori / cay /

The refrain of this text (first stanza) begins with an anomalous short verse that does not fit the *chaṛā* pattern; this manner of beginning is common and is often reflected in the musical structure, which will be discussed in some detail in the last chapter. For the moment it may be noted that when sung, the refrains frequently have an ABA structure; either the first refrain verse may be so constructed, or the stanza, or both the first verse and the stanza. In the poem just quoted, the return of A occurs when the first half of the first line (*guru bhajo re*) returns at the end of a stanza; the musical setting of the refrain is somewhat uncommon, though not unique, in that this return is not reflected in it. Also uncommon is the fact that in the setting of this refrain, there is no cadence at the end of the first verse, and this necessitates repeating the entire refrain couplet after each stanza. Normally only the first verse is sung as an internal refrain, the couplet being reserved as the final refrain.

The *chaṛā*-like texts are close to doggerel verse in the simplicity of their prosody; other texts reveal a considerable sophistication in their construction. The couplets quoted next, for example, are quite complex in comparison to the preceding ones.

kēno kul hārāli gowr rūpe nayon kēno dili gōdhonī
tui gowr bhōgī/e jagat mājhi/kalaṅkhinī holi gōdhonī/

kuler kulobodhugon / tōrāi āmār kathā śon /
premer pathe koris nā gamon /
tor nanodinī / kāl sāpinī / diben karotāli gōdhonī /

tōrā thāk / dhoirẏo dhori / ẏās nā gharer bāhire /
gowr pāne cās nā gō phiri /
ō se hāl se behāl / diner kāṅāl / pāy se carondhūli gōdhonī /

se ẏe rosik rasomay / gowr hori raser hāṭe ray /
gowr hori raser kathā kay /
se raser kathāi/hoȳe śrōtā/lājer māthā khāli gōdhonī/

These pairs of verses resemble the type of meter called *tripadī*; they are odd, however, in that they appear to combine a verse in *dīrgho tripadī*—8-8-10 or 12 *mātrās*—with one in regular *tripadī*—6-6-8 *mātrās*. Despite this irregularity, the prescription for rhyme is followed; this requires that the first two *parbo*s in each verse rhyme. Normal *tripadī* also requires that the last syllable of each verse rhyme with its mate; in this poem each couplet ends with the same word. As in the *chaṛā* example, the first verse of the refrain is short and irregular in that it does not conform to the pattern in which the first verses of other stanzas are set.

Besides being relatively free in meter, the song texts are also subject to further distortion by the addition of extra words during performance. These words are usually inserted before a verse or phrase and are set to upbeats; two- or three-syllable exclamations are often used, such as *ō re* or *ā re* (simple attention getters, like "hey!"), *ō bhāi* (oh, brother), *hori bol* (a Vaisnava exclamation and greeting, "Say Hari!"). The same exclamations and longer ones like *ō bhōlār mon* (oh, forgetful mind) and *pāgol* (or *khēpā*) *mon āmār* (mad mind of mine) are also given longer melodic settings than the short upbeat phrases. Although these longer phrases may occur anywhere, they most often come at points which do not interrupt the flow of the text and melody phrases but rather at points which reinforce their articulation.

CHAPTER SEVEN

Instruments

The various instruments used by Bauls and non-Bauls to accompany Baul-*gān* may be divided into a basic and an adjunct group, the division being based upon the frequency with which a particular instrument is used, its importance for the Bauls, and the likelihood of their playing it themselves. Each group contains chordophones, idiophones, and membranophones, but only the adjunct group contains aerophones.

The basic group consists of six instruments: chordophones: *gōpīẏantro, khamak, dōtārā*; idiophones: *ghuṅur, nūpur*; membranophone: *ḍuggi*.

Basic Chordophones

Gōpīẏantro

Like many other forms of Indian music, classical or folk, Baul-*gān* is often sung to a drone, and for the Baul, the most common drone instrument is one that is frequently called *ēktārā*. The instrument itself is a metonymical symbol for Bauls, although, in fact, many other mendicant singers of various religious sects use it throughout India. Since a number of such sects in Bengal is popularly included in the Baul group simply because their adherents sing similar songs, the common equation of *ēktārā* and Baul is understandable.

Ēktārā means "one-string," and the instrument to which it refers has only one string; one end of the string is attached to a tuning peg while the other end passes through a membrane and is tied to a twig that is pulled against the membrane by the tension of the string. With this instrument there is a problem of nomenclature as there is another type of folk instrument called *ēktārā*, which also has one string. This, too, is used to produce a drone, but since the instrument is of the lute type, it appears to be a more sophisticated instrument than one used for droning. The fairly numerous descriptions and drawings or photographs of these two types of instru-

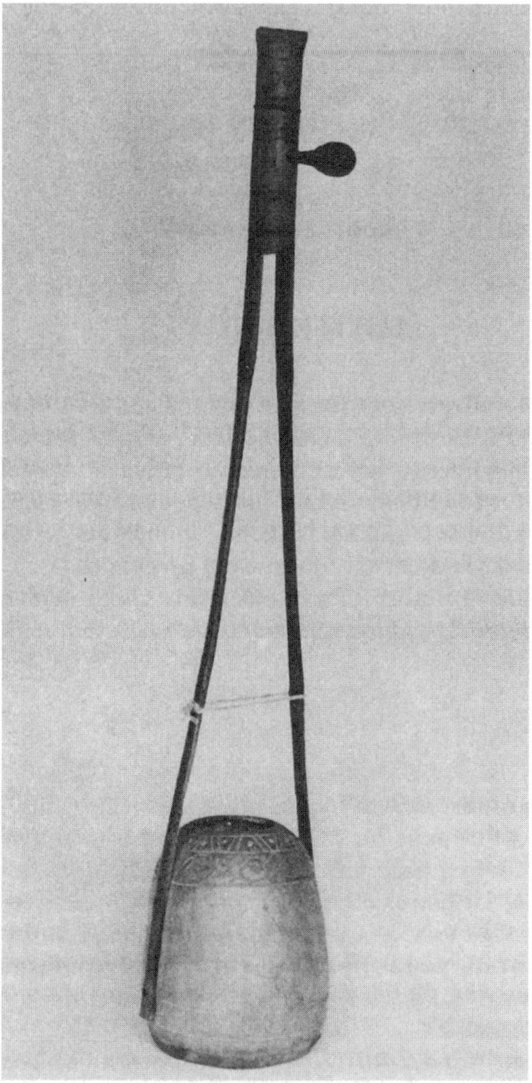

Fig. 23. *Gōpīýantro*.

ments have created a lot of confusion as to which instrument is called what, particularly as each is called by names given another instrument as well. Not infrequently, the description of one instrument, which even may contain an illustration, better fits the construction of the other.

The instrument of the non-lute type, is illustrated in figure 23 and is hereafter referred to as *gōpīẏantro*. It has also been called *gōpīcạd* (Krishnaswamy 1971, 84), *khamak* (Ray 1973, 107), *ānandolohori* (Deb 1966, 526; Kothari 1968, 79, no. 3284), and *lāuẏā* (Monsur Uddīn 1942, liii; S. K. Bose 1967, 56), as well as *gōpīẏantro* (D. Sen 1911, 164; S. Das Gupta 1969, 369, 369 n. 1; Mahillon 1978, 1:121, no. 76, also 1:140 which includes a drawing; Kothari 1968, 79, no. 283; Sachs 1923, 78–79) and *ēktārā* (Deb 1966, 525; Kothari 1968, 79, no. 283)—not to mention its other names in other regions of India (Kothari 1968, 78–80, Group Ia, division 2, class IV [chordophones]). Although the name *ēktārā* is commonly applied to this instrument, it is also commonly used for the lute type of instrument; *gōpīẏantro* is the preferable name for the former, since among the Bauls, at least, it is always used to mean the non-lute type of instrument. The lute type of *ēktārā* is not favored by the Bauls, if, indeed, they use it at all.

The name *gōpīẏantro* is a compound of two words: *gōpī-ẏantro*. The latter means "instrument," while a hasty guess would lead one to assume that the former refers to the cowherd girlfriends of Krishna, the *gōpīs*, as Curt Sachs was misled into believing (1923, 78–79). But according to Dineshchandra Sen, the Bengali literary historian, "The one-stringed lyre which was used by a ballad-singer while singing the glories of Gopi Pal, is still known as the Gopi-yantra, after the name of that monarch" (1911, 164). The magico-spiritual adventures of Gopi Pal, or Gopi-candro are the subjects of a very old tradition of balladry throughout Hindustan. In many places, the balladeers are Saivite yogis who revere the guru of Gopi Pal's guru, Goraksanath, as their first guru; in Bengal the descendants of such yogis have become a caste, the *ẏugi* caste, some of whom have been in the past and may still be itinerant singers of the Gopi-candro legend.[30]

The connection of *gōpīẏantro* with the Gopi-candro ballads has been questioned, however, by S. Das Gupta (1969, 369, 369 n. 1), who reports that this etymology was suggested by the Irish-born follower of Swami Vivekananda, Sister Nivedita, from whom D. Sen adopted the name. Das Gupta himself doubts this etymology but does not offer any further explanation. Whatever may be the explanation for the name, we will use *gōpīẏantro* only in reference to the non-lute instrument and will reserve the name *ēktārā* for the instrument of lute construction. The plucked string of the lute instrument passes over a bridge which rests on a membrane covering a hollow gourd; the string can be tuned to the singer's tonic by the peg at the end of the stick opposite the resonator gourd which the string pierces. A single pitch is all the instrument produces as only the open string is used.

In contrast with the *ēktārā,* the *gōpīýantro* is constructed to allow for altering the pitch. The sound produced by the string of the *gōpīýantro* passes directly to the membrane without the intermediary of a bridge; that is, the string passes through the membrane and is secured on the other side with a twig or something similar (fig. 24). In a way, this twig or knot acts like a bridge as it transmits the tension and vibrations of the string to the membrane which magnifies the sound. The membrane is attached to the wider end of a truncated-cone type of wooden or gourd resonator,[31] the opposite end of which is open. Passing through this end the string is attached to a peg inserted into the small, intact portion of a bamboo cylinder, part of whose tubular sides have been removed to leave two long thin slats which are attached to opposite sides of the drum at its narrower, open end. The string is usually tuned with the peg, but a secondary tuning device, for smaller gradations of pitch, may also be used; this consists of a thread wound around the bamboo slats whose tension may be adjusted by moving the string toward the drum or toward the peg to lower or raise the pitch slightly. Most frequently, the instrument is grasped by one of the bamboo

Fig. 24. *Gōpīýantro,* bottom view.

Fig. 25. *Gōpīẏantro* played with one hand by Lakṣ-m̃aṇ Dās.

slats in a manner which allows the index finger of the same hand to pluck the string (fig. 25); sometimes a wire plectrum may be worn on this finger. This manner of playing limits the instrument to producing the tonic drone.

An alternate manner of performance allows the pitch to be changed. In this manner, the index finger of one hand plucks the string, but the thumb and fingers of the other, instead of encircling a single slat, rest on both slats (fig. 26). Squeezing the slats toward one another decreases the tension on the string and lowers its pitch; no distinct pitch is aimed at, since immediately after being plucked in this position the string is normally returned to its basic tension by releasing pressure on the slats. The result, a rapid, swooping portamento from an indeterminate pitch up to the tonic, can be used most effectively to create catchy rhythms.

Fig. 26. *Gōpīýantro* played with two hands by Lakṣ-m̃aṇ Dās.

Khamak

In place of the *gōpīýantro,* another instrument, which is played with both hands, has become popular with Bauls, particularly in the Birbhum area of West Bengal. This instrument, like the *gōpīýantro,* has a variety of names, but they may all be applied with equal validity to the same instrument. Among the Bauls from whom information was gathered for this book the name most commonly used is *khamak*. This name, like *gubgubi*—another name for the same instrument—is onomatopoeic; *khamak* seems to represent the sound of a sharp sforzando accent (*mak*) preceded by a quick but equally forceful upbeat (*kha*), while *gubgubi* characterizes the less tense, crooning rhythmic sounds the instrument is capable of producing. Still another name refers to the undulating portamenti the instrument produces, but is not onomatopoeic—*ānandolohori* (wave of bliss).

In essense the instrument is similar to the *gōpīýantro;* that is, the *khamak* is a plucked "drum," but the tension of its string, or, more frequently, its pair of strings, is maintained or altered directly by hand rather

Fig. 27. *Khamak.*

than by being fixed by a peg. The end of the string is attached to the head of another tiny drum (figs. 27–29) that is held in the fist of the left hand, while the large drum is suspended from the player's shoulder by a cord and is pressed against the side with the left elbow (fig. 30; see also fig. 5). With slight flexing of the wrist, the performer can greatly vary the tension of the strings of the *khamak,* which he plucks with a pointed, elliptical plectrum that has a finger hole in the middle (fig. 31). With its double strings, usually of nylon, greater tension, and a heavy plectrum, both the dynamics and ambitus of the *khamak* are much greater than those of the *gōpīýantro.* The *khamak,* too, is often used to produce a tonic drone, but its greater resources allow it to be used for a much livelier and compelling style of accompaniment than is possible for the *gōpīýantro.* Although many Bauls play the instrument, few can match the subtle virtuosity of Pūrṇo Dās and his brother Lakṣm̃aṇ; they claim that their paternal grandfather Okrur (Ananto) Ģōsāi was the first to add the second string to the *khamak* and to make it popular in Baul-*gān.*

Dōtārā

The *ghuṅur* or *nūpur* (see p. 100) are always used in conjunction with *gōpīýantro* or *khamak,* as they leave the hands free. They may also be used

Fig. 28. *Khamak.*

with the most common stringed instrument among the Bauls, the *dōtārā* (figs. 32 and 33). Although the name literally means "two-strings," this instrument possesses four strings. The two middle strings are tuned to the same pitch, the tonic; the higher string, nearest the player's face, is a fourth lower, and the lowest string is tuned a fourth higher. The body, about two and a half to three feet long, is of the lute type, although neither that of the short- or long-necked lutes; that is, the neck, longer than those of short lutes in which the belly is the larger part, is also not distinctly articulated from the belly as in most long lutes. Both belly and neck are carved from the same piece of wood with little indication, viewed from behind, where one leaves off and the other begins; viewed from the front, the skin covering the belly makes evident the division between resonator and fingerboard. Some examples of the instrument may be waisted at this division, with barbs at the end of the fingerboard, which is fretless and often covered with a sheet of metal or glass in order to facilitate sliding the fingernails along the strings. The plectrum, small, thick, and blunt, is made of bone and is ordinarily attached to the instrument with a cord.

Although the "traditional" *dōtārā* available from manufacturers is relatively standardized and never has sympathetic strings added to it, one often encounters versions of the instrument, made by Bauls or other folk musicians, which do have sympathetic strings and which therefore resemble more closely the sarod used in classical Hindustani instrumental music.

Fig. 29. *Khamak.*

Fig. 30. *Khamak* played by Tinkoṛi Dās.

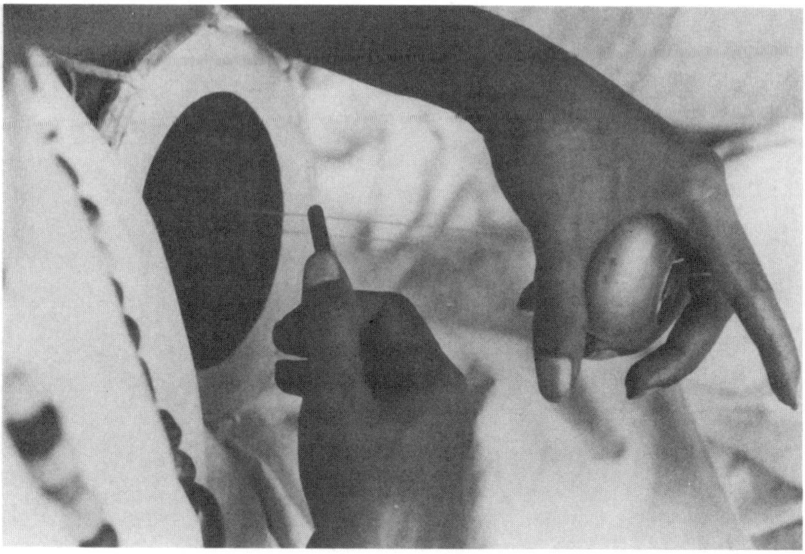

Fig. 31. Plucking *khamak* strings.

Fig. 32. *Dōtārā* played by Ýotin Dās.

Fig. 33. *Dōtārā* played by Nārāyoṇ Dās.

It is the manufacturers who provide instruments for the trained urban performers who have kept the "traditional" form, while the rural folk musicians continue to experiment with the instrument.

Like the *khamak,* which seems to be favored by Bauls of the Birbhum area, the *dōtārā* is an instrument with some regional associations, namely, with the Bangladesh area; and within Bangladesh, it is associated more with North Bengal around Dinajpur, Rajshahi, and Rangpur than with other areas (S. K. Bose 1967, 47). Although there is consensus about the association of the *dōtārā* with North and East Bengal, the instrument is easily found everywhere including Birbhum, in West Bengal; nevertheless, it appears that in North and East Bengal a more melodic accompaniment of folk song is preferred to the percussive and rhythmic accompaniment more common in the western and southern areas of the province.

Basic Idiophones

Ghuṅur and *nūpur*

Among the idiophones used in Baul-*gān,* the most popular for self-accompaniment are two types of ankle bells. The first type, *ghuṅur,* are similar to western sleigh bells, small, slit, spheres of metal with a single loose pellet inside. Many of these spheres are tied to a length of cord and then wrapped around the ankles in the same manner as in Kathakali, Kathak, Bharata Natyam, or numerous other styles of Indian dance, classical and folk. So basic is the gentle jangle of ankle bells to the rhythm of Baul-*gān* that even if a singer does not dance but performs seated on the ground, he is apt to wrap the bells around his big toe and tap his foot on the ground to accompany himself.

A still softer jangle than that of the *ghuṅur* is produced by the *nūpur,* a slit tubular anklet loosely filled with shot (fig. 34). It has a more feminine quality about it, perhaps because it is more ornamental looking than the *ghuṅur* and resembles the brass anklets some Indian women wear. The feminine associations of the *nūpur* are accented when, as occasionally happens, a Baul colors the rim of the sole of the foot with *mehdi* (henna), a cosmetic used in this manner by Indian women.[32]

Basic Membranophone

Ḍuggi

Although the *gōpīýantro* is often used alone, its modest volume of sound is insufficient to accompany the livelier and occasionally raucous performances some Bauls enjoy giving, for which reason it may be paired with a small kettledrum, the *ḍuggi.* The *gōpīýantro* alone may symbolize mendicant singers of religious songs, including Bauls, but the paired *ḍuggi* and *gōpīýantro* seem to be associated more specifically with the Bauls. The occasional drawings of Bauls seen in magazines or books, for example, frequently show them dancing to their own *gōpīýantro-ḍuggi* accompaniment, and the crude clay figurines illustrating the various peoples and costumes of India which the Government Cottage Industry shops sell include among them a Baul, complete with *geruỳā ālkhāllāh* and with one hand plucking a *gōpīýantro* while the other beats the *ḍuggi* strapped to his hip. Despite the common association of these instruments with Bauls, the *ḍuggi* is less common than the *khamak* now; perhaps the *ḍuggi* (fig. 35) was more common in the past.

The *ḍuggi* has a bowl-shaped clay body about 9 inches in diameter covered by a membrane to which a circle of hard paste has been permanently affixed to give it a deeper and more resonant tone. It is a smaller folk

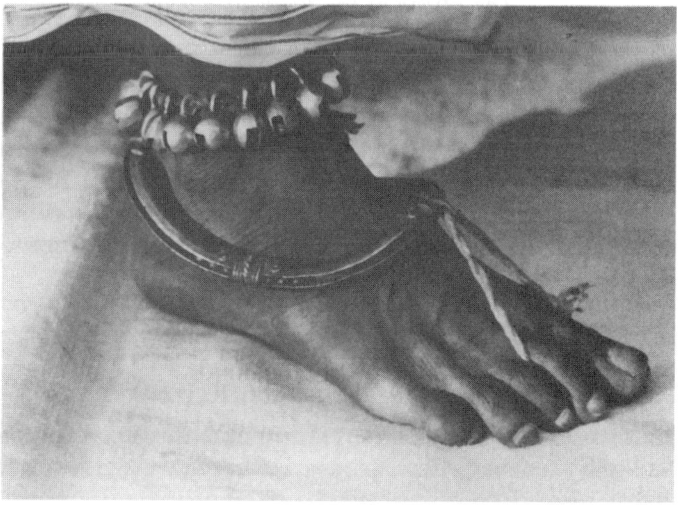

Fig. 34. *Ghuṅur* (*above*) and *nūpur*.

Fig. 35. *Ḍuggi* and *bā̦yā* (*right*).

version of the *bāyā* (left) drum which is paired with a *dāhinā* (right) to form the *tablā* used in the accompaniment of Hindustani art music; sometimes one still finds the name *ḍuggi* used in reference to the *bāyā*. In performance, the *ḍuggi* is tied in front of the left hip with the waist sash that forms part of the Baul's full dress. This leaves the left hand free to strike the drum while the other holds and plucks the *gōpīyantro;* in this way the singer can accompany himself while standing or dancing.

ADJUNCT CHORDOPHONES

The instruments discussed thus far, although not uniquely associated with Baul-*gān,* are those which are most commonly used; the instruments discussed in this section are more varied and may have more intimate associations with types of music other than Baul-*gān*.

Violin

The violin, which has long been a standard accompanying and solo instrument in Carnatic art music, and which has acquired a secure position as a solo instrument in Hindustani art music as well, has become a significant rival to its indigenous North Indian equivalent, the *sārindā,* in music like *padāboli kīrton* where it is used to accompany the *kīrtonīyā* and to play solo interludes. Its strings, usually of metal, are tuned to the lower tonic, fifth, higher tonic, and fourth. The one Baul I met who played the instrument, Monorām Dās, used it both to accompany himself, in alternation with singing, and others.

Since the violin is used in so many types of Indian music, it is not necessarily a sign of Western influence except in the purely organological sense, and even then, the tuning has been accommodated to Indian practice. In art and folk music contexts the violin is used to produce Indian music; in film music, Western influence may be more evident. In another context, the violin may be used for "Orientalized" music, too, as a busker I once heard in Calcutta made evident. The busker was a native of Chandernagore, a one-time French colonial city in Bengal where he had learned to play violin in a Western type ensemble. His repertoire consisted of fixed tunes with a Western sense of phrasing but with an Indianized feeling for ornament; modality was a hybrid, an Orientalized major-minor.

Sārindā

The uses of the *sārindā* are far more circumscribed than those of the violin. The instrument is confined to folk music; for art music, its more elaborate relative, the *sāraṅgī*, is used. In the *History of Musical Instruments,* Curt Sachs introduces these two instruments with the following sentence: "Short fiddles in India have a really fantastic shape" (1923, 227).[33] The *sāraṅgī* is not only fantastic but clumsy and ugly; the *sārindā,* on the other hand, is fantastically beautiful. Its belly is an elliptical bowl which has been pinched to create an exaggerated waist. The large barbs above the waist are hollow and uncovered; only the narrower and less pointed part, below the waist, is covered with parchment on which the bridge rests. It has a short neck and three gut strings which are bowed in the underhand manner of viols. If, in the imagination, one greatly reduces the size of the barbs, enlarges the size of the parchment-covered belly, and allows the neck to extend into a fingerboard covering the barbs and reaching to the belly, it is easy to see the relationship between the bowed short lute, *sārindā,* and its plucked equivalent, *rabab,* of which we have already met an example in the waisted *dōtārā.*

Although Cittorañjan Deb says in his description of the *sārindā* that it has "been used a great deal in ascetic and Vaisnava Baul sects" (1966, 530), it does not seem to be used much outside Vaisnava *kīrton,* and would appear to be infrequently used by Bauls. There is, however, an excellent film record of a lively and entertaining performance by a Baul singing and accompanying himself on *sārindā.*[34]

In folk performance, including Baul-*gān,* both violin and *sārindā* are used not only for melodic accompaniment and solo passages but also to give rhythmic impetus to the performance. K. S. Kothari (1968, 77, no. 6) gives this as a characteristic of folk *sāraṅgī* playing: "A notable feature that distinguishes the sarangi of Folk Music from the one used in Classical Hindustani Music is its manner of bowing. The former emphasizes rhythmic bowing for accentuating the rhythmic movement of the musical piece." Although he does not mention it in his description of *sārindā,* rhythmic bowing applies equally well to that instrument and to the violin. Often this rhythmic quality is due merely to an imitation of textual articulation, even when the instrument is playing solo during a refrain, for example. At other times, the rhythmic emphasis is due simply to a desire on the part of the performer to make the pulse and meter more perceptible.

Keyboard zither

This instrument is something of a freak; made in Japan, it consists of a few zither-mounted strings strummed with a plectrum and stopped with a keyboard mechanism to produce a melody. It is essentially an autoharp except that its function is melodic rather than harmonic. This instrument was played by a non-Baul to accompany performances at the *utsab* for Lakṣmaṇ Dās's *māmā.*

Fig. 36. *Kartāl.*

ADJUNCT IDIOPHONES

Kartāl/mandirā and *premjuṛi*

Of all the instruments used to accompany Baul-*gān*, only two idiophones, *kartāl/mandirā* and *premjuṛi,* to be discussed in this section, are commonly used by women; I met only one Baulini who regularly accompanied herself on *gōpīýantro,* and she was clearly considered eccentric, though much appreciated (see fig. 6). Male Bauls, too, may play *kartāl/mandirā* and *premjuṛi,* but this is uncommon.

Kartāl/mandirā are two different types of cymbals. The first of these names, *kartāl,* is that most frequently used for knobbed, disc-shaped cymbals of bell metal and fairly small diameter, about 5 inches (figs. 36 and 37). The name means "handclap" and refers to their use mainly as time keepers with only slight rhythmic interest. Similar cymbals are still used in Carnatic music for Bharata Natyam dance and in the accompaniment of the large oboe *nāgaśvaram* to indicate the *ghāṭa* or clapped beats with an open sound and the *visarjita* or throwaway beats with a damped sound.

As with many other widely dispersed instruments in India, nomenclature is difficult to sort out in the case of *kartāl.* Sachs gives this name to a pair of wooden clappers with jangles (1923, 15), which, as will be seen, I call *premjuṛi.* Sachs's designation is supported by K. S. Kothari (1968, 23, no. 17), but the instrument to which he refers comes from Rajasthan, not Bengal. The name *kartāl* will be reserved in this study for the cymbals.

A second type of cymbals, having a smaller diameter than the *kartāl* and a cup or bowl shape without a rim, is much rarer than the *kartāl*. It is called *mandirā*, at least by Cittorañjan Deb (1966, 524) in his book on Bengali folk music, where he clearly distinguishes this type from the *kartāl*.[35] Sachs gives the name *mañjirā* as the Hindi variant (1923, 19), but Deb (1966, 525) inexplicably applies this name to the frame drum which the Bauls call *khañjoni*. Even more puzzling is Deb's use of *khañjoni* for the wooden clapper with jangles that the Bauls call *premjuṛi* (fig. 38), and which, as Sachs correctly indicates, are widely called *kartāl* in Hindustan. The word *prem* in *prem-juṛi* means love and perhaps refers to the context of devotional music singing in which this instrument, as well as the *kartāl* and *mandirā*, are most apt to be found. It should be remembered that Baul-*gān* is not devotional music in the participatory sense; it is sectarian, soloist music performed by professional folk singers for an audience. Devotional music refers to the popular group singing of an inclusive nature like *bhajan* or *nām-kīrton*, in which simple percussion like *kartāl*, *mandirā*, and *premjuṛi* can increase devotional fervor without distracting the devotees with difficult or subtle music. As these instruments are so closely linked to group devotional singing, they are not basic in Baul-*gān*; but, as they require the least technique, they are suitable for use by the few female Bauls who sing and who are not apt to seek the same soloist status as performers as their husbands.

Fig. 37. *Kartāl, khōl, and khamak* played by (*left to right*) Brajobālā Dāsī, Sarot, and Lakṣmaṇ Dās.

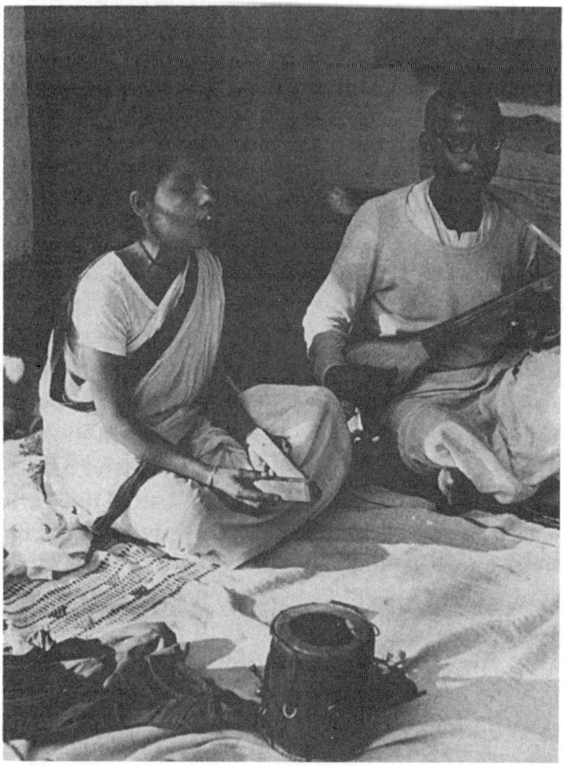

Fig. 38. *Premjuṛi* (*left*) played by Prem Dāsī; *dōtārā* played by Ýotin Dās.

Saucer and spoon; match and matchbox

It was a female Baul who performed on one of the more unusual instruments used as accompaniment to Baul-*gān,* and hers was the only such performance I encountered in my two years among these people. Perhaps one could consider her instrument, a saucer and a spoon, a sign of Westernization in Baul music since these utensils are the paraphernalia of tea drinking, a habit borrowed from the British. In the last few generations, tea drinking has overcome a prejudice against the practice to acquire wider popularity. Like alcohol, tea is a foreign drug in beverage form, the drinking of which has sociological significance as well as a physiological effect. The most common vessel for tea is a small, disposable, baked clay, handleless cup—the Indian version of the Dixie cup—like those made by the family of potters in back of Ýotin Dās Baul's house in Jiyaganj. Glasses are often used, too, but china, however crude, adds "class" to tea drinking, and occasionally a cup and saucer are to be had even at a rural tea stall. However the female Baul I observed had come by the saucer and spoon she used to accompany her husband, the Baulini played them in a manner nearly indistinguishable from that used to play *kartāl / mandirā*, except for the lack of difference between open and damped sounds.

Another percussion instrument was improvised from usual materials by Ŷotin Dās to accompany his wife in a performance at Santiniketan. His instrument was made from the smaller type of wooden matchbox and a match. Placing half the length of a wooden matchstick on top of the box lengthwise and securing it lightly with a finger or two, he would strike the half extending over the edge of the box with several fingers of his other hand, creating a series of accented beats with rolled upbeats somewhat similar to the way a *khamak* can be played but with nothing like its timbre or dynamic range.

Adjunct Membranophones

Khōl

Among the percussion instruments in this group, the most important is the *khōl,* used in the accompaniment of *kīrton.* The *khōl,* because of its Vaisnava associations and the heavy Vaisnava influence on the Bauls, is sometimes included in the accompanying ensemble for Baul-*gān,* although it appears not to be used by Bauls either for self-accompaniment or for accompanying someone else. Lakṣm̃aṇ Dās, nevertheless, had a *khōl,* which was played mainly in the village *nagar kīrtons* (processional *kīrtons*) in which he took part.

Like the use of the greeting phrase, *hori bol,* the adoption of the basil necklace, and the veneration of Caitanya, the use of the *khōl* is another sign of the assimilation of Vaisnava customs by the Bauls. At the same time, the peripheral role this instrument plays in their music is similar to the peripheral role of Vaisnavism in their doctrine. Perhaps the extremely intimate connection between the *khōl* and Vaisnava devotional singing has helped to prevent its becoming a primary accompanying instrument in Baul-*gān.*

Khōl, meaning "shell" or "covering," is the usual name for this drum, but it is sometimes also called by the fancier Sanskrit name *mṛidaṅgo,* which is used as a general term for all double-headed barrel drums. Unlike the *pākhōŷāj* used in Hindustani *dhrupad* and the *mṛidaṅgam* of Carnatic classical music, the *khōl* is actually made of clay, as the Sanskrit name *mṛidaṅgo* (earth-body) suggests (figs. 39–41; see also fig. 37).

Fig. 39. *Khōl.*

Fig. 40. *Khōl*, treble head.

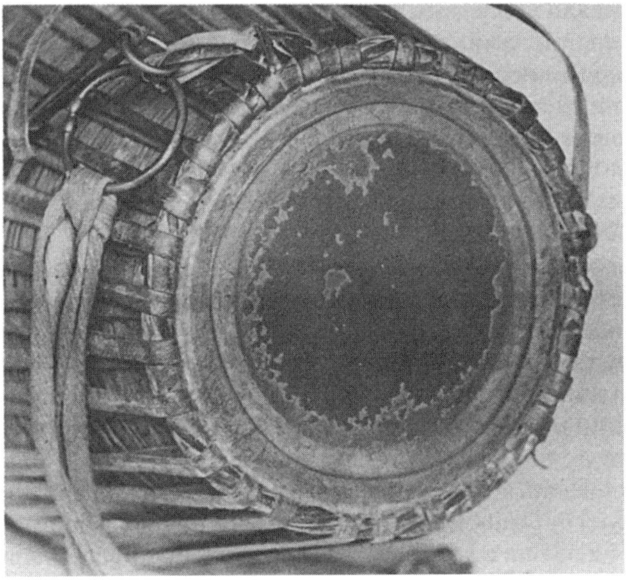

Fig. 41. *Khōl*, bass head.

The drum is about three feet long, and its smaller right head—considerably smaller in relation to the left head than on the *pākhōȳāj* or *mṛidaṅgam*—gives the drum its characteristic brittle, ringing tone, which contrasts sharply with the dry crack of the *mṛidaṅgam* and the booming resonance of the *pākhōȳāj*. The smaller right head has a spot of tuning paste permanently attached to it like the other drums; in my experience, the left head has been free of paste, but according to K. S. Kothari (1968, 42) the "broader left head is pasted with flour" as are those of the other *mṛidaṅga*s. A large number of rawhide laces is used to secure the heads to the body and to help protect the fragile clay body.

In the more refined style of *kīrton*, which was in the past associated with art music, the two-hand technique required for playing the *khōl* is considerable, and its repertoire of meters and rhythmic patterns is large and complex. For Baul-*gān*, no such elaborate accompaniment is required; the few simple patterns used are easy and repetitious enough to be picked up by anyone with a modicum of interest and ability.

Tablā

Another drum whose primary association is with music other than Baul-*gān* is the *tablā*; this name refers to a pair of single-headed drums called *bāyā* and *dāhinā* used in the accompaniment of most forms of Hindustani art music, both vocal and instrumental. The *bāyā* is a larger version of the *ḍuggi* kettledrum described earlier; the *dāhinā* is a small conical drum about 10 inches tall, slightly taller than the *bāyā*, and with a smaller head diameter (about 5 inches as opposed to 9 inches). Both drums have permanently fixed spots of tuning paste. Inexpensive *bāyā*s are made of clay, just as the *khōl* and *ḍuggi* are.[36] Better ones are made of nickel-plated copper; *dāhinā*s are made of wood.

As *tablā* are now the most important drums in Hindustani art music for solo recital, in the rhythmically complex Kathak dance style, and in the accompaniment of instruments and voice, the skill and technique required for playing them is formidable; in the accompaniment of Baul-*gān* only minimum skill is needed, since only a couple of simple meters are used and neither artful improvisation nor fixed compositions are a part of the performance.

Like the *khōl*, the *tablā* are peripheral to Baul-*gān* and are not normally played by Bauls. Since they are ubiquitous among non-Bauls, however, it is likely that wherever a *melā* or *utsab* is in progress, someone will have "picked up" enough *tablā* to accompany various kinds of folk and / or popular music. Because of their art music associations, the *tablā* have a degree of prestige among professional folk musicians like the Bauls, but the drums remain essentially alien; it is not so surprising that Lakṣmaṇ Dās, for example, possesses a *khōl* even if he does not use it to accompany himself, but it would seem a bit affected for him to own a set of *tablā*, and, in fact, he does not.

Pūrṇo Dās, exceptional in this as in other things, is almost always accompanied by *tablā*—and harmonium—because the other members of his troupe sing types of popular religious music for which these instruments are now standard. When Pūrṇo sings Baul-*gān*, however, his own dynamic *khamak* accompaniment often overshadows the steadier and blander rhythmic background of the *tablā*.

Khañjoni

In the group of less commonly used percussion instruments to which the *khōl* and *tablā* belong, the *khañjoni* is one which is played by the Bauls themselves both for self-accompaniment and for accompanying others. The *khañjoni* is a small frame drum with a relatively broad rim about 3 inches wide and a glued-on head about 6 to 7 inches in diameter. Apparently because the rim slants outward slightly towards the open side and

Fig. 42. *Khañjoni* with jangles.

because it is relatively broad in relation to the diameter of the head, Sachs classifies the drum as conical. The player grasps the drum by placing the rim in the palm of his hand and putting his thumb on the inside while lightly resting two or three fingers on the outer surface of the head. By exerting and relaxing tension on the head with these fingers, he can alter the pitch of the drum somewhat, and timbre and dynamic changes can be made by different placement of the striking fingers of the other hand or by use of the whole palm. Like the *khamak,* the *khañjoni* can provide a most attractive and exciting accompaniment.

Unlike the *khōl* and *tablā*, the *khañjoni* has no association with art music or those more elaborate types of devotional music which approach art music in complexity. It is, nevertheless, one of the instruments commonly used by other mendicant singers of religious songs, and in the hands of some can attain a remarkable degree of subtle musical expression.[37] But only in Carnatic music has it become an instrument suitable for the accompaniment of art music.[38] In the Carnatic *kañjira,* a single pair of jangles is ordinarily added, but these may be omitted in the northern folk instrument (fig. 42).

Adjunct Aerophones

Harmonium

This is the only group of instruments to be considered which has no counterpart among the basic instruments for Baul-*gān* accompaniment—not surprisingly since it is difficult to blow and sing at the same time. The harmonium, of course, gets round this difficulty nicely, but it is quite expensive for one thing, and rather heavy and awkward, which makes dancing difficult and transportation clumsy. As it has no dynamic expressiveness or possibility for sharp, clean articulation, it does not lend itself to rhythmically enlivened performance or accompaniment of melody as do the bowed, plucked, or struck instruments. Although the instrument derives from the harmonium introduced by missionaries, it, like the violin, should not be considered as evidence of Westernization; the harmonium has been thoroughly Indianized. Even the instrument's construction has been altered to provide it with a compacter bellows, manually rather than pedally operated, which allows it to be used by performers seated on the floor in the Indian manner (fig. 43).

By now the harmonium has become a fixture in Hindustani classical and popular art music and is used in preference to the *sāraṅgī,* which has disreputable associations, by many Hindustani vocalists, particularly males. The harmonium is also to be found in many middle-class homes where amateurs may accompany their own performances of *robīndrosoṅgīt, ādhunik, philmi-gīt,* and other types of composed popular and art songs.

Being such a popular instrument, one is always within easy access of any organized occasion at which Baul singing is apt to occur. But regular use of the harmonium by a Baul is rare. Only Sadānando Dās accompanies himself, quite competently, on harmonium; the type of song he chose to sing for me to record was a well-known sentimental song such as one might hear an amateur of the city sing. Perhaps he thought this more suited for taping by a foreigner than a presumably less appealing Baul-*gān* which he probably would have accompanied on *dōtārā*, an instrument he also played.

While Sadānando's technique on the harmonium was fairly polished, in another performance recorded at the home of Lakṣmaṇ Dās, the need for playing technique was eliminated altogether by reducing the harmonium to a drone instrument. The performer, a neighbor who happened in, not only had no technique but no ear as well, for he would sometimes accidentally, and persistently, in attempting to play an octave drone, depress a key adjacent to the drone pitch, making it a long sustained semitone dissonance to which he was perfectly oblivious. The use of an unbroken

Fig. 43. Harmonium.

drone is characteristic of Indian art music of both the North and the South; a modified version of the harmonium which has no keyboard but a system for opening or closing particular reeds is used especially in the South. In Baul music the *gōpīyantro* and *khamak* also provide a drone, but it is somewhat intermittent; their role is rhythmic as well as tonal, the various plucking patterns, dynamic changes, and portamenti complementing the drone function.

The only Baul who is regularly accompanied by harmonium is Pūrṇo Dās, who sings for urban audiences in contexts where Baul-*gān* has become a form of popular entertainment music. The other members of his troupe are not Bauls and perform other types of song for which harmonium is the most appropriate accompaniment.

Flute

Other than the harmonium, the only aerophone used is the transverse bamboo flute (*āṛ bą̄si*); partly because singing is the primary folk musical activity and instrumental music is used mainly for accompaniment, flute playing is relatively rare. Despite the central place it holds in Vaisnava imagery as the instrument with which Krishna intoxicates the souls of his devotees, as far as the Bauls are concerned, it is just another of the instruments which is welcomed as accompaniment if there should happen to be someone in the vicinity who can play it and cares to join in. Recently, it would appear that Sonāton Dās Ṭhākur has acquired a flute-playing disciple who regularly accompanies him, as the flute player was evident in tape recordings Carol Salomon made of Sonāton in 1975.

Concluding Observations on Instrumentation

The manner in which a flute may just happen to join an ensemble accompanying a Baul is characteristic of the partly unpredictable nature of such ensembles. Although some rather odd combinations have been mentioned in these ensembles, such as the match and matchbox or spoon and saucer, the possibilities have probably not been exhausted; I have discussed only those of which I have certain knowledge. There are some possibilities, however, which are most improbable; perhaps they are impossibilities. The various double reeds (*sānāi*) for example, would be incongruous as Baul-*gān* accompaniment, not only because they are too loud to serve as vocal accompaniment, but also because they have very specific connections with festivities like weddings or with particular functions such as marking the hours at temples and *dargā*s. Since it requires a good deal of practice to play the *sānāi* well and since it has a special repertoire, *sānāi* players are a professional class unto themselves, and it is not likely that where Bauls are singing an amateur performer would just happen to be in the vicinity who would join in as a flutist might.

Neither would a *ḍhāk* be used. This large barrel drum is played vigorously with sticks and is quite loud; also, like the *sānāi*, it has a specialized role since it is played in *pūjā*s using particular patterns is signal different sections of the ceremonies.[39] Therefore, although there is serendipity in the constitution of instrumental groups accompanying Baul-*gān*, there are some instruments which would probably never be included. On the other hand, it should be reiterated that a few instruments, such as the *gōpīẏantro, khamak,* and *ḍuggi*, are particularly appropriate for Baul-*gān* and are the instruments most likely to be played by Bauls themselves. This does not necessarily mean, however, that such instruments will invariably be used; the use of the *ḍuggi*, for example, is now infrequent, and the *khamak* and *dōtārā* may have greater currency in one area than another, but such instruments are the ones most clearly associated with Baul-*gān*.

CHAPTER EIGHT

Temporal Organization

The most significant rhythmic features of Baul music concern: 1) an unmeasured introduction that may precede the performance of a song; 2) use of only two types of meter; and 3) the change of meter that may occur during the performance of a song. Each of these features will be discussed and illustrated in this chapter.

Unmeasured Introductions

Before a Baul begins the measured part of a performance, he may first sing an unmeasured introduction, which may in its turn have been preceded by an unmeasured instrumental introduction. Vocal introductions are rendered in a rhapsodic manner and are of two types. In the first and shorter type, the singer merely hums or sings the vowel *ā* to a few notes around the tonic before starting with the measured song; in the second type, he sings the refrain, or parts of it, which he will later sing in measured rhythm. For the instrumental introduction that precedes the vocal, the performer, usually the singer himself, will also render the refrain in free rhythm if he plays a melodic instrument such as the *dōtārā;* otherwise he will play a series of fast rhythmic patterns on the *khamak*. In the introductions, instrumental sections are apt to be longer than the vocal sections; the two together rarely reach a length equal to a fifth of the length of the measured song.

The total performance times for the songs I recorded for this study range from about three minutes to more than fourteen minutes. This difference in performance times was determined by the length of the text, the competence of the performer, the context of the performance in which he performed, and, perhaps, by where the singer and song came from. *Nitāi āmār nāker bēśor,* for example, lasts less than three minutes in the version sung by Brajobālā Dāsī; its text is short and it was sung by an old woman seated in the courtyard of her village home during an impromptu recording session at which her son and a couple of friends were present. My recording of *tēmon ēkjon pāgol,* on the other hand, lasts twelve minutes forty seconds. Its text is exceptionally long; it was sung in the same locale as the previous song by a vigorous young man, who danced as he sang before an audience of other Bauls and villagers gathered to commemorate the death anniversary of another Baul.

The Meters of Baul-*gān*

The meters of Baul-*gān* tunes are limited to 6/8 and 4/4. Tunes in 6/8 meter frequently alternate or mix 3×2 and 2×3 (ex. 1), while those in 4/4

Example 1 ⁀ indicates metric shift to 3/4 (*sab lōke kay lālon ki jāt*)

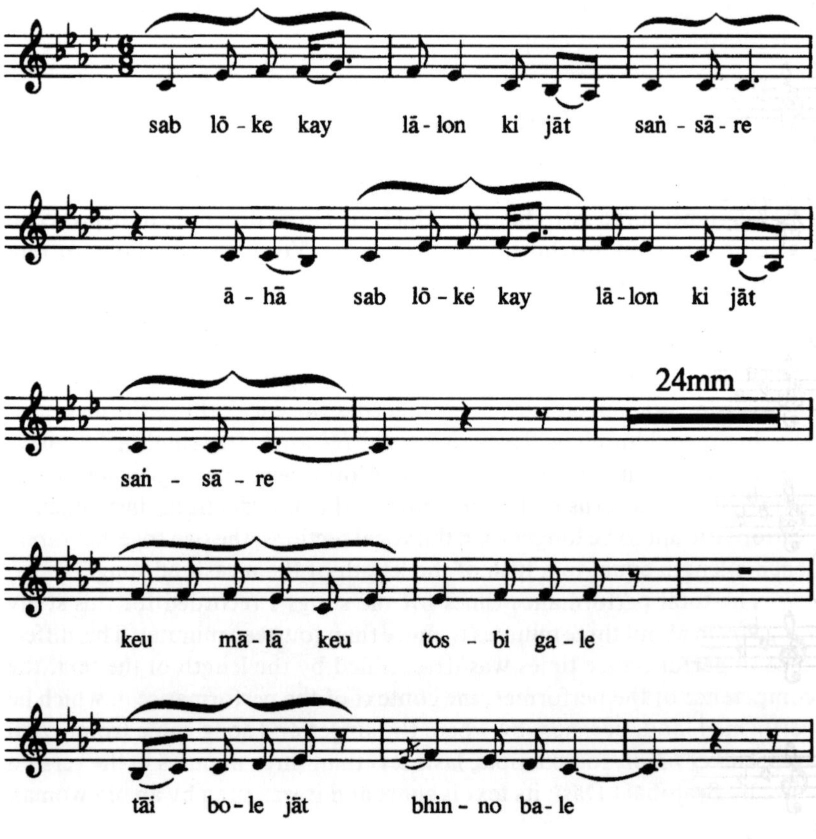

meter often exhibit an additive rearrangement of its four-square measures, such as ♩. ♩. ♩ (ex. 2). These two rhythmic characteristics are often linked to verbal accents but are not wholly dependent on them, because the same rhythmic characteristics are regularly found in the accompaniment figures of instruments like *khamak, khañjoni, gōpīÿantro,* and *ḍuggi.* These accompanimental figures may either coincide or contrast with rhythmic pat-

Example 2 (*tumi se nā deśer kathā re mon bhule giÿecho*)

terns of the tune accompanied, or even do both simultaneously if the performer uses two or more accompanying instruments together, such as *gōpīyantro, ḍuggi,* and *ghuṅur* (ex. 3). The melodic accompaniment played on an instrument like the *dōtārā* is more apt to be cast in rhythmic patterns that reinforce the meter as do those of the accompaniment in example 2. The use of hemiola in 6 / 8 and the use of additive rhythmic patterns in common time, though characteristic of Baul-*gān,* are not unique to it; they are both found in many types of Indian music.

Distribution of the Two Meters, Tempi, and Metric Change

According to Ŷotin Dās, who was unusual among Bauls for the amount of musical terminology he employed, the two meters of Baul-*gān* are called *lōphā-dādrā* (6 / 8) and *karphā* (4 / 4). The former name is a paradox as it combines *lōphā,* the name of a four-beat meter associated with *kīrton,* and *dādrā,* the name for (6 / 8) in light classical music of folk origin. The second name is probably a Bengali version of Hindustani *kaharvā,* the common time of light classical music.

The number of Baul-*gān* in the two meters appears to be about equal, with a slight favoring of compound duple. Tempi for both groups commonly are within the ♪ = 200–300 MM range; Lakṣm̃aṇ Dās's performance of *kēno kul hārāli,* in which ♪ = 160, and Tinkoṛi Dās's performance of *bhāṅā ghare,* in which ♪ = 360, are exceptional. In the former song, such a slow tempo is probably associated with the song itself, since the same singer performs other 6 / 8 songs, like *tēmon ēkjon pāgol,* at the more common and quicker tempo, ♪ = 280. In *bhāṅā ghare,* however, the exceptionally quick tempo is at least partly attributable to Tinkoṛi's characteristically brisk manner of performance.

The tempo of a song increases during its performance, and those tempi given for songs mentioned in the preceding paragraph are representative of the first half of a performance; Lakṣm̃aṇ Dās, for example, began *tēmon ēkjon pāgol* about ♪ = 270, but reached nearly ♪ = 390 by the end of the song. The tempo ♪ = 390 exceeds even that of the fast beginning of *bhāṅā ghare,* which Tinkoṛi started at ♪ = 320 and finished at ♪ = 400.

Once a performer has begun a measured song, he usually continues to the end in the same meter. There are, however, two common exceptions. In the first, the singer changes from measured rhythm to parlando rubato to deliver a short passage of text, normally the end of a stanza (ex. 4); during this time the accompanists are silent. After this parlando passage, the singer starts the refrain in measured rhythm and the accompaniment returns. The second exception involves a sudden change in meter, called *tāl phertā*

Example 3 (*mon ēkbāre hori balo*)

Example 4 (*tēmon ēkjon pāgol pelām nā*)

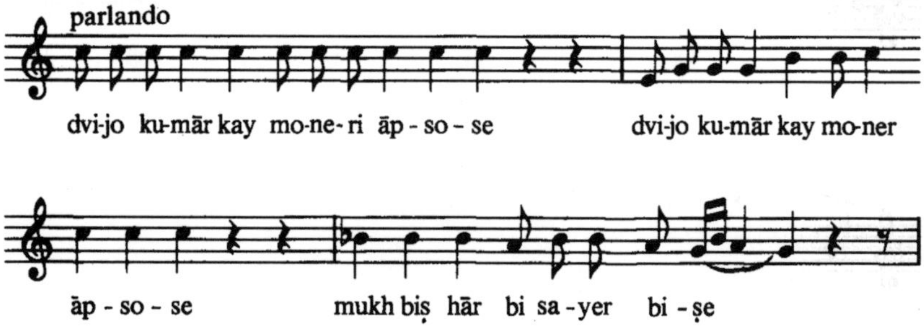

(meter change), a term borrowed as, perhaps, was the device itself from the more sophisticated style of *kīrton* (*padāboli*). The *tāl phertā* normally occurs nearer the end than the beginning of a performance, is followed by a return to the original meter, and is more often a change from compound to simple duple than the reverse, although the latter does occur.

Example 5 illustrates *tāl phertā* in a) Tinkoṛi's performance of *bhāṅā ghare,* b) Nārāyon Dās Odhikāri's performance of *mānob deho mōṭor gāṛi,*

Example 5a (*bhāṅā ghare uri diẏe thākbo kato din*)

ās - be bar - ṣā kar - be phar - sā re
bhō-lār mon

Example 5b (*mānob deho mōṭor gāri cālāō sādhon rāstāte*)

2
ō gō sad gu - ru - ro
bāk-ȳe-te ā-bār mon ḍrāi-bher-ke ō tōr
mon drāi-bher- ke
2mm
mon ḍrāi - bher-ke neo ṭhik kore
khē-pā sad gu - ru - ro bā - kȳe-te

Example 5c (*sukher dhān bhāṅā*)

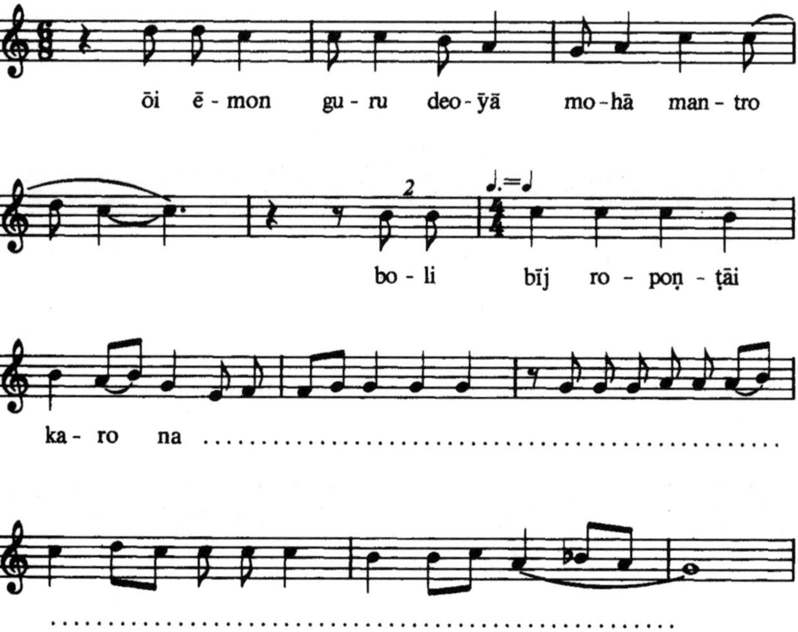

and c) Lakṣm̃aṇ Dās's performance of *kēno mānob jomin ābād korli nā*, in each of which the change is from 6 / 8 to 4 / 4. In the last excerpt, the *tāl phertā* takes place quite early in the performance (m. 120 of 257), and there is no return to the original 6 / 8. As Lakṣm̃aṇ also changed the scale in the middle of performing this song, it may be that he decided to change to a tune that was more familiar to him for singing this text, so the *tāl phertā* is merely fortuitous.

Ýotin's performance of *bṛindābone tin raṅgete* is also an unusual example of change in meter; throughout the performance there is frequent alternation between two meters instead of a single change followed by a return to the original meter. Although the Lakṣm̃aṇ and Ýotin examples illustrate exceptional uses of *tāl phertā*, they also illustrate the unpredictability of Baul behavior, which typically extends to their musical performances as well as to other aspects of their culture. As Jogendra Nath Bhattacarya remarked in 1896, "Their songs are characterized by a kind of queerness which makes them very amusing" (1968, 381).

CHAPTER NINE

Pitch Use and Tonality

Because the Bauls have no body of consciously formulated musical theory, the principles governing the use of pitch material, as proposed in this chapter, are based on my own observations of musical behavior. The Bauls, of course, are not aware of the principles I propose, and so they frequently "violate" them; in this regard, the phrase *uḷto pathik* (contrary pilgrim), which is used to describe the unorthodox social and religious behavior of the Bauls, may just as well describe their musical behavior. An account of the contradictions evident in Baul performances would require much verbal description of particular musical details and, if given here, would obscure the discussion of the general theory that is the topic of the chapter; consequently, I will concentrate on a description of the principles governing the selection and use of pitches and not on the many specific ways in which those principles are transgressed.

Pitches and Scale Degrees

As a body of song, Baul-*gān* uses all twelve chromatic pitches available within the octave. While the intonation of some of these, in reference to a tonic,[40] is variable, it is, nevertheless, clear that the octave is divided into twelve pitch positions that are roughly equidistant.[41] With one possible exception, there is no differentiation between varieties of scale degrees that are less than a semitone or more than a whole tone apart. The possible exception is the type of third degree—midway between the flatted and natural third degrees—that Pūrṇo Dās employs in his performances of a tune to which he sings several different texts.

The relationship of the pitches to scale degrees is governed by a variety of restraints; there is no universally applicable procedure within the system, such as that employed in Western music to create five pitch varieties (𝄫, ♭,

♮, ♯, 𝄪) of each degree by the uniform application of accidentals. Some of the relationships between pitches and scale degrees in Baul-*gān* correspond to those of Hindustani theory, however, and in the discussion that follows, agreement and divergence will be noted. A handy summary of the elements of Hindustani theory which are pertinent to this comparison may be found in N. Jairazbhoy (1971, 32–64).

Every Baul-*gān* uses a heptatonic scale, and of the twelve or thirteen pitches used, two may occur enharmonically as pairs of scale degrees; these are the natural third / flatted fourth, and the sharped fourth / flatted fifth.[42] Thus there is in Baul-*gān* a total of fifteen functionally distinct notes, that is, pitches, functioning in the seven degree positions of the scale (see table 1).

TABLE 1
The Scale Degrees of Baul-*gān* and Their Associated Pitches

heptatonic degrees	*chromatic pitches functioning as degrees*		*total number of notes*
VII	12	B♮	15
	11	B♭	14
VI	10	A♮	13
	9	A♭	12
V	8	G♮	11
	7	G♭	10
IV	7	F♯	9
	6	F♮	8
	5	F♭	7
III	5	E♮	6
	4a	E?	5
	4	E♭	4
II	3	D♮	3
	2	D♭	2
I	1	C	1

Of the seven degrees of the scale, the first, alone, is invariable. In Hindustani theory both the first degree and the natural fifth degrees are invariable and are named *acal svar* (immoveable notes). Though the flatted fifth degree is encountered in Baul-*gān,* it is rare and never supplants the natural degree as a primary scale degree; it is used only ornamentally. In Hindustani musical practice the fifth degree is, despite its classification as an *acal svar,* moveable to its flatted position, in which form it is used not only ornamentally in *rāg bhoirobī,* but also as a primary scale degree in *rāgs* like *lolit* and *śuddh basant,* where it is the only form of the fifth degree; in such contexts, because of the limitations of Hindustani theory, it must be named a sharped fourth degree.

Although the sharped fourth degree does occur in performances of Baul-*gān,* it is, like the flatted fifth degree, merely ornamental and is never a primary scale degree, a rank reserved for the natural form only. The flatted fourth degree, too, is an ornamental tone in Baul-*gān*, but it is nonexistent in both the practice and theory of Hindustani music; in the latter, the fourth degree is the only one that may be sharped, and in some of the *rāg*-generating scales (*thāṭ*), such as *kalyāṇ, mārōyā, pūrbī,* and *tōṛī,* the sharped rather than the natural fourth degree is used.

All the remaining degrees, the second, third, sixth, and seventh, are capable of being moved from their natural to their flatted positions, in both Hindustani theory and practice, where they are called *cal svar* (moveable notes), and in Baul-*gān.* Strictly speaking, the fourth degree is also a moveable pitch in Hindustani theory because it may be sharped. The one possible exception in Baul-*gān* is the extra position for the third degree suggested in table 1.

Of the seven scale degrees, the first, both as tonic and tonic octave, and the natural fourth and natural fifth degrees above the tonic function as the major tonal goals and points of repose, so melodic activity centers primarily on them (table 2). The importance of these pitches is indicated by the fact that a singer will seek them out in his *khamak* accompaniment. This instrument, it will be recalled, is capable of producing clear pitches as well as percussive noise. Because clear pitches are only intermittently used, even

TABLE 2
Primary Tonal Goals

the occasional use of the tonic seems more significant than does its more continuous use in *gōpīÿantro* accompaniment. Rather than functioning merely as a drone, the tonic, when sounded in *khamak* accompaniment, often helps articulate the song structure. In Example 6, for instance, the syncopated *tihāi*-like rhythmic pattern in the *khamak,* which concludes a statement of the refrain, clearly sounds the tonic, reinforcing the tonal ca-

Example 6 (*ēmon cāsā buddhi nāsā*)

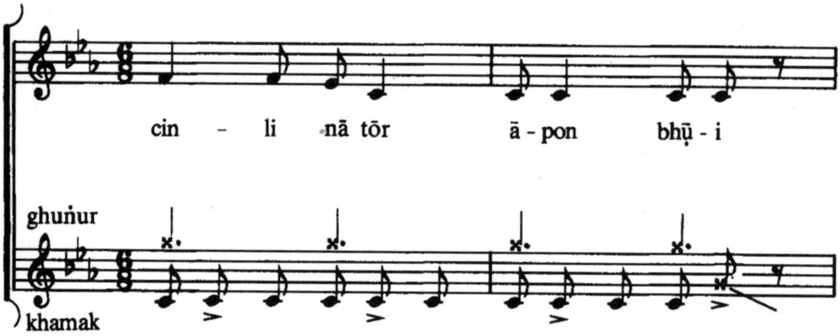

dence as well as creating a rhythmic one.[43] When the setting of a new line of text emphasizes the fourth degree, which is often the case, this pitch will be supported in the *khamak* accompaniment, too (exx. 7a and 7b).

Example 8 is an extended illustration of a sensitive use of the pitch-producing capacity of the *khamak* to reinforce the conventional cadence progressions of the melody phrases. Starting with the tonic-octave cadence of the voice in m. 46, the *khamak* emphasizes this note in the succeeding measures. At m. 50 a new melodic phrase descends from the tonic octave and comes to rest on the fifth degree, which note is echoed in the *khamak* accompaniment of the following measures. The vocal melody, going back to the flatted seventh degree in m. 56, descends further and concludes with an implied cadence on the tonic which is approached by an incomplete portamento from the third degree in m. 57. In the following measure (58), the descent from the flatted seventh degree is reiterated in the *khamak* with a long tremolo glissando that dramatically reintroduces the tonic for the return of the refrain in m. 59.

Tonalities

Since the tonic, its octave, the natural fourth, and the natural fifth degrees play a similar structural role in every Baul-*gān,* it is upon the re-

Example 7a (*ēmon cāsā buddhi nāsā*)

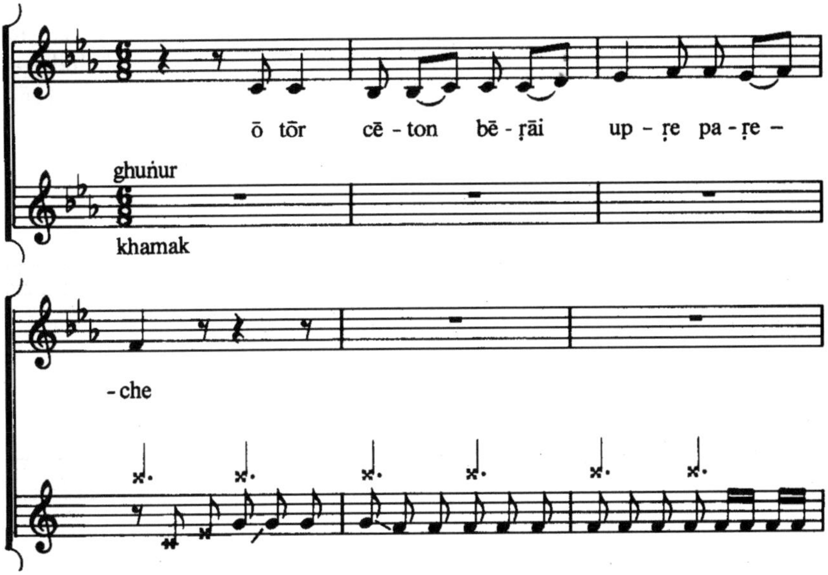

Example 7b (*ki aścaryo majār kathā*)

Example 8 (*ki aścarýo majār kathā*)

maining degrees, the second, third, sixth, and seventh, that the tonality of a song depends. Among these degrees the type of third particularly characterizes a tonality; therefore, the tonalities of Baul-*gān* may be said to be basically of two types, that with a natural third degree and that with a flatted third degree, with, possibly, a subsidiary type having a third degree between these two.

Tonality with a Natural Third Degree

In songs of this tonality, the natural third degree is used exclusively, or predominantly if the flatted third is also present; either way, the presence of the natural third degree exerts an influence on other moveable notes, so that the second and sixth degrees are always natural. The two augmented seconds between the flatted second and natural third degrees and the flatted sixth and natural seventh degrees, characteristic of so many *rāg*s, are nonexistent in Baul-*gān.*[44]

The seventh degree appears more independent of the influence of the natural third degree than the second or sixth degrees because it has two alternative uses: one is its occurrence exclusively in flatted form, the other is its occurrence in both flatted and natural forms in the same song. Consequently, the scale degrees of the tonality with a natural third degree can be listed as in table 3. The sharped fourth degree, which may occur in performances of songs in this tonality, has been omitted from the table since its occurrences are rare, unpredictable, and uncharacteristic; it is used only as the fourth above the tonic (not in the position an octave higher).

Since both the third and seventh degrees have two alternatives, some examples will be given to illustrate the contexts in which the one or the other alternative is encountered. Example 9 is taken from a performance whose ambitus spans a minor seventh from the tonic, and which consequently has the flatted seventh as its highest pitch; it is therefore also an example of what appears to be the smallest ambitus used in Baul-*gān.* The extreme ambitus is about two octaves from a fifth below the tonic. The song from which example 9 is taken is typical of *bhāōāiȳā,* a genre of North Bengal folk songs dealing with love themes. It is a type of Baul-*gān* in that such songs are sometimes sung by Bauls. Because the singer neither goes

TABLE 3
Primary Scale Degrees in the Tonality with a Major Third Degree

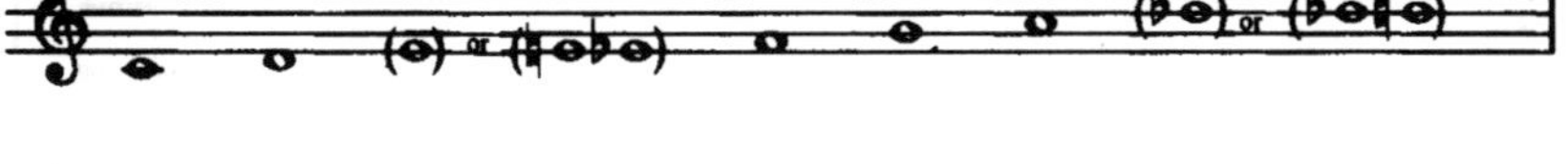

below the tonic nor rises to its octave, the seventh degree is never converted to a leading tone but, remaining flatted, always leads to a cadence on a lower degree such as the fifth. A phrase in which the flatted seventh degree is held a long time and creates a charming dissonance with an actual or implied tonic drone before falling to the consonant fifth degree, as is done in example 9, is said to be characteristic of *bhāṭiẏāli,* the East Bengal boatman's song (Cakrobortī 1962, 678).

Example 9 (*naylā bandhu re kato din pābo tōmār dēkhā*)

The same type of *bhāṭiẏāli* phrase with the flatted seventh degree is illustrated in example 10. The phrase following it in the example descends exceptionally low, to a perfect fifth below the tonic, and thus gives this song a greater ambitus than the previous one. The seventh degree included in the extension of the ambitus below the tonic is also always flatted in this performance, even though it sometimes rises to the tonic.

When the ambitus of a song in the tonality with a natural third degree extends below the tonic and / or reaches to its octave or beyond, both the

Example 10 (*ā re ō jībon chāriẏā nā jāō mōre*)

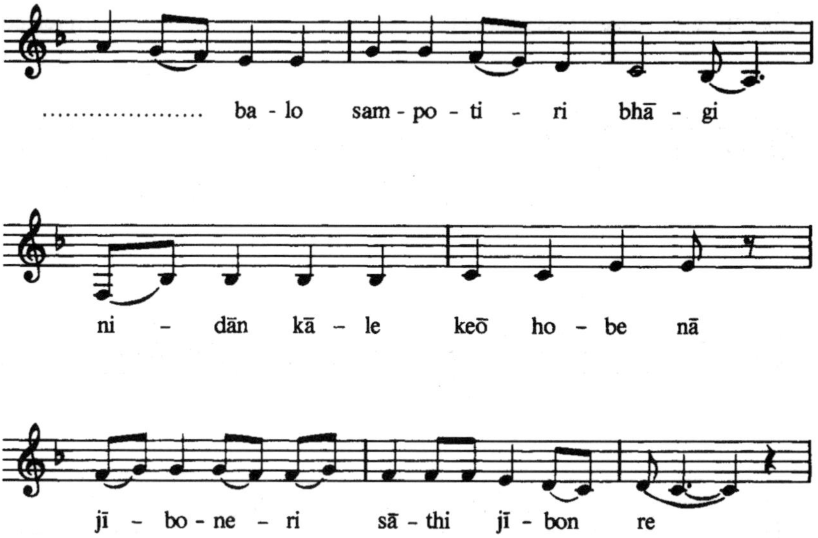
.... ba - lo sam - po - ti - ri bhā - gi
ni - dān kā - le keō ho - be nā
jī - bo - ne - ri sā - thi jī - bon re

natural and flatted seventh degrees will be employed. Frequently, the choice of one or the other, particularly in the higher octave, depends on the melodic goal. When, for example, the melody emphasizes the tonic octave, the seventh is most often natural, even when it does not resolve directly to that note (ex. 11). In such circumstances as these, if the flatted seventh degree is introduced, it initiates a movement away from the higher tessitura centering on the tonic octave and toward a cadence on some lower note, perhaps the fifth degree or the third, in preparation for an eventual cadence on the tonic (exx. 12a and 12b).

Below the tonic, the natural seventh degree is most often used as a lower neighbor embellishment to a tonic cadence (ex. 13). When the flatted seventh degree is used below the tonic, its most characteristic appearances are 1) in a phrase which descends to a temporary cadence on the lower sixth degree before ascending to cadence on the tonic (ex. 14), and 2) in a redundant cadential phrase that rises from the lower sixth degree to conclude on the tonic (ex. 15).

Similarly to the way in which the seventh degree is used in alternative manners, the third degree is used in its natural form in some songs and in both its natural and flatted forms in others. In the songs in which both forms appear, despite the appearance of the flatted third degree, the tonality is described as that with a natural third degree, since that degree is predominant and continues to influence the intonation of the second and sixth degrees. Typically, the alternation between the two types of third degree takes place in the lower octave (ex. 16). The use of the two forms of

Example 11 (*tōrā āi ke jābi re*)

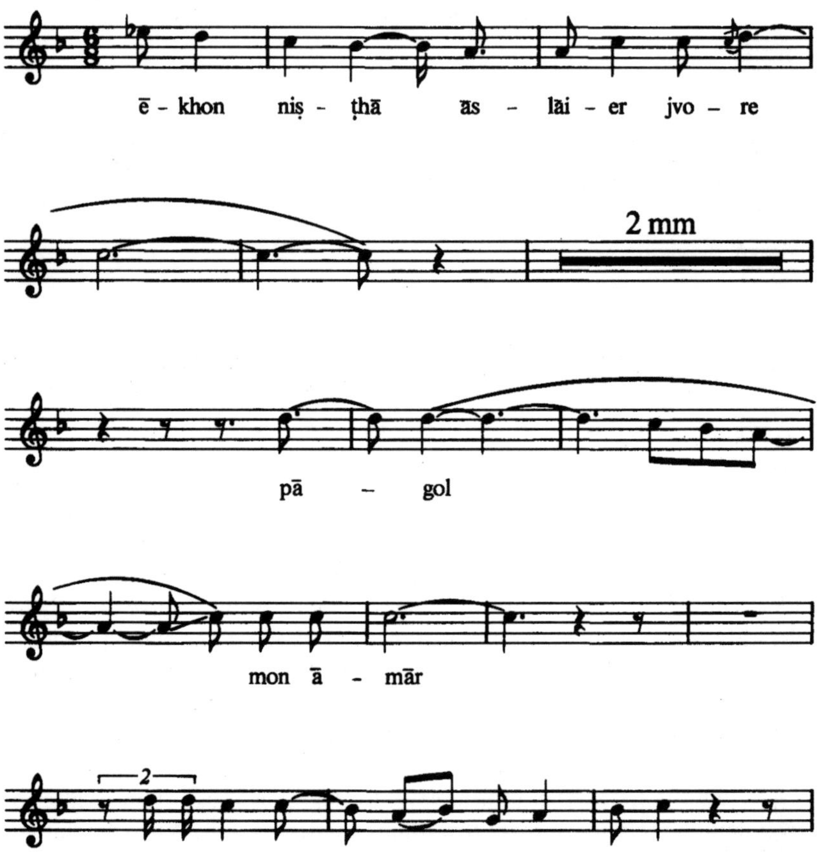

the third degree and the descent to the lower sixth degree lend a quality to the tune from which the example has been extracted that is characteristic of tunes from East Bengal. The presence of these regional characteristics in the tune is no doubt explained by the fact that the singer, Ýotin, immigrated to West Bengal from an area of Northeast Bengal now in Bangladesh.

Tonality with a Flatted Third Degree

When the flatted third degree is used virtually to the exclusion of the natural, it becomes the characteristic pitch of the tonality. The remaining

Example 12a (*tēmon ēkjon pāgol pelām nā*)

bo - li de - śer lō - ke
de - śer pā - gol ci - ne uṭh - te ke - ō pār - le nā
ār sā - gor pā - re nā - ri na - re
āj - ō ka - re sā - dho - nā sā - gor pā - re
2 mm
bo - li sā - gor pā - re
nā - ri na - re āj - ō ka - re sā - dho - nā
tē - mon ēk - jon pā - gol pe - lām nā

Example 12b (*sukher dhān bhāṅā*)

2
ō ḍhi - ki col - be ḍhi - ki col - be
nā bhāi ke pā - gol ke
pā - gol ke pā - gol col - be ḍhi - ki col - be
nā su- kher dhān bhā - ṅā

Example 13 (*gowr prem niṣṭā cinir ras karā*)

niṣ - ṭhā ci - nir ras ka -
- rā gowr prem

niṣ - ṭhā ci - nir ras ka - rā

Example 14 (*thākite pār ghātete*)

thā - ki - te pār ghā - ṭe - te
tu - mi ghā - ṭer nāi - ẏā di - no
ban - dhu re
ā - mār din ki ēm - ni ẏā - be
bāi - ẏā

Example 15 (*ēmni kore thākli dūre bạci kēmone*)

primary scale degrees are the same as those of the tonality with a natural third degree (excluding, of course, its characteristic pitch); in addition to these pitches; the flatted forms of the sixth and second degrees are available. The scale degrees of the tonality with a flatted third degree, consequently, can be listed as in table 4. Although the sharped and flatted fourth, flatted fifth, and even the natural third degrees are to be heard in this tonality, they are rare and ornamental and never occur except in the positions closest to the tonic.

Because of the primary importance of the flatted third degree, the two

Example 16 (*gowr cą̄d ki guṇo jāne gō*)

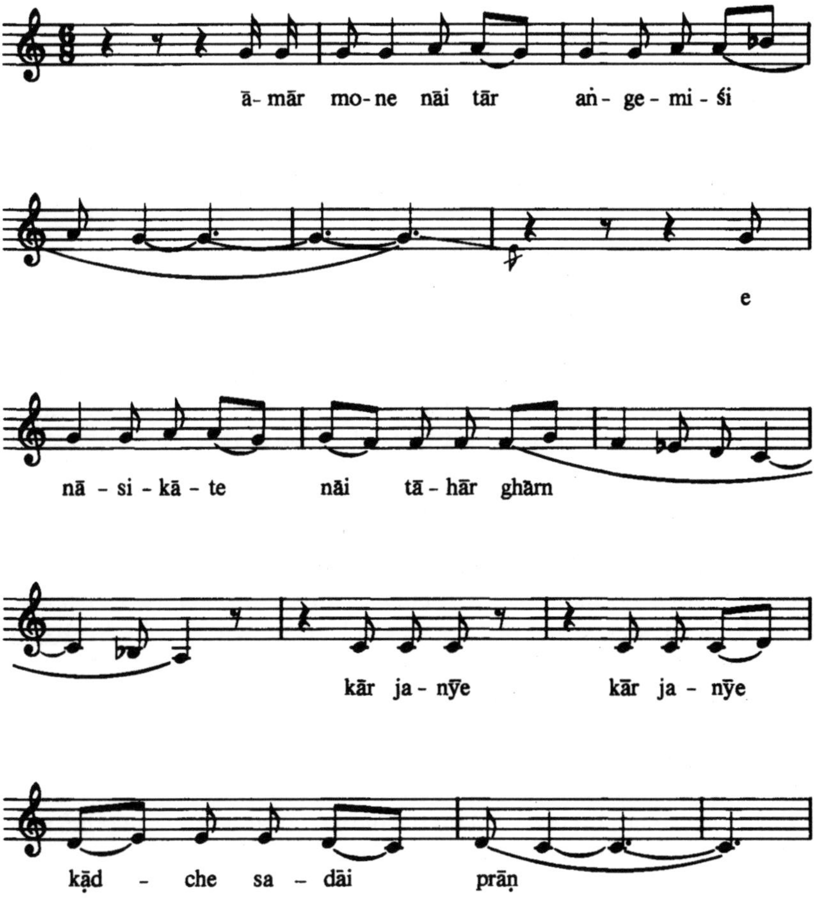
ā- mār mo- ne nāi tār aṅ- ge - mi - śi
e
nā - si - kā - te nāi tā - hār ghārn
kār ja - nȳe kār ja - nȳe
ką̄d - che sa - dāi prāṇ

new forms of the second and sixth degrees become available in this tonality, for only when the third degree is consistently flatted is the flatted sixth degree used, and only when the latter is the primary form of that degree is the flatted second degree used (cf. table 4). Also, because only the flatted third degree is used, the flatted form of the seventh degree is more characteristic of this tonality than is the natural form.

In the tonality with a flatted third degree, ambiguity of intonation of the moveable notes is more common than in the opposite tonality; indeed, in songs such as *ēmon ulṭā deś* and *mānob deho mōṭor gāṛi,* the intonation

TABLE 4

Influence of Flatted Third Degree on Inflection of Second and Sixth Degrees

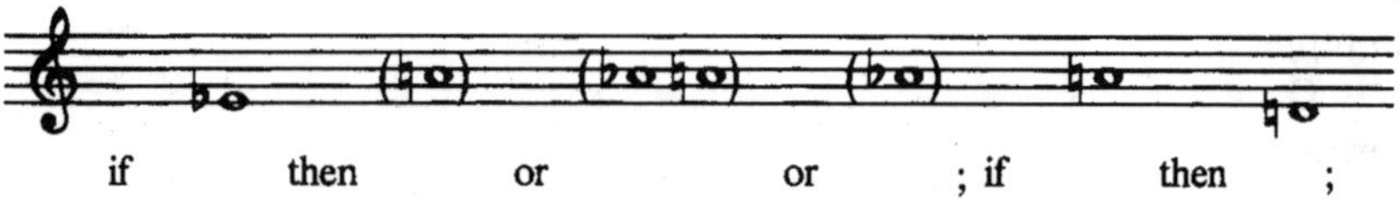

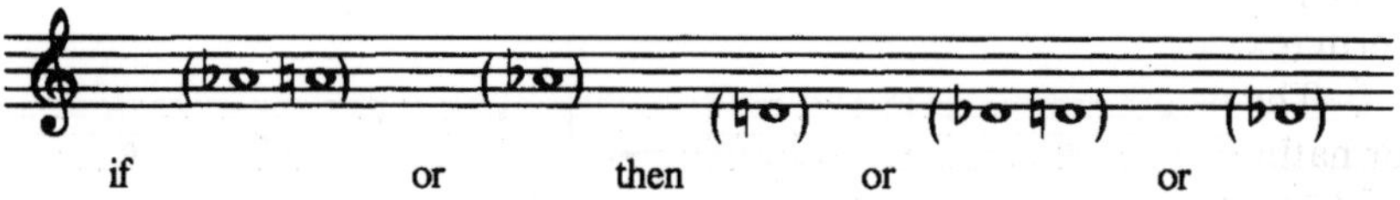

of the third degree itself is often closer to being natural than flatted. This wide intonational flexibility is one of the characteristics that sets this kind of performance apart from that in the tonality with a natural third degree; in the latter there is, in those songs using both forms of the third degree, more an impression of contrasting two notes than of varying the intonation of a single note.

Contrasting two forms of the same degree in one song occurs in this tonality, too, but not, of course, with the different forms of the third. Examples 17a and 17b illustrate the circumstances under which singers alternate the flatted and natural forms of the seventh, sixth, and second degrees.

While the flatted seventh degree can be considered the basic form in songs of the tonality with a flatted third degree, the natural form is used ornamentally as a chromatic lower neighbor in many of them. In a few, such as *nirma korle, gowr prem* (as sung by Monorām), or *rādhār prem tarańgo,* it is used in a characteristic phrase that raises the tessitura from the mid-range to the higher range centering on the tonic octave (exx. 17a and 17b). These songs, however, retain the flatted seventh degree in other contexts, namely, in descending phrases or as the top note in an ascending phrase.

Example 17a (*nirmā korle marlām ýodi*)

Example 17b (*bahu diner prāner sakhā*)

Songs in which the flatted forms of the sixth and / or second degrees are primary may also use the natural form as a lower neighbor tone (ex. 18). The opposite usage appears less common, and the flatted forms seem rather to replace, temporarily, the natural degrees as in example 19.

Occasionally the second degree may be equally important in both its forms. In singing *āmār ei rudhir dhārāy*, for example, Phokir Dās regularly uses the natural second degree in the phrase that ascends to initiate a new verse, while in the following descent to the tonic, he uses the flatted second form (ex. 20).

The sixth degree, too, may sometimes be equally important as a flatted or natural degree, as is illustrated in the performance of *tumi se nā deśer kathā* (ex. 21). The sixth degree is flatted when it is the top note of a phrase cadencing on the fifth degree, and natural when part of a quite similar phrase that, however, rises to the flatted seventh degree.

Although the alternation of the flatted and natural forms of the sixth and second degrees may be characteristic of many songs in this tonality, most do favor one form or other of those two degrees. Pūrṇo Dās's performance of *ẏā re ẏā tel digā tōr āpon carkhāte,* in which he adheres unswervingly to the flatted forms of both, is perhaps atypical and may be compared,

Example 18 (*sab lōke kay lālon ki jāt*)

Example 19 (*rādhār prem taraṅgo beri brajo bheseche*)

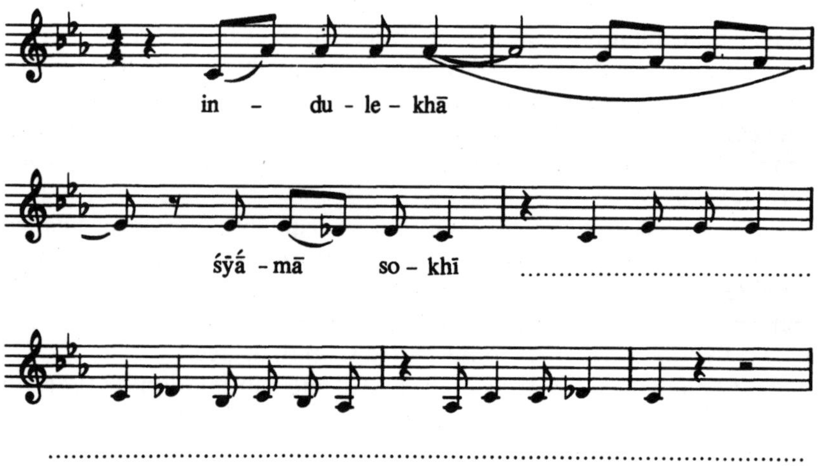

Example 20 (*āmār ei rudhir dhārāy dhuye jak tōr moner maylā*)

Example 21 (*tumi se nā deśer kathā re mon bhule giẏecho*)

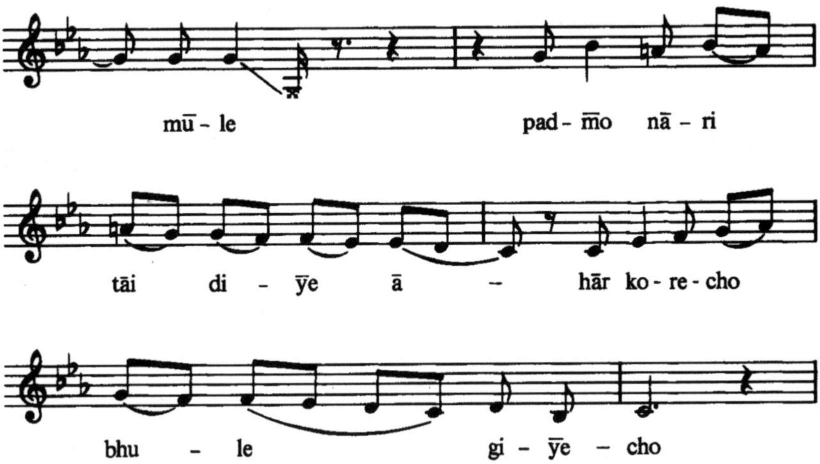
mū - le
pad - m̃o nā - ri
tāi di - ȳe ā - hār ko - re - cho
bhu - le gi - ȳe - cho

for example, with Ẏotin's performance of *kālo biṛāl* and *tumi se nā deśer kathā*. In each of these the sixth degree is almost always natural (and because of this, the second degree is too); the possibility of using the flatted sixth, possible in any song with the flatted third degree, is realized just once, very clearly in each performance. Likewise, as pointed out in table 4, in any song in which the flatted sixth degree is primary, the second degree, if natural, has the possibility of being flatted.

Hypothetical Tonality with a Neutral Third Degree

The use of the neutral third degree in some of the performances recorded for this study is my chief reason for postulating a third type of tonality, but the existence of a peculiar relationship between the second and sixth degrees in these performances has also played a part in supporting this suggestion. Only one of the recorded tunes represents the tonality, that to which Pūrṇo Dās sings *ẏā ẏā śokhī* and *ēto lōk periẏe gelo* and to which his brother Lakṣm̃aṇ sings *hṛidayo piñjore*. Pūrṇo also sings the same tune to the text *śeṣer dine sejon bine* on a commercial disc, *The Bauls of Bengal* (Elektra EKS 7325), and it is in this performance that the third is most consistently sung with a neutral intonation. Among those performances I recorded, the third is not so stable in its neutrality, and were this degree alone to be considered, those performances might be included in the tonality with a minor third degree. In the latter, it will be recalled, the flatted third in some performances is also frequently inflected very high, but there was also the condition that the predominant use of the natural sixth degree blocks use of the flatted second, a condition that is not fulfilled

Example 22a (*ẏā ẏā śokhī ẏā phire ẏā*)

ghā-ṭe ese bo - rāy kar - te

Example 22b (*ẏā ẏā śokhī ẏā phire ẏā*)

bo - li soi – bār kē – mon

in a characteristic phrase of the tune in question as rendered by Pūrṇo in *ēto lōk periẏe gelo* (exx. 22a and 22b). Here the natural sixth degree is emphasized at the beginning of the phrase, while at its end the flatted second degree, often intoned a bit sharp, is used where one might expect the natural degree.

While Pūrṇo's performance of the tune sounds quite different from other performances of Baul-*gān,* that of his brother Lakṣm̃aṇ might easily be added to examples of the tonality with a flatted third degree; the curious use of the natural sixth and flatted second degrees, for example, is absent, and the third degree is basically flatted. For this reason, the suggestion of neutral third tonality in Baul-*gān* is offered tentatively, since it may be that the characteristics that make Pūrṇo Dās's rendition of the tune so odd are merely idiosyncracies and that other performers might render the tune in a way more in harmony with the tonality having a flatted third degree. It is certain, at least, that the tune did not originate with Pūrṇo Dās because S. Cakrobortī recognized it as similar to one commonly used in the *monohorśāhi* style of *kīrton* prevalent in the area of West Bengal where Pūrṇo Dās was raised, and I heard it sung in processional *kīrton* at Jayadeva *melā* by a group of non-Bauls.

Baul-*gān* Scales As Bengali Writers Describe Them

Bengalis write about folk songs like Baul-*gān* by referring to other folk songs and to *rāg*. They assume that the readers understand such references and do not employ the verbal conventions of Western musicological description and analysis in their writings. It is generally agreed among them that Baul-*gān,* being widely cultivated in Bengal, has acquired a variety of types that derive from the influence of the regional songs of Bengal, and at least one writer, Āśutōṣ Bhaṭṭācārẏo (1962a, 20), goes so far as to deny that there is any such thing as a Baul *sur* (tune), since the Bauls have adopted whatever tune is common to the area in which they live. Thus, *bhāṭiẏāli* and *sāri* are said to provide the tunes for East Bengal Baul-*gān, bhāōẏāiẏā*—itself considered a variety of *bhāṭiẏāli*—the tunes for North Bengal Baul-*gān,* and *jhumur* and *kīrton* the tunes for West Bengal Baul-*gān* (S. K. Bose 1967, 55). But Bengali writers have devoted little attention to the specific characteristics of each of these types of song.

Bengali writers are mostly concerned with types of Baul-*gān,* which, in this chapter, are characterized as being in the tonality with a natural third degree. The reason they have limited their interest to songs of this tonality may be that in a discussion of the more elaborate types of folk song, like Baul-*gān,* they often draw attention to *bhāṭiẏāli.* Sukumar Ray has observed that "Bhatiyali has extended its influence on all types of songs" (1973, 111), and Ā. Bhaṭṭācārẏo (1962a, x) has speculated that *bhāṭiẏāli* is the source for most Bengali folk song. In discussing the scale material of *bhāṭiẏāli,* Ray has been careful to make a distinction between pitch selection and use. The upper octave, he says, is in *bilāval ṭhāṭ* (i.e., C scale with occasional use of the minor seventh degree), "and appears to be a blending of Ragas like Behag-Pahadi-Jhinjhoti, etc.," while below the tonic a change to *khamāj ṭhāṭ* (G scale) is said to occur, and further, that, "For the use of the notes below C (Sa) and for some other characteristics the tune is considered as Raga Jhinjhoti . . . which Suresh Chandra Chakraborty refers to as Rag kausauli jhinjhit" (1973, 111). The point Ray makes here is that while *bhāṭiẏāli* uses what we would call the major mode with the occasional addition of the minor seventh (i.e., *bilāval* and *khamāj ṭhāṭ*s), its characteristic melodic patterns often use gapped ascents, such as those in *rāg*s like *behāg* (no fourth or seventh degree in ascent)[45] or *jhinjhōṭi* (often omits third and seventh degrees in ascent), and sometimes emphasizes the tonic by cadencing upward from the lower sixth, as does *jhinjhōṭi* (c′-b♭-a-c′).

Sureś Cakrobortī (1962, 680) agrees with Ray that *jhịjhịṭ* (*jhinjhōṭi*) is popular in Bengal because it is used in almost all folk songs and even in *kīrton;* he also increases the number of pitches to be considered to equal that which I have included in the tonality with a natural third degree. This he does by observing that while many songs admit the use of *khamāj ṭhāṭ* (G scale), they are mainly *bhimpalāśī* or *kāphi* (*rāg*s in *kāphi ṭhāṭ,* D scale). Cakrobortī (1962, 684) also mentions, as does N. K. Bose (1960, 488 n. 2) specifically in connection with Baul-*gān,* that *rāg bibhāṣ,* like *jhinjhōṭi,* is particularly characteristic of Bengali folk song. This *bibhāṣ*, however, is not the common one of the Hindustani tradition but is peculiar to Bengal; instead of having, like the Hindustani, a flatted second and a flatted sixth degree, the Bengali *bibhāṣ* uses only natural degrees. It is basically pentatonic, omitting the fourth and seventh degrees, although, "because of the habit of using *komal ni* (the flatted seventh degree) *jhịjhịṭ* often intrudes" (Cakrobortī 1962, 684).

One of the most characteristic features of *rāg jhịjhịṭ* is the direct ascent from the natural sixth degree to the tonic; this cadence is generally preceded by a descent to the sixth degree—one that includes the flatted seventh degree and may first reach the fifth degree before rising to the cadence. Although many examples of gapped phrases omitting the seventh degree in ascent to the tonic are to be found in songs in the tonality with a natural third degree, ascent from the sixth to the tonic generally includes the seventh degree, as in the refrains of *thākite pār ghāṭete* or *ese ēk rosik pāgol*, and thus a salient phrase of *jhịjhịṭ* is obscured. As for the nearly pentatonic *bibhāṣ* type, songs like *tōrā āi ke ẏābi re* certainly contain many phrases of a purely pentatonic type that would conform to *bibhāṣ;* yet the frequent use of both kinds of seventh degree and of the natural fourth degree succeed in straying from it.

Although one who is acquainted with Hindustani *rāg* music may hear the *chāyā* (shadow)[46] of a *rāg* from time to time in Baul-*gān,* Ray's comment about the relation of *rāg* to *bhāṭiẏāli* is equally true of Baul-*gān*: "On the whole, it does not satisfy the condition of the structure of a Raga. Therefore, bhātiyāli maintains an individuality of its own in tune pattern" (1973, 111). Ray reiterates this point later when he discusses other types of Bengali folk song, and though his English is somewhat awkward, his words are worth reproducing since in them he corrects the impression often given by other writers that we may take for granted a close relationship, whether evolutionary or coexistent, between *rāg* and folk song.

> We refer to these Ragas for proper understanding of the nature of the phrases [i.e., certain melodic phrases which give a *rāg* its modal identity may occur in folk songs]. It should be remembered that these phrases, similar to those of the base part of bilawal group [i.e., using natural notes and with a propensity toward gapping in rising to the fifth degree], upper part of *khamaj* group [i.e., use of the natural seventh degree in ascent and the flatted in descent], and middle portions of *kafi* and *kalingaḍa* [i.e., alternation of flatted and natural third degrees in *kāfi—kālingāḍā* with the natural third and flatted sixth degrees does not occur in Baul-*gān*], do not indicate the true character of the Raga in any way. It is not also of any use to connect musical forms of these folk songs with Ragasangit [*rāg* music] excepting some references to *That* [scales] or portions of Ragas as appear in songs. . . . A prabhati-sangeet or rural morning

> hymn may represent [i.e., employ] a few phrases from the *bhairavi* That or Raga kalingada performed in a monotonous [i.e., stereotyped] manner, but such . . . should be considered as . . . having nothing to do with the conception of these Raga frames. Similar is the case of Raga bibhas often referred to be in use in folk songs. A raga does never take shape in a few fixed and monotonous patterns. . . . So for folkmusic, it is idle to establish any relationship with Raga music, as is often done. (1973, 114)

I will conclude this chapter with a brief summary of the principles I believe underlie pitch use and tonality in Baul-*gān* with the caveat that while I have derived these principles from observation of practice, they are broad generalizations, and a study of the particularities of performance would reveal many exceptions indicative of the flexibility every Baul takes for granted in solo singing.

The pitches used in Baul-*gān* correspond roughly to those of the chromatic scale with the possible addition of a neutral third. These pitches are used in such ways as to create permutations of the diatonic scale in which the structurally important degrees are the first and its octave and, secondarily, the fourth and fifth. The remainder are used in their natural or flatted forms to produce two common tonalities and an uncommon one with a neutral third. In the first tonality, the third degree is natural, and as a result, the second and sixth degrees are always natural. In the second tonality, the third degree is flatted and the second and sixth degrees are sometimes flatted, sometimes not. The seventh degree is normally raised if the third is natural though it is often flatted, while if the third is flatted, the seventh is normally, too, though it may be raised. A regular chromatic succession of intervals and the augmented second, both common in *rāgs*, are unknown in Baul-*gān* except for the experiments of Sonāton Dās Ṭhākur. Regarding the latter, though the contents of the experiments may be exceptional when compared with general practice, the attitude that brought them about may be considered typical of the individuality Bauls are said to bring to all their endeavors as *ulṭo pathiks*.

CHAPTER TEN

The Structure of Baul-*gān* and its Realization in Performance

Nearly all Baul-*gān* are based on the same musical structure. The following account begins with an outline of the structure of Baul-*gān* texts and their musical settings; thereafter, a particular performance is examined in detail to illustrate how the hypothesized structure relates to the actual rendition of a Baul song.

Summary of Structural Principles

The structure of Baul-*gān* is intimately linked with that of the texts. These are composed of stanzas, each a couplet, which alternate with a refrain. Verses commonly have caesurae that divide them into two or in some cases three phrases. The first verse of the refrain, however, is a frequent exception, often being somewhat shorter than the other verses and without a caesura.

The musical setting is organized into three units: A) a group of phrases that sets only the first verse of the refrain; B) a group of phrases that sets the second verse of each couplet, including that of the refrain; C) a group of phrases that sets the first verse of each couplet but not that of the refrain. Each of the three units may be characterized in the following way. A is used to hover around and, with few exceptions, to cadence on the tonic (ex. 23). When used to set a short unbroken line of text, A will make up a single musical phrase (ex. 24); a line of text with a caesura may be set to a single phrase, or to two phrases in succession (ex. 25), or the line of text may be set to two phrases arranged in the pattern aba (ex. 26). The first phrase of B is usually employed to ascend from the third, fourth, or fifth degree either to cadence on the tonic octave or, having touched it, to turn back to cadence on the fourth or fifth degree (ex. 27). The second phrase of B is used in

Example 23a (*kēno rākhite nārili premojal*)

Example 23b (*āi ke ýābi re gowr cạ̄der hạ̄spaṭāle*)

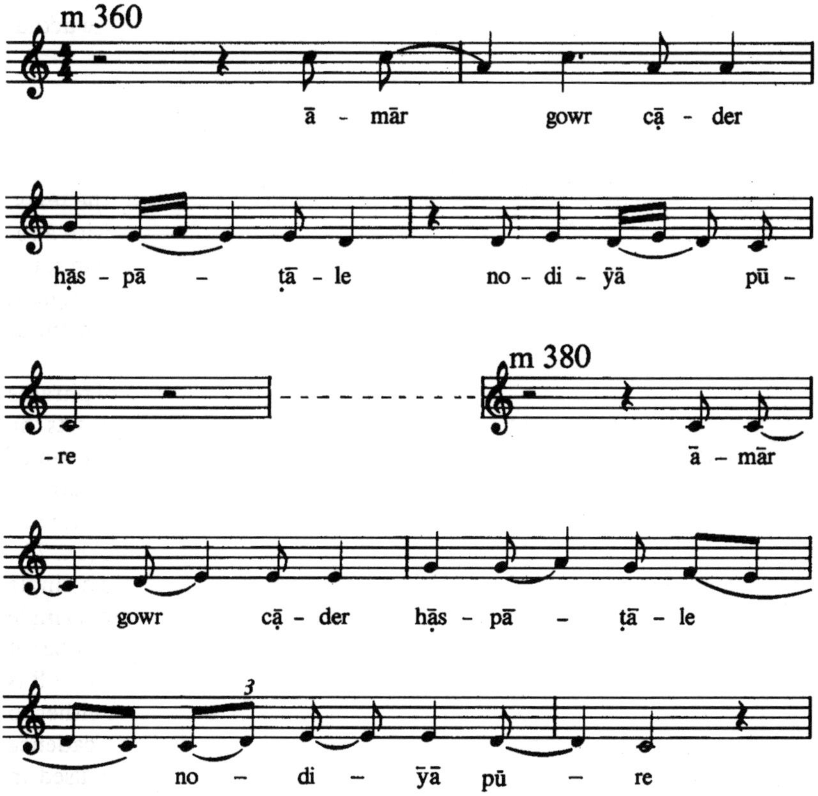

Example 23c (*mon ēkbāre hori balo*)

mon ēk - bā - re ho - ri ba - lo
mon ēk - bār ho - ri ba - lo
din phu - rā - lo ṭi - ki - ṭer
ghaṇ - ṭā ho - lo ā - mār mon
ho - ri ba - lo

Example 24 (*bhāṅā ghare uri diye thākbo kato din*)

bhāṅ - ā gha - re u - ṛi di - ẏe
thāk - bo ka - to din bhā - ṅā gha - re
u - ṛi di - ẏe thāk - bo ka - to din

Example 25 (*ēmon cāsā buddhi nāsā cinli nā tōr āpon bhụ̄i*)

ē - mon cā - sā bud - dhi nā - sā
cin - li nā tōr ā - pon bhụ̄ - i

Example 26 (*mon ēkbāre hori balo*)

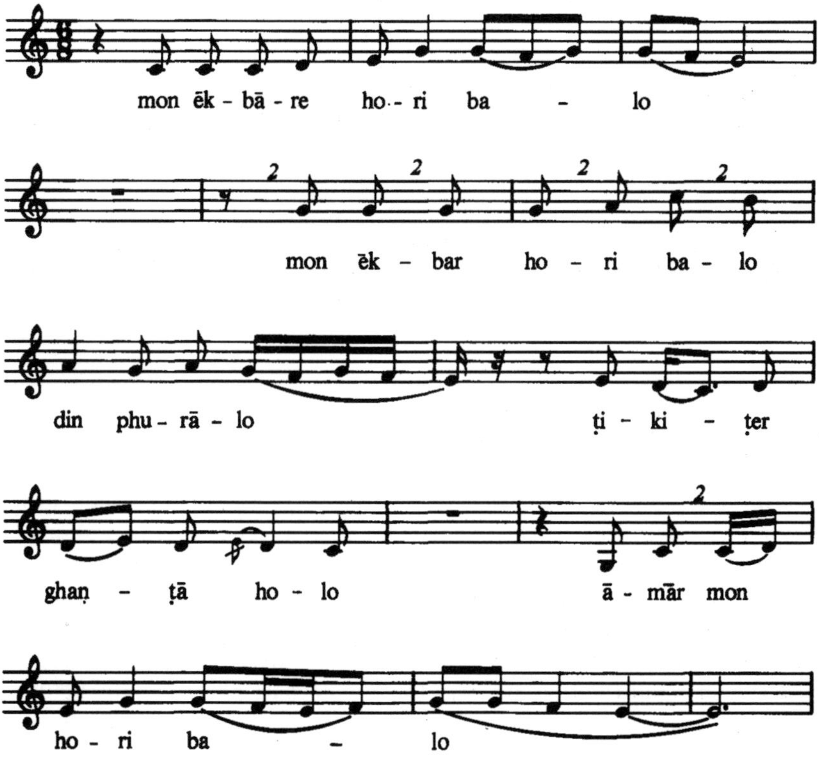
mon ēk - bā - re ho - - ri ba - lo
mon ēk - bar ho - ri ba - lo
din phu - rā - lo ṭi - ki - ṭer
ghaṇ - ṭā ho - lo ā - mār mon
ho - ri ba - lo

Example 27 (*ēmni kore thākli dūre bāci kēmone*)

Example 28 (*ēmni kore thākli dūre bāci kēmone*)

descending from the cadence pitch of the previous phrase to the starting pitch of the refrain, which is often the tonic (ex. 28). C often consists of two alternative groups of phrases, whose components may either be mixed indiscriminately with one another or may occur in one or the other form alone. The difference between one phrase and its alternative is a question of tessitura. With the first phrase, a singer may rise from the area of the tonic on which he concluded the preceding refrain, cadence on the third, fourth, or fifth degree, and go on to a second phrase which turns toward a cadence on or near the tonic (ex. 29); or with the alternate first phrase he may begin on a higher pitch than he did with the counterpart phrase and conclude with a cadence on the tonic octave, after which he may proceed to the

Example 29 (*gowr prem niṣṭā cinir ras karā*)

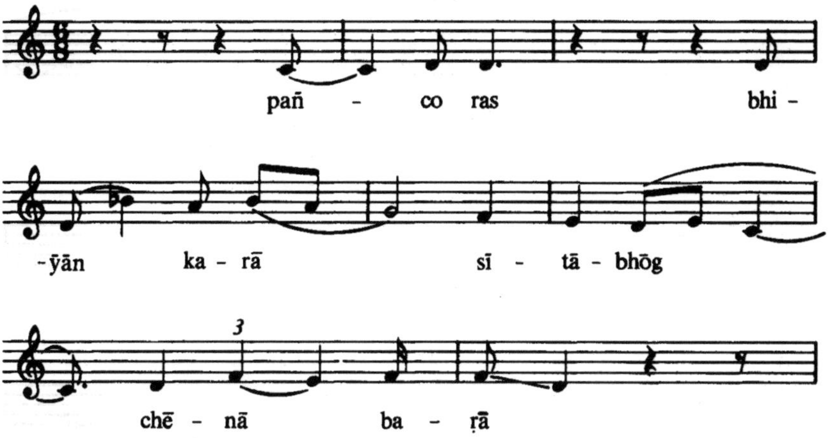

Example 30 (*gowr prem niṣṭā cinir ras karā*)

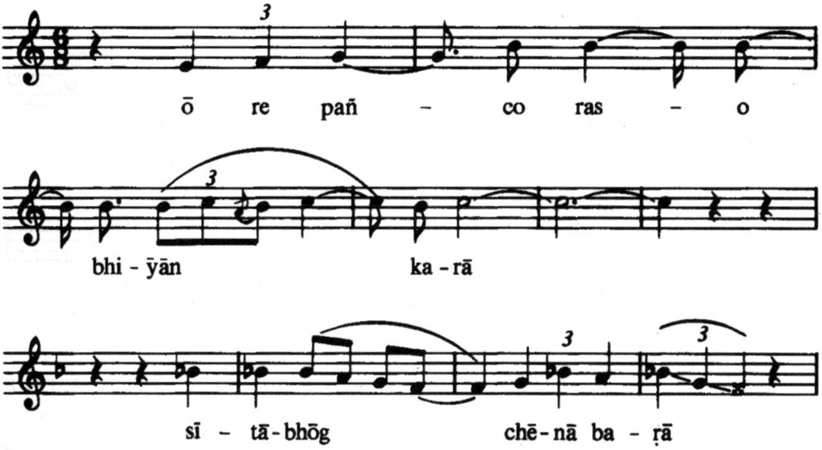

alternate second phrase and thereby descend to a cadence on the fifth degree (ex. 30). Commonly, if both alternatives are used, the higher tessitura phrases follow the lower ones, as in examples 27 and 28. When the verse that is set to C is of the type having two caesurae, C will then comprise three phrases, and these, too, may have alternate forms (ex. 31).

With few exceptions, Baul-*gān* combines a rounded form with the simpler one of refrain and stanza alternation. A special use of the refrain

Example 31 (*mānob deho mōṭōr gāri*)

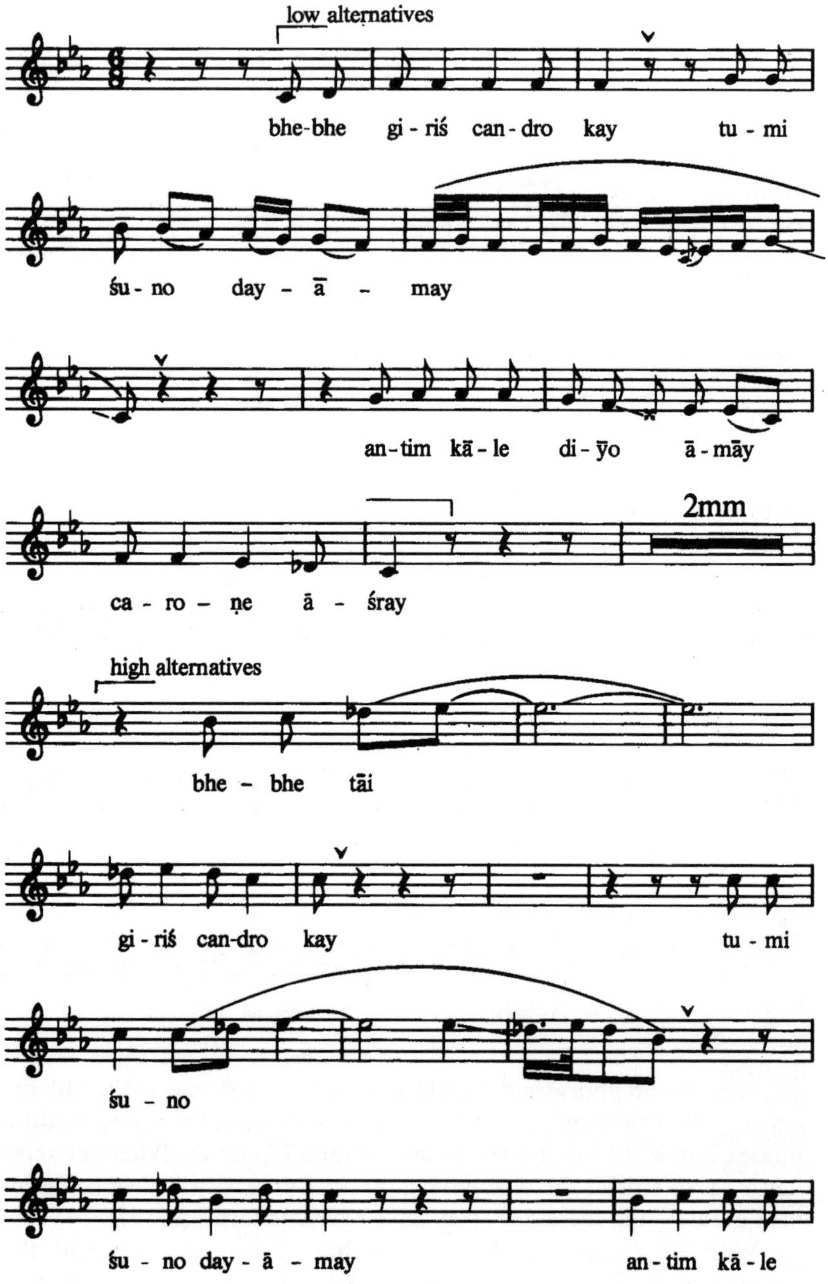

accounts for both these aspects of form: the great majority of the internal refrains is limited to the first verse of the refrain-couplet (hereafter called refrain-verse), and the refrain-couplet is generally—but not invariably—reserved for the opening and closing of the song. Since the refrain-verse occurs after every stanza and usually after the full refrain, the initial and closing refrains are normally rounded (ABA——ABA), and as pointed out, the common practice of having the beginning of the refrain-verse return at its end results in a rounding within A (A = aba). In the last appearance of the refrain-couplet, the first A serves the simultaneous function of setting the refrain-verse which follows the last stanza and beginning the final statement of the complete refrain.

In setting a Baul-*gān* text, then, the three groups of phrases usually occur in the following sequence: ABA, CBA, . . . CBABA.[47] Since only the refrain-couplet is used in the rhythmically free introductions that may precede measured song and are analogous to *ālāp* in art music, only the music associated with the refrain (A and B) is to be heard in them. An instrumental introduction may precede a vocal one; if the instrument is capable of producing a melody, as the *dōtārā* or *sārindā* are, the performer will render on it phrases of A and B music. Whether or not a performer gives an introduction of these sorts depends largely on his own preference and habit, but rarely does he commence without at least perfunctorily sounding his instrument once or twice and singing a little turn around the tonic to the vowel *ā*.

An Example of Baul-*gān* Structure as Realized in Performance

The previous section was devoted to presenting a theory of Baul-*gān* structure; what follows demonstrates the competence of that theory to make comprehensible the basic structure of a particular performance of Baul-*gān* and illustrates the incidental additions to the structure that typically occur during a performance. The performance chosen is that of *jīber bujhi sudin āj holo* by Śaśāṅko Dās. The text and a translation of this difficult song are given in number 17 of appendix A, and a complete transcription is provided in appendix B.

In the singing of this text restatements of the three sections of music involved in its setting, the A, B, and C discussed on pages 146–51, are not apt to be exactly like their first statements. The constituents of these sections continually change because their texts are fragmented, parts repeated, or phrases interrupted, and the melodic materials are multiform. This quality of melodic multiformity is illustrated in example 32, in which every setting of the words *jīber bujhi sudin āj holo,* the second half of the refrain-verse, has been placed one above the other for ease of comparison. While no two settings are precisely alike, they are all forms of the same melodic root, a phrase that ascends slightly from some pitch above the tonic and soon turns back to descend to a cadence on the tonic.

The phrase in example 32, which ends with a tonic cadence, is one of two used to set the complete refrain-verse (A); the second phrase is used to set the remaining text of A, *hori nām prem dite nitāi elo* (actually the first half of the verse), and must be followed by a return of the first phrase,

Example 32 (*jīber bujhi sudin āj holo*)

66
jī - ber bu-jhi su - din ho - lo
79
jī-ber bu-jhi su-din āj ho - lo
136
jī-ber bu - jhi su-din āj ho - lo
141
jī-ber bu - jhi su - din ho - lo
159
jī-ber bu-jhi su-din ho- lo
198
jī- ber bu - jhi su-din āj ho - lo
203
jī- ber bu - jhi su - din
217
jī-ber bu - jhi su-din āj ho - lo
223
jī - ber bu - jhi su-din ho-lo

because the second has an inconclusive cadence. The two phrases are thus in the pattern aba, and Aa has the text of the *second* half of the verse (ex. 33). In varying the content of this pattern, Śaśāṅko sometimes takes the unusual liberty of omitting part of the refrain text (that set to Ab) and substituting a short exclamation (*holo re*) that radically alters the musical content of Ab, as in example 34, without altering its function as a bridge between Aa and its return.

Example 33 (*jīber bujhi sudin āj holo*)

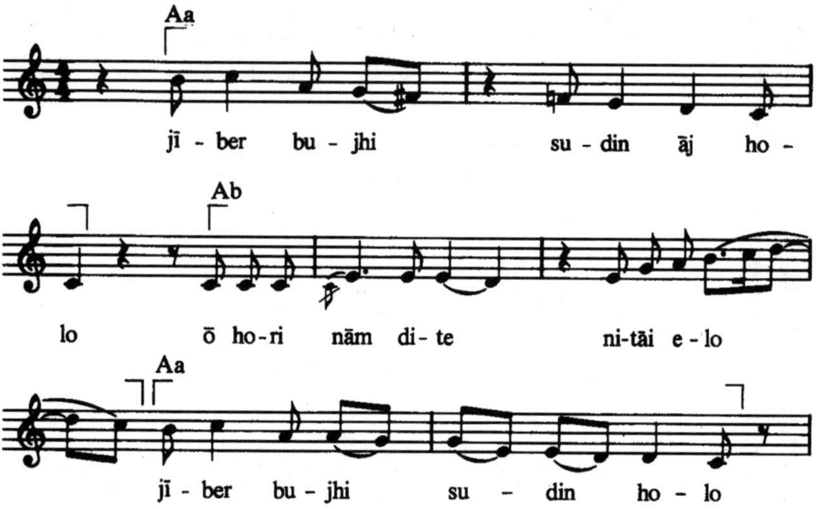

Example 34 (*jīber bujhi sudin āj holo*)

In this performance of *jīber bujhi,* Śaśāṅko follows the usual procedure of singing the complete refrain only at the beginning and end and follows both the refrain-couplet and the stanzas with the refrain-verse. The music for the second verses of both refrain and stanzas (B) consists of two phrases that also occur in a multiplicity of forms and are fragmented and interrupted with interpolations in the manner already described for A. All the performance techniques of B are illustrated in example 35. Each half of a

Example 35 (*jīber bujhi sudin āj holo*)

verse is sung once and then repeated to a slightly altered form of the same musical phrase (Ba mm. 8–10, 11–12; Bb 13–14, 21–22). After the first Bb, a short fragment (*āmār gowr*) of the text for Ba is immediately appended, as though Śaśāṅko had intended to return to that phrase, as he does to the phrase *āmār nitāi ẏe nām enechilo* in similar circumstances nearer the end of the song (ex. 36); instead, he is silent for two measures (ex. 35, mm. 16–17), and then inserts a phrase with words unrelated to the song text (mm. 18–20) before singing Bb a second time.

Because the stanzas of *jīber bujhi* have first verses of the type with two caesurae (C), their musical setting consists of three phrases. In performance, Śaśāṅko sometimes repeats the portion of text after the second caesura to a modified form of the previous musical phrase, so that C takes the shape abcc′ as in example 37. This c′ is not the sort of alternative phrase described in the general account of structure given at the beginning of this chapter; both Cc and Cc′ have similar endings and consequently have the same tonal goal, the tonic. An alternative phrase, besides having a different melodic contour from that of its mate, aims at a different tonal goal as well.

Example 36 (*jīber bujhi sudin āj holo*)

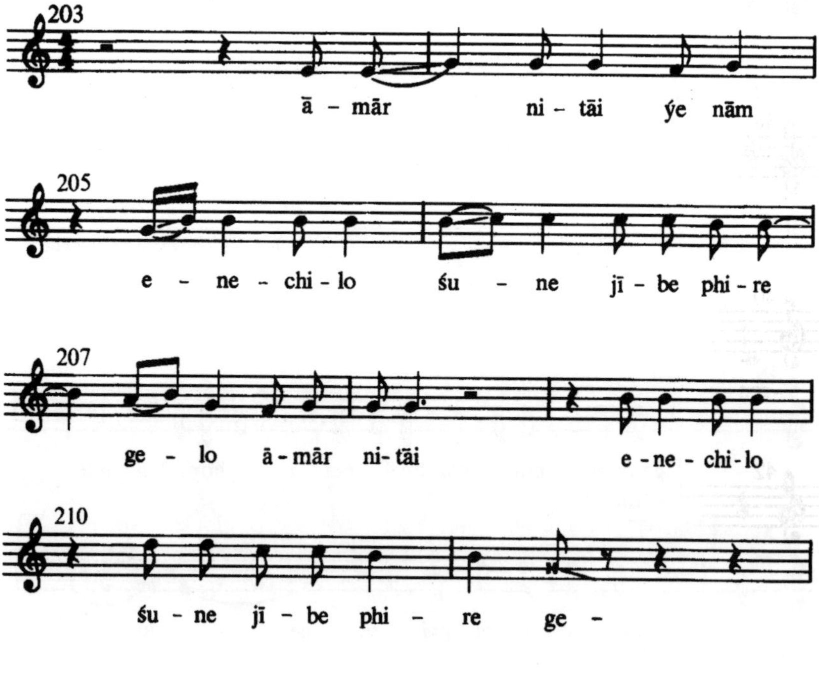

Example 37 (*jīber bujhi sudin āj holo*)

The Cc′ phrase of Śaśāṅko's performance of *jīber bujhi* appears, instead, to be a kind of recapitulation of the overall melodic movement of Cabc.

Since both Ba and Ca, generally speaking, may have phrases that cadence on the upper octave of the tonic, sometimes, as in this performance, the same phrase may be employed to achieve that cadence (cf. ex. 35, mm. 8–10 with ex. 37, mm. 30–33). More commonly, a phrase like those in examples 38a and 38b is used to cadence on the tonic octave; such a phrase is, in fact, used once in the performance of *jīber bujhi* (see ex. 36, mm.

Example 38a (*ō mon mayrā re kēno bhiȳān śikhli nā*)

ō re ci - ṭer - gu - ṛe pāk lā - gā - le

Example 38b (*tēmon ēkjon pāgol pelām nā*)

bo - li nā - nā ra - ṅer
nā - nā ḍha-ṅer ke ka - re tār ṭhi - kā - nā

203–6). In his performance of *mon mayrā,* Sonāton used this type of phrase in both Ba and Ca positions (ex. 39), just as Śaśāṅko used the phrase illustrated in example 35; in both songs, despite the musical similarity of the Ba and Ca phrases, each Ba is differentiated from its soundalike Ca phrase by context, that is, by the particular group of phrases with which each commences, and by its function, namely, the setting of a prescribed part of the text.

In addition to the basic text of *jiber bujhi* and the three major groups of musical phrases that set it, Śaśāṅko has included other fragments of unrelated text in his performance, and these may require either the expansion of some of the basic musical phrases or the inclusion of new phrases.

Example 39 (*ō mon mayrā re kēno bhiẏān śikhli nā*)

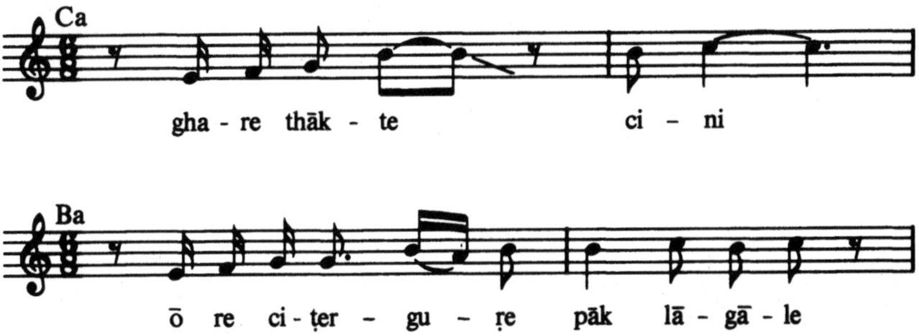

Many of the additional fragments of text are conventional apostrophes or exhortations used by most Bauls, such as *mono re* (oh, mind), *ābār* (again), *boli* (I say), and *bhāi re bhāi* (hey, brother); these may be prefixed to a verse of the song text and be simply set to integrate musically with the phrase which follows and sets the verse (ex. 40). Similar to this type of addition is the unusual substitution for the Ab phrase often employed by Śaśāṅko (see ex. 34, p. 156), in which the substituted element is joined smoothly with the following Aa, but is distinct enough to serve the same purpose as the original Ab, that is, to make the second Aa sound like a return rather than a simple repetition.

Another manner of setting added apostrophes and exhortations makes them more independent, even detaches them from the verses and their music. As the added texts are normally quite short, their musical settings (designated x) usually acquire the necessary length for a measure of independence by being made melismatic. In example 35, mm. 18–21 Śaśānko has, instead, employed repetition of syllabically set text as a means of

Example 40 (*jīber bujhi sudin āj holo*)

lengthening the insertion; melismatic settings of additional text in his performance of *jīber bujhi* are found only in the introduction (ex. 41); in the measured part of the song, similar melismatic phrases take their text from the initial portion of a verse that is then restated and the verse completed (ex. 42).

Example 41 (*jīber bujhi sudin āj holo*)

Example 42 (*jīber bujhi sudin āj holo*)

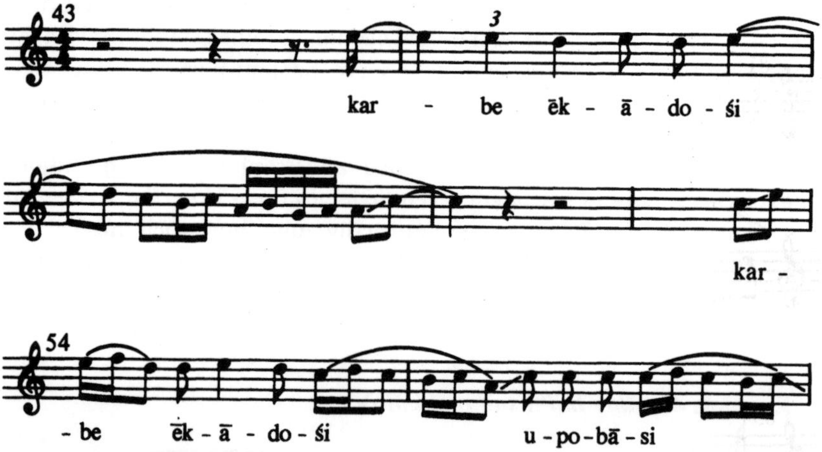

Besides having interpolated bits of conventional text into his performances, Śaśāṅko also added an extensive section of text. Whereas the music setting bits of interpolated text is integrated with the phrase or group of phrases in which it occurs, the music of this unusually long section of added text contrasts with that which precedes and follows it. Instead of the logical arrangement of the A, B, and C groups of phrases, there is a meandering succession of new phrases that emphasizes the sixth degree as a temporary tonal center and that momentarily evokes a type of *kīrton* singing (ex. 43, mm. 99–113). When, at last, in m. 114, Śaśāṅko returns to the text of *jīber bujhi,* the feeling of return after a suspenseful digression is quite strong. Such a digression is exceptional but may have the unexceptional explanation of a lapse of memory. Bauls seem to experience such lapses with moderate frequency, and two performances of a song, or of a spoken and a sung text, may have different numbers of stanzas. Of course, some of these differences may be attributable to choice, but obvious lapses account for some, as may be observed when a Baul commences a verse and then, without finishing it, repeats the music with a different text, or, having broken down in mid-phrase, starts up again after being prompted by someone, often his wife.

Śaśāṅko's presumed lapse of memory begins at the start of the second stanza (*elen abodhowto rāy*), where he sings text which recalls the first verse of the first stanza to appropriate music, namely, Ca (ex. 43, mm. 81–83). Apparently not wishing to interrupt the flow of music, Śaśāṅko

Example 43 (*jīber bujhi sudin āj holo*)

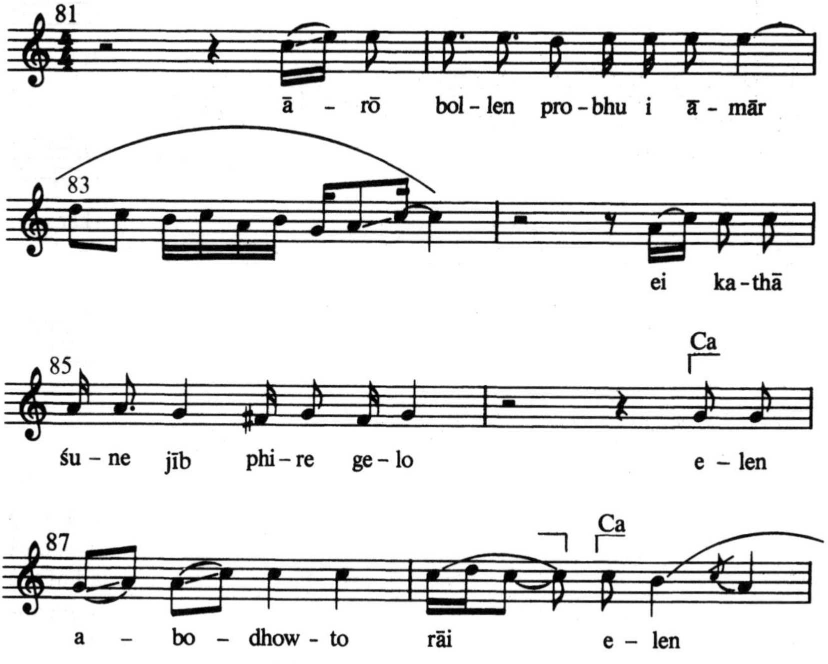

89
Cb
a - bo - dhow - to rāi pro-bhui ā -
91
- mār ba - ṛo day - ā - may
Cb
93
pro- bhui ā - mār ba - ṛo day - ā -
95
Cc
- may ke ni - be ke
97
ni - be bo - le ḍāk-chen ō re
99
āi bol-len bol-len āi āi ho - ri
101
nām ni - se - ri ā - mi ko - re lā - gi
103
nā - me bo - li ēk - bār muk-he

105
ho - ri bo - le ko-re lā - gi nā - me bo - li
108
.... āmi
110
ko - re lā - gi nā - mer
Ca
112
ēk-bār mu - khe ho - ri e-len a - bo-dhow-to
115
rāi
Cb
118
pro - bhui ā - mār ba - ṛo day - ā -
Cc
120
- may ke ni - be ke
122
ni - be bo - le ḍāk - chen ō re

then fills in with another misplaced phrase, borrowed from the refrain (mm. 84–85), after which he performs the first verse of the second stanza with the group of phrases Cabbc (mm. 86–99). At this point, he makes the digression in *kīrton* style (mm. 99–113) and follows it with a return to the first verse of the second stanza, restated in its entirety, but, as though there had already been enough delay, with no repetitions (mm. 114–23). Only at this point does he complete the second stanza by singing its second verse to appropriate music (Baabab, mm. 124–34).

Despite the interpolations, the presumed lapse of memory, the frequent repetitions, and a nearly Schoenbergian quality of continuous variation, Śaśāṅko's performance makes a coherent whole that may easily be comprehended in terms of the general description of Baul-*gān* structure given at the head of this chapter and that may conveniently be represented in diagrammatic form (table 5). Not every performance of Baul-*gān* is as complex as this one of *jīber bujhi,* as may be confirmed by comparing its diagram with that of a performance by Gaṅgādhar Dās of *gōlōk hote gōlōker nāth* (table 6). Gaṅgādhar uses no interpolations, apparently has no lapse of memory, and uses musical repetition only once (st. 2, Cabab). Though he repeats text at the beginnings of stanzas 1 and 3, he avoids musical repetition by using alternative phrases for the repeated text (ex. 44).

In a performance of *tēmon ēkjon pāgol,* a song whose text is exceptionally long, Lakṣm̃aṇ Dās uses both repetition and alternative phrases in C, none of whose constituent series of phrases is exactly like that of another, although each maintains the syntactical sequence abc:

mm. 40–66	Cabc, a′b′c
101–23	Caʼb′c, abc
170–201	Caaʼb′c, abc
260–83	Cabcaʼb′c
328–54	Cab′c, aʼb′c
398–427	Cabʼbc, aʼb′c
475–93	Ca′aʼb′cxc
539–68	Caʼb′c, aʼb′c
611–25	Ca′aʼbʼb′c

Throughout this presentation of a theory of Baul-*gān* structure and its relation to actual performance, it has been maintained that three principal sections constitute the gross structure. Since this is at variance with the way some Bengali musicologists interpret the structure, an account of their views will be given in the next section, and an attempt made to reconcile them with what has here been maintained about the structure of Baul-*gān.*

TABLE 5

The Structure of a Performance of *jīber bujhi sudin holo*

(Words not part of the song text are capitalized. The listing of text by lines corresponds to its division in performance by musical rests.)

Refrain	*Component of musical structure*	*Location in transcription*
line 1, first half		
mono re	Ba	ph. 1
hori nām prem dite		2
hori nām		3
hori nām prem dite nitāi elo		4
hori hori bolo		5
hori nām prem dite nitāi elo		6

Refrain	*Component of musical structure*	*Location in transcription*
line 1, second half		
jīber bujhi sudin āilo	Aa	mm. 1-2
holo re	Ab	3-4
E jīber bujhi sudin āilo	Aa	4-5
line 2, first half		
ĀBĀR gowr ýe nām lenechilo	Ba	8-10
BOLI gowr ýe nām lenechilo		11-12
line 2, second half		
śune jībe phire gelo / ĀMĀR gowr	Bb	13-15
GOWR BOL HORI BOL HORI BOL BOLE	x	18-21
śune jībe phire gelo	Bb	21-22
Refrain verse		
jīber bujhi sudin āilo	Aa	23-24
HOLO RE	Ab	25-26
jīber bujhi sudin āilo	Aa	26-27
Stanza 1		
line 1, first part		
probhu bollen trisandhȳā snān	Ca	30-33
line 1, second part		
korbe ēk sandhȳā bhōjon	Cb	34-36
line 1, third part		
(sālȳo?) anno nebe sabe tel matsȳo bāroṇ	Cc	37-40
(sālȳo?) anno nebe sabe tel matsȳo bāroṇ		40-43
line 2, first part		
korbe ēkādośī	Ba	43-46
korbe ēkādośī thākbe upobāsī		46-48
line 2, second part		
Ō BHĀI preȳosīr bāroṇ chilo	Bb	48-50
[Stanza 1]		
line 2, first part		
korbe ēkādośī upobāsī	Ba	54-56
line 2, second part		
preȳosīr bāroṇ chilo	Bb	57-58
HORI NĀMER MĀJHE BHĀIRE	x	58-59
preȳosīr bāroṇ chilo	Bb	60-61

Refrain	*Component of musical structure*	*Location in transcription*
Refrain verse		
jīber bujhi sudin āj holo	Aa	mm. 62-63
holo re	Ab	64-65
jīber bujhi sudin āilo	Aa	65-66
(instrumental passage)		
jīber bujhi sudin āj holo	Aa	78-80
Stanza 2		
wrong text, recalls stanza 1		
ĀRŌ bollen probhui ĀMĀR	Ca	81-82
music and text of refrain, line 2, second part		
EI KATHĀ śune jībe phire gelo	Bb?	84-85
line 1, first part		
elen abodhowto rāi GŌ elen abodhowto rāi	Ca	86-88
line 1, second part		
probhui āmār baṛo dayāmay	Cb	90-92
probhui āmār baṛo dayāmay		93-95
line 1, third part		
ke nibe ke nibe bole ḍākchen ōre āi	Cc	96-99
BOLLEN BOLLEN ĀI ĀI HORI (NISERI?)	x	99-101
ĀMI KORE LĀGI NĀME		101-103
BOLI ĒKBĀR MUKHE HORI BOLE		103-105
KORE LĀGI NĀME		106-107
(. . . . .)		108-109
ĀMI KORE LĀGI NĀME		109-110
ĒKBĀR MUKHE HORI		112-113
line 1, first part		
elen abodhowto rāi	Ca	114-116
line 1, second part		
probhui āmār baṛo dayāmay	Cb	118-120
line 1, third part		
ke nibe ke nibe bole ḍākchen ōre āi	Cc	121-124
line 2, first part		
ŌI āmār nitāi pūrṇo brahmo jñāni	Ba	124-126
āmār nitāi pūrṇo brahmo jñāni		127-128
line 2, second part / first part		
brahmomay jagot dekhilo / āmār nitāi pūrṇo	Bb	129-130

Refrain	*Component of musical structure*	*Location in transcription*
	/Ba	mm. 130-131
brahmo jñāni		132
brahmomay jagot dekhilo	Bb	133-134
Refrain verse		
jīber bujhi sudin āj holo	Aa	135-137
o hori nām dite	Ab	137-138
nitāi elo		139-140
jīber bujhi sudin āilo	Aa	140-141
(instrumental passage)		
jīber bujhi sudin āilo	Aa	148-149
Stanza 3		
line 1, first part		
ĀRŌ bollen	Ca	160-162
bollen māgur mācher jhōl		162-164
māgur mācher jhōl		164-166
māgur mā—		167-169
line 1, second part		
ār bhōr ýubotīr kōl	Cb	170-172
line 1, third part		
jīber bale ebār marā bolbo hori	Cc	173-175
jīber bale ebār marā bolbo hori bol		179-182
line 2, first part		
gōsāi gowr balen e kathāke	Ba	185-187
Ō RE gōsāi ĀMĀR gowr balen e kathā		188-190
line 2, second part		
e ýe gōlemāle rohilo	Bb	190-192
ANDHO JĪBṬĀ BUJHBE KĒNOI ẸṬE		193-194
gōlemāle rohilo		195-197
Refrain		
line 1, second part		
jīber bujhi sudin āj holo	Aa	197-199
line 1, first part		
hori nām dite nitāi elo	Ab	199-201
line 1, second part		
TĀI jīber bujhi sudin	Aa	202-203
line 2, first part / second part		
āmār nitāi ýe nām	Ba	203-204

Refrain	*Component of musical structure*	*Location in transcription*
enechilo / śune jībe phire gelo / āmār nitāi	205/Bb	206-7/Ba 207-8
enechilo / śune jībe phire ge—	209/Bb	210-211
BALO E NĀM (. . . . .)	Ba	211-213
line 2, second part		
śune jībe phire gelo	Bb	214-216
Refrain verse		
jīber bujhi sudin āj holo	Aa	216-218
O hori nām dite nitāi elo	Ab	218-220
jīber bujhi sudin holo	Aa	221-223

TABLE 6

Structure of Performance by Gaṅgādhar Dās of *gōlōk hote gōlōker nāth*

refrain	Ba (ph. 2)	
	Ba (ph. 3) Bb (phs. 4–5)	Aa (ph. 6–m.1) Ab(2-4) Aa(4-5)
	Ba(6-8)	
	Ba(10-12)Bb(12-14)	Aa(14-16)Ab(17-19) Aa(19-21)
st. 1 Ca(24-27)Cb(29-32)	Ba(43-45)	
Ca′(34-37)Cb′(38-42)	Ba(46-47)Bb(48-50)	Aa(50-51)Ab(53-55) Aa(55-56)
st. 2 Ca(59-61)Cb(62-67)	Ba(76-79)	
Ca(68-71)Cb(72-75)	Ba(80-82)Bb(83-85)	Aa(85-87)Ab(88-89) Aa(89-92)
st. 3 Ca(96-99)Cb(100-103)	Ba(118-120)	
Ca′(107-111)Cb′(113-117)	Ba(122-124)Bb(125-128)	Aa(130-131)Ab(131-132) Aa(133-135)
ref.		
[Aa(130-131)Ab(131-132)	Ba(135-137)	
Aa(133-135)]	Ba(137-139)Bb(140-142)	Aa(142-144)Ab(144-146) Aa(146-149)

Example 44 (*gōlōk hote gōlōker nāth elen bujhi dharāte*)

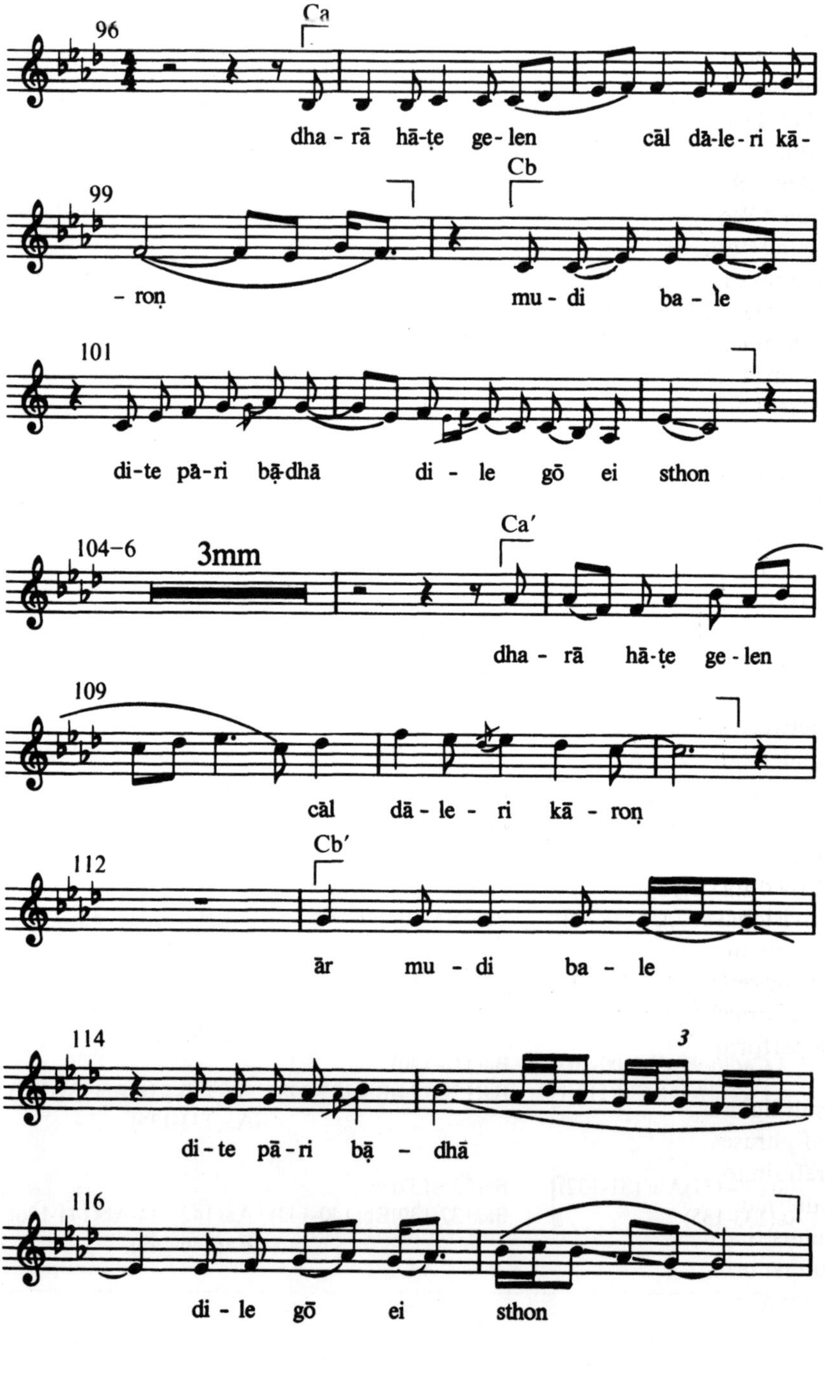

Structure of Baul-*gān* as Described by Bengali Musicologists

Bengali musicologists consider the structure of Baul-*gān* as consisting of two sections rather than three. Sureś Cakrobortī (1962, 681–82) says that the two *tuk* (phrase-group) construction is almost universal in Indian folk song except for recitative types. In his book on the music of Tagore, Śāntideb Ghōṣ has the following to say about the structure of Baul-*gān:* "We see two divisions in the tunes of Baul-*gān.* Ordinarily, however many stanzas there may be in these songs, the only difference to be noted in the tunes is that between the first stanza and the second. All the remaining stanzas are set like the second one, and except for the first stanza, the poetic rhythm of all the others is the same also" (1962, 104). In this passage "stanza" is a translation of the word *koli,* which can refer either to a stanza of text or to the music used to set it; in this latter sense it is equivalent to *tuk.* It should be understood that the first couplet is repeated after each of the others as a refrain. The difference in poetic structure Ghōṣ finds to exist between the first couplet and the others is, no doubt, based on the often-found short first verse of the refrain, a feature discussed in chapter 6.

The names *asthāȳī* and *antarā* which Cakrobortī, among others, gives to the two *tuk* or *koli* of Baul-*gān* are, like the latter terms, derived from the theory of art music and are now applied to the two groups of phrases, differentiated by tessiture and tonal goals, that constitute the *gat* of instrumental music and the *bandiś* of *kheȳāl.* As there is often a musical rhyme between *asthāȳī* and *antarā* of compositions in *rāg*-based music, it is easy to understand why those two terms are used in referring to the AB, CB musical structure of the refrain and stanzas of Baul-*gān* when the return to A (ABA, CBA) is omitted in both. This bipartite division of Baul-*gān,* though it is convenient for prescriptive notations such as that done by Subhāṣ Cowdhurī in example 45, overlooks the fact that the latter half of each division is the same (cf. mm. 11–15 with mm. 28–32). When performance is based on such prescriptive notations, furthermore, it results in the refrain being repeated in its entirety after every stanza, which is exceptional in Baul performance. While exceptional, such use of the full refrain was evident in a performance of a song I recorded at Jayadeva *melā* in January 1970.

When the refrain-verse alone is used for the internal refrains, the resulting musical unit, the stanza plus the refrain-verse, is a tripartite group of phrases, CBA, but in prescriptive notations that require the complete refrain to be performed after every stanza, the music for each is a unit that alternates with a fellow, CB for the stanzas, ABA for the refrains; it is these units that Bengali musicologists call *tuk, koli,* or, differentiating the two units, *asthāȳi*/*antarā,* and these terms refer to a higher level of structural organization than that which isolates the individual groups of phrases constituting each *koli.* Since in actual Baul performances, the alternation of

Example 45 (*sab loke kay lālon ki jāt*)

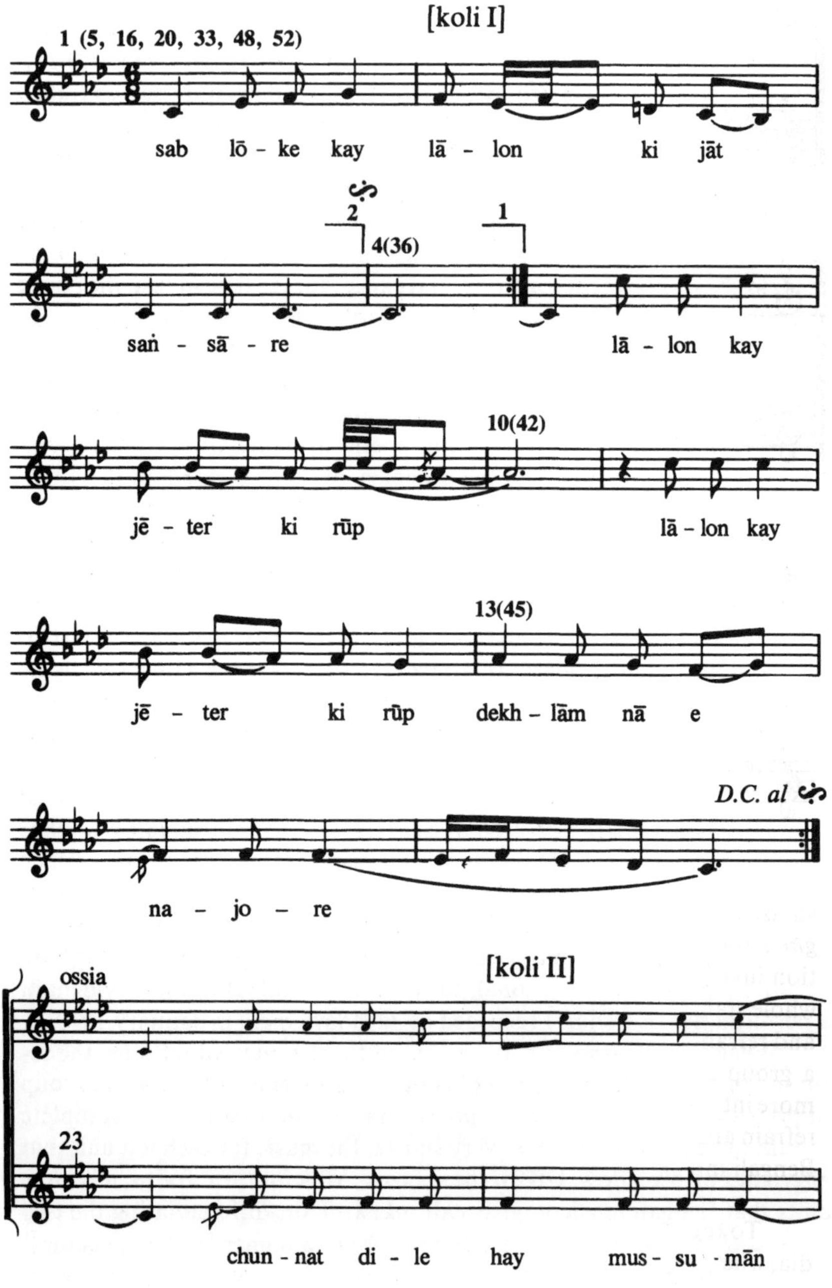

26
nā - rā lō - ke ki hay bi - dhān
29
bā - mon ci - ni pai - tār pro - mān
bām - ni ci - ni ki ko - re
32
[repeat Koli I]
The remaining koli are sung like the second.

stanzas with the complete refrains is relatively rare, the description of Baul-*gān* structure given in this chapter emphasizes the lower level of organization involving the groups of phrases setting individual verses rather than whole stanzas; such an emphasis makes evident the fact that while stanzas and refrains each have an individual group of phrases, they normally share a group as well, and as performed by Bauls, Baul-*gān* generally have a more intricate structure than the simple alternation of *asthāyi* and *antarā*—refrain and stanzas—implicit in the discussion or notation of Baul-*gān* by Bengali musicologists.

To those acquainted with relatively sophisticated types of song in India, whether art or folk, the structure of Baul-*gān* as described in this chapter will certainly have seemed familiar with its *asthāyi* / *antarā,* or refrain / stanza, components, and their association, respectively, with low and high tessiture. This familiarity makes it evident that some basic principles of music-making are both old and widespread in India, and that Baul-*gān* is part of an Indian musical lingua franca with a venerable past and every indication of prospects for a lengthy future.

The venerable past from which Baul-*gān* stems is hinted at in the thousand-year-old *caryāpad*s of the Buddhist Siddhacaryas. The *rāg* names preceding the texts of these songs suggest their tunes were part of a canonical musical tradition just as the tantrik slant of their texts suggests a connection with a ubiquitous religious tradition; but their language, considered the oldest form of Bengali, already indicates a tendency toward regional parochialization that was no doubt accomplished long before Baul-*gān* came into being as the musical expression of a peculiarly Bengali sect. The connections of the *caryāpad*s with *rāg* music, too, have withered, and this has allowed the tunes of Baul-*gān* to appear to have sprung from native soil as the spontaneous encapsulation of the Bengali soul.

During the nineteenth century, when the confrontation between indigenous and colonial peoples in Bengal was most active, the development of a new Westernized class of natives and of an intelligentsia brought about new perspectives on the traditional elements of Bengali culture, among them the Baul sect and their peculiar songs. The new focus upon the sect included elements of ridicule by the more Westernizing group who condemned things native as naive and backward while enthusiastically adopting things foreign as enlightened and liberating. But the more moderate attitude of the intelligentsia allowed for the adoption of the Bauls and their songs as vehicles for self-representation in both a nationalistic and a regional ethnic mode.

Today the Bauls speak, or rather sing, not just for themselves but for Bengal, and their new emblematic role emphasizes more than ever the dichotomy between their being both public figures and members of an "obscure religious cult." While the idiosyncratic and esoteric beliefs of the Bauls may never achieve widespread popularity, there can be little doubt that the non-doctrinal texts of Baul-*gān* combined with their infectious and captivating tunes will continue to make them a popular medium for cultural performance.[48] Unlike many types of participatory religious folk song, Baul-*gān* has always been performer / audience oriented, which has helped these songs make a smooth transition from being the expression of an obscure cult to being a musical emblem of a large ethnic group; the dichotomy between private and public attitudes is inherent in Baul performance and although modern contexts of performance may continue to exaggerate the dichotomy, this does not necessarily invalidate it for the

Bauls. Thus Pūrṇo Dās can be a successful world-traveled "artiste" and yet maintain he continues to be a Baul. The success with which Baul-*gān* fulfills the new role initiated for it by men like Rabindranath Tagore and Kshitimohan Sen is due not only to its attractive qualities but also to the ability of the Bauls to adopt to the new requirements made of them as the carriers of a cultural emblem. It is this ability which should guarantee the continuation of the Bauls' significant role in the life of modern Bengal.

APPENDIX A

Song Texts

ORIGINAL BENGALI WITH ENGLISH TRANSLATIONS AND NOTES

Index of First Lines

Words followed by a question mark and enclosed in parentheses are uncertain transcriptions.

Words in square brackets represent the author's amplification.

Ellipsis points indicate unintelligible text.

[1]

Singer: Sonāton Dās Ṭhākur

āge gharer khabor nā jene   kēno geli bhajon sādhone
bhajon sādhon sahoj nay mon   āge damon karo madone

ghare chay ripute bēṛāy ghure   sādhon pathe bighno kare
tārā tōr ghare basot kare   tōr kathā se kay śone

ghare thākte jñān nayon prohorī   din dupure hacche re curi
tui hay mānūṣ emni behuś   moner mānūṣ hārāli ajatone

basot karo ālgā ghare   kapāṭ nāi tār nayṭā dvāre
pañco bhute nityo kare   hāsāy kādāy svapone

madnā bētā baṛoi duṣṭo   mon maynāṭā karle naṣṭo
madan nāg tōr durodṛiṣṭo   kṛiṣṇo pābi kēmone

Before knowing your own business,[1]
  why have you gone in for *bhajon-sādhon*?[2]
Bhajon-sādhon are not easy, mind;
  first restrain Madan.[3]

Six enemies[4] roam about at home;
  they obstruct the path to *sādhon*.
They dwell in your house;
  they speak and hear your words.

Even though the eye of knowledge is on guard,
  the theft goes on in broad daylight.[5]
Being a man so unaware,
  you have lost the *moner mānūṣ*.[6]

You dwell in a ramshackle house;
  there are no doors in the nine doorways.[7]
The five elements continually
  make you laugh and cry in dreams.[8]

That boy Madan is very naughty;
  he has destroyed the mind-mynah.[9]
Madan Nag, Your fate is hard;
  how will you obtain Krishna?

1. *gharer khabor,* "news at home"; i.e., knowledge of the body, *dehotattvo.*
2. Worship and religious discipline.
3. Eros.
4. Desire, anger, greed, infatuation, pride, envy.
5. Theft of one's eternal substance.
6. Man of the Heart, the eternal substance.
7. Eyes, ears, nostrils, mouth, anus, and urethra.
8. Earth, air, fire, water, and ether.
9. The eternal spirit which, like a bird, flies in and out of the cage of the body.

[2]

Singer: Phokir Dās

āmār ei rudhir dhārāy dhuȳe ẏāk tōr moner maylā
mār kheȳe nām bhulibo nā re nitāi bol hori balāy

snān kere āi gaṅgā jale nāmer tilok paṛo kopāle
mantar di tōr koriṇo mūle ghuche ẏāk tōr tritāp jvālā

bṛithā ahaṅkār cheṛe triṇādopir bhāb dhore
hori nām japo antare paṛāiȳe di nāmer mālā

rādhār sẏām tōr ār bhay nei hori bole ḍāk sadāy
hori bole ḍāk re sadāy bhabo nodīr pather dhuloy

Let the filth of your heart
be washed in my blood.
Though beaten, will we forget the name?
Ever say the name of Hari.[1]

Go bathe in Ganges water,
put the name *tilok*[2] on your forehead.
Give the mantra to your inmost ear,
Let your threefold wants[3] be extinguished.

Leaving false egoism,
take on the humble nature of grass.[4]
Recite the Hari-name within you,
put on the garland of names.

Radhasyam, there is no more need to fear,
always cry out saying the Hari-name.
Always cry out saying the Hari-name
on the dusty path along the river of life.

1. Perhaps the refrain refers to Jogai and Madhai, two disciples of Caitanya, who had mocked him before being converted.
2. Sectarian mark on the forehead.
3. *tritāp jvālā,* spiritual, material, and supernatural afflictions.
4. The Vaisnava ideal of pacifism expressed in the willingness of grass to be trodden upon without revenge.

[3]

Singers: Prem Dāsi, Ẏotin Dās

ā re ō jībon chāṛiȳā nā ẏāō mōre
tui jībon chāṛiȳā gele ādor korbe ke (jībon re)

bhāi balo bhātijā balo sompottir bhāgi
nidān kāle keō habe nā jīboneri sāthi (jībon re)

kā̦cā bā̦ser khā̦ṭ pālaṅko   sukhnā pā̦ṭer doṛi
cārjonete kandhe loẏe   bolbe hori hori (jībon re)

ei nā mukhe khāccho kato   kṣīr ār sar noni
se nā mukhe jvālāiẏā dibe   jvalanto agni (jībon re)

śmaśān ghā̦ṭe niẏā tōmāy   puṛiẏā karbe chāi
ẏābār bēlāy diẏā ẏābe   rām nāmer dōhāi (jībon re)

This text as sung by Prem and Ẏotin preserves older verb forms and pronunciations typical of East Bengal, such as *chā̦ṛiẏā* and *jvālāiẏā* for *cheṛe* and *jvāliẏe,* and *koirbe* and *khātso* which have been transcribed as commoner forms *korbe* and *khāccho* (i.e., *koribe* and *khāitecho*).

O hey Life! Don't go and leave me.
If you leave me, Life, who will care for me? (Hey Life!)

Whether you call your brother or your nephew heir,
At the end no one will be a life's companion.

Four pall bearers, saying "Hari, Hari" will take upon their shoulders
The cot of green bamboo and dried jute ropes.[1]

In that very mouth with which you now eat so much curd, and cream, and butter,
They will place burning fire.[2]

They will take you to the burning ground and burn you to ashes.
While going there, they will give out Rama's name as a pretext.

1. Hindu corpses are burned on such cots.
2. Before lighting the pyre, the son first touches fire to the lips of the corpse.

[4]

Singer: Tinkoṛi Dās

bhāṅā ghare (uri?) diẏe thākbo kato din
ẏe din āsbe barṣā karbe pharsā   rākhbe nā tōr konoi cin

e ghare nāi ēkṭiō jhā̦ṭi   hiṅsā rui pōkāte koreche mā̦ṭi
āmār bhajon sādhon duṭi khuṭi   tāō hoẏeche śoktihin

e ghare nāi ēkṭiō pēlā   ā̦j āche kāl ẏābe poṛe āmār sāder ā̦ṭcālā
tokhon dekhbi pañco bhuter khēlā   bhay koriś nā konoi din

(murdhoni?) āche muriri jore   (kā̦ci konāi?) gēche cheṛe kon din ẏābe re poṛe
doṛ kowpin mālā nebe cheṛe   rākhbe nā tōr konoi cin

cowddo pōẏā māper ghar khānā   tār bhitore birā̦j kare ōi ṣōlojōnā
dvijo tinkaṛ bale e sab ghare   bās karā holo kaṭhin

How long will you stay in a ruined house (by patching it up?)
That day the rain comes, it will clean up and leave no
trace of you at all.

In this house, there is not even a single broom;
the envy-termites have made everything mud.
My two *sādhon-bhajon* pillars[1]—
those, too, have become weakened.

In this house, there is not even a single prop;
today it stands, my mansion of desires; tomorrow it will collapse.
Then you will see the play of the five elements,[2] don't you
doubt it for a moment.

The (roofbeam?) stands on the strength of the drainpipe;
the (crossbeams?) have loosened; on what day will they fall?
They will take your *dor̤, kowpin,* and *mālā*[3] and tear them
and keep no trace of you at all.

The house measuring fourteen quarters[4]—within it reside
those sixteen people.[5]
Dvijo Tinkori says, "It is difficult to live in such houses."

1. Religious practice and worship.
2. You will be dissolved into the elements at death.
3. Constituents of Vaisnava Baul dress.
4. That is, fourteen hands in measure, the body.
5. For possible meaning see the explanatory note to song no. 6.

[5]

Singer: Ŷotin Dās

br̤indābone tin raner tin phul phoṭe   nīl jarod sādā
kon phule śrī kr̤iṣṇo āche   kon phule śrī rādhā

phul phoṭe bāro batsor pare   māse māse se phul jhor̤e
phuler kathā bolbo kāre   rosik bine kaite bādhā

anŷeri phaler kāmonā   phule maje rosikjōnā
jībe tār sandhān jāne nā   phule madhu phale sudhā

phalete ei jībi bhuleche   phulete rosiki meṭeche
madhu pāne madhubone   matto brajer balāi dādā

āmār gọsāi gurucạd bale   phul phoṭe se nirguṇ ḍāle
phuler kathā karṇe śunle   rādhāśŷām tōr lāgbe dhạdhạ

In Vrindavan[1] bloom three flowers of three colors—
blue, yellow, and white.[2]
In which flower is Sri Krishna,
in which flower is Radha?

The flowers bloom after twelve years;
month by month those flowers fall.

To whom shall I speak of the flowers—
  except to the *rosik*,[3] it is forbidden to speak.

Others is the desire for the fruit;
  the *rosik* delights in the flower.
Creatures don't know its whereabouts;
  in the flower is sweetness, in the fruit is intoxication.

This creature has forgotten himself in the fruit;
  the *rosik*s revel in the flowers.
Drinking honey in Madhuban,[1]
  Vraja's[1] Balai[4] is ecstatic.

My Lord Gurucad says, "The flowers bloom on that
  qualityless branch.
"If you hear about the flowers, Radhasyam, you will
  be puzzled."

1. Place significant in the life of Krishna.
2. Colors associated with the three days of ritual coitus during menstruation.
3. See discussion of this word on p. 11.
4. Elder brother of Krishna.

[6]

Singer: Ýotin Dās

c̣ā̤der gāy c̣ā̤d legeche   āmrā bhebe karbo ki
jhiȳer peṭe māȳer janmo   tāre tōmrā balo ki

tin māser ēk kanȳā chilo   nay māse tār garbho holo
ēgāro māse tinṭi santān   konṭā niben phokiri

ṣolo bahu battriś māthā   garbhe chele kay go kathā
kebā tāhār pitā mātā   ei kathāṭi jijñāsi

ghar āche tār duȳār nāi   mānūṣ āche tār bākȳo nāi
ke bā tāhār āhār ýōgāy   kebā kare sandhā bāṭi

lālon śā phokire bale   māȳe chule putro mare
ei ýār kathār māne hole   tāri hobe phokiri

One moon has touched the body of another;
  what shall we do, having thought of that?
The mother's birth is from the daughter's womb;
  what do you call her?

There was a girl of three months;
  in nine months she conceived.
In eleven months there were three offspring;
  which one will the fakir take?

Sixteen arms, thirty-two heads;
  the child speaks within the womb.

Who are its mother and father?
  That's a question to be asked!

There is a room with no doors;
  there is a man who doesn't speak.
Who furnishes his food;
  who lights the evening lamp?

Lalon Shah, the fakir, says,
  "If the mother touches, the son dies.
"He to whom these words have meaning,
  to him, indeed, belongs fakirdom."

This song is of the *hẹȳāli* (riddle) type; what exegesis I received from Ȳotin I offer without much hope of unravelling the riddle completely.

The first line refers to the mystery of conception. The second line contains two involved puns. The word *jhi,* daughter, may also mean maidservant, and little girls are often affectionately called *mā,* mother; thus, there can be confusion between daughter / mother, and mothers can be thought of as maidservants to their offspring.

The three months refer to the three residences of man: 1) in our fathers' heads (storage place of immobilized semen); 2) in our mothers' wombs (after conception); 3) in the material world (after birth). Three months are needed for the distillation of semen in the father's head. Nine plus three make twelve, the years of the girl's first menses. The term of pregnancy is supposed to be ten months and ten days. Three offspring are the three attributes we have at birth: 1) *jñān;* 2) *buddhi;* 3) *bal* (consciousness, intellect, physical capacity); or 1) *kṣudhā;* 2) *śabdo;* 3) *bhay* (hunger, vocal sound, fear); or the three deities Vishnu, Shiva, Brahma; of these Vishnu is a fakir because he is a *sādhok* (ascetic devotee).

The sixteen arms are: five *jñānendriȳo* (sense organs)—eyes, ears, nostrils, tongue, skin; five *karmendriȳo* (physical organs)—speech, hands, feet, anus, genitals; and six *ṛipu* (enemies)—desire, anger, greed, infatuation, pride, envy. The child who speaks in the womb is the *adhor mānūṣ,* the Elusive Man. He has neither mother nor father because he is the Eternal Substance.

The room (or house) of the body cannot be entered by any door to discover the individual personality. Man, as seed, cannot speak.

Many potential children die (as seed) at the touch of the mother. He who understands these riddles has the knowledge of fakirs.

[7]

Singer: Gaṅgādhar Dās

emni kore thākle dūre bạci kẽmone
āmi pathohārā andho pathik tōmār kathā nāi mone

andhojōnār nayon tumi andho pathik hay gō āmi
anābādi āmār jōmi ār bibādi chayjōne

āśi lakṣo janom pare   āmāy enecho soṅgi kore
tōmāy ḍākte gele bhōlāy mōre   āmār kāmini ār kañconi

guru kumud kānto hoȳe saday   narāke loiȳo ōi rāṅā pāy
āmi cāi nā bhokti cāi nā mukti   dēkhā diȳō maroṇe

If you remain distant like that,
  how will I survive?
I am a blind pilgrim who has lost the path;
  I have not kept your words in mind.

You are the eyes of the blind;
  I am a blind pilgrim;
My land lies fallow;
  and there are six plaintiffs.[1]

After eighty lakh births,[2]
  you have brought me as a companion.
If I go to call out to you,
  Woman and Gold make me forget.

Guru Kumud Kanto, being charitable
  take Nara to those beloved feet.[3]
I want neither devotion nor liberation;
  show yourself when I die.

1. *chay ṛipu* (six enemies): *kām, krōdh, lōbh, mad, mōho, mātsarýo* (desire, anger, greed, infatuation, pride, envy).
2. Lakh 100,000; i.e., having achieved incarnation as a human being.
3. That is, lead the singer to proper devotion.

[8]

Singer: Tinkoṛi Dās

ēmon cāṣā buddhi nāśā   cinli nā tōr āpon bhụi
tōr mānob jōmi pākā dhāne   legeche chayṭā bābui

bohu kaṣṭe korli ki re svāmi   cowddo pōȳā māper jōmi nām dehokhāni
tāte tōr bhokti phasol janmechilo   kheȳe gelo hiṅse coṭui

cēton bēṛāy upṛe poṛeche   ālgā peȳe pākā phasol kheȳe giȳeche
gọph phulāiȳe bose āche   mācā bharā bighno bhụi nikoṣer samay

minse mōṭā kụṛe (bhāture?)   jōmir āli bạdhli nā kụṛe
ēkhon cinta jvore morbi puṛe   tōr peṭe hobe re pilui

phasol gelo ghoṭlo bhīṣon dāy   ṭhekbi ýe din śikhbi se din nikoṣer samay
gọsāi gowr bale āmi kubirer   pade monke ṭhui

Such a witless peasant,
  you haven't known your own land.[1]

Six weaver-birds[2] have attacked
  the ripe paddy of your human-land.

What have you accomplished, master, with such difficulty?
  The fields of fourteen quarters measure, named the body—
In those, your devotion-crop took root;
  the envy-sparrows have eaten it up.

The attention-fence has fallen down;
  being unprotected, the crop has been eaten.
He sits twisting his moustaches—
  the obstacle land, full of storage platforms.

Fat, lazy, sluggish fellow,
  you didn't build the dikes.[3]
Now you will burn up and die with worry-fever;
  your spleen will swell into your stomach.[4]

The crop is finished, terrible difficulties have arisen;
  you will learn on the day you get stuck,
  at the time of testing.
Gosai Gowr says, "Let me place my heart at the feet of Kubir."

1. That is, the body.
2. *chay ṛipu* (six enemies): *kām, krōdh, lōbh, mad, mōho, mātsarýo* (desire, anger, greed, infatuation, pride, envy).
3. The dikes are the divisions between one paddy field and another; they are narrow pathways of raised earth which retain the irrigation water. The yogic implication is that the singer has not attained the physical control needed to retain and immobilize semen.
4. A symptom of malaria.

[9]

Singer: Gaṅgādhar Dās

ēmone gowr pābi kise
tōr gowr pālāy mon āne ýāy   tōr mone nā miśe

lōk dēkhāno tilok mālā   kono kāje nāhi āse
ḍub dile jal khele   ki habe ēkādośir upobāse

bāhire tōr kọcār patton   chụcōr kīrton bāse
dekhli nā jñān cokṣu mile   māyā mad kheẏe roẏecho behụśe

onurāg nā hole pāy nā gowr   bolechilen horidāse
rāger ghare śikṣā karo   onurāgir guru pāse

How will you obtain Gowr[1] that way?
Your Gowr flees, your mind goes elsewhere;
  He doesn't merge with your mind.

If you display *tilok*[2] and *mala*[3] to people,
  it doesn't matter at all.
If you drink water while taking a dip,
  what will happen to your eleventh-day fast?

In public the folds of your dhoti are elegant;
  at home there's a muskrat's revival meeting.[4]
You haven't looked with the eyes of knowledge;
  you have drunk the wine of illusion and remained unconscious.

"One doesn't get Gowr without affection,"[5]
  said Hari Das.
"Learn in the house of attachment[6]
  from a guru of affection."

1. Caitanya.
2. Sectarian mark on forehead.
3. Rosary.
4. Though your public life is proper, your private life is a scandal.
5. *onurāg*—one of a variety of emotional states (in Vaisnava theology) in which the devotee experiences growing attachment to Krishna.
6. *rāg*—see note 5.

[10]

Singer: Pūrṇo Candro Dās

ēmon kore ār bā̃śori bājāiȳō nā śȳā̃m
āmi guru jōnār madhȳe bose   lajjāte morlām

prem jāno nā kālo sōnā   rādhār boi ki nām jāno nā
majāȳō brajer brajaṅgonā   brajer guṇodhām

mukundo dās bolchen hori   majāiȳo nā kulonāri
e kalaṅke kṛipā kori   caroṇe diȳō sthān

Pūrṇo Dās, who sings this song, tends to omit *r* in consonant clusters (*Cr* becomes *CØ*) as in *pem* for *prem* or *kipā* for *kṛipā*. This is common in Birbhum.

Don't play the flute like that any more, Syam.[1]
Sitting among my in-laws,
  I died of shame.

You don't know love, Kalo Sona;[1]
  don't you know any name but Radha?
You intoxicate the women of Vraja,
  O Vraja's abode of virtues!

Mukundo Das says, "Hari[2]
  don't intoxicate the women of good family.

"Mercifully give this sinner
  a place at your feet."

1. Krishna.
2. Of whom Krishna is an avatar.

[11]

Singer: Ýotin Dās

ēmon ulṭā deś gō guru kon jāygāy āche
se ýe hẹ̄ṭo muṇḍo urdho pade   se deśe bās korteche

se nā deśe ýato lōker bās   mukhe āhār kare tārā nāker nāi niḥśvās
tārā mal mūtro tÿā́g kare nā   ābār āhār kore jībon bā̩ce

se nā deśe ýato nad nodī   urdho mukhe jaler srōtoḥ bay nirobodhi
jaler niche ākāś bāyu   tāte bāmon bās korteche

din sarot bale holam camotkār   candro śurýer tāp nāi sekhāne ghōr andhokār
ābār se deśer mānuṣ ei deśete   abirato āsiteche

Verb forms such as *korteche* (for *korche*) and *āsiteche* (for *āsche*) are typical of East Bengal dialects. Ýotin, who sings this song, preserves some elements of East Bengal pronunciation as in *kon zāygāy āse* (for *kon jāygāy āche*).

In what place, dear guru, is there such a topsy-turvy land?
With bowed head, raised feet,
  Men reside in that land.

However many people live in that land,
  they eat with their mouths but in their noses is no breath.
They neither defecate nor urinate,
  but they eat and survive.

However many rivers and streams there be in that land,
  the currents of water ceaselessly flow upstream.
The sky and air are beneath the water;
  in them the brahman lives.

Din Sarot says, "I was surprised;
  the moon and sun have no heat; there is impenetrable darkness there.
"But the people of that land,
  are coming uninterruptedly to this land."

This song is a riddle about gestation. The Bauls consider the foetus to be performing yoga in the womb by resting in a head down position (*śirṣāsana*) and arresting respiration (*kumbhaka*).

[12]

Singer: Sambhu Dās

ese ōi rosik pāgol bā̦dhāle gōl noder mājhe dekse gō tōrā
pāgoler soṅge ýābo pāgol habo herbo raser nabo gōṛā

nitāi pāgol gowr pāgol caitanȳo pāgoler gōṛā
advoito pāgol rase ḍube prem eneche jāhāj porā

brahmā pāgol biṣṇu pāgol ār ēk pāgol nā dēy dharā
koilāśer śib ō pāgol kheȳe pāgol sār koreche bhāṅ dhuturā

ýato sab boirāgi boiṣṇob bhek niȳe nām bāṛāile bāul ō nēṛā
kubir cā̦der bacon pābi caroṇ hobi re jiȳanto marā

That *rosik*[1] madman came and created an uproar in Nodia,[2]
  go and see yourselves.
I will go with the madman, become mad myself;
  I will behold the new source of *ras.*[1]

Nitai[3] is mad, Gowr[4] is mad;
  Caitanya is the root of madness.
Advaita[5] became mad and sank into *ras;*
  he brought a shipload of love.

Brahma is mad, Vishnu is mad,
  and another madman doesn't allow himself to be caught.
Shiva of Mt. Kailasa is mad from eating—
  for he lives on *bhāṅ*[6] and jimson weed.

However many have taken the dress of the ascetic Vaisnava,
  they have magnified their names as Bauls and Neras.[7]
Kubir Cad's words: "You will obtain the feet,
  when you will be dead-in-life."

1. See discussion of *rosik* and *ras* p. 11.
2. The town in which Caitanya began his revivalist movemen
3. Chief companion of Caitanya.
4. Caitanya.
5. Caitanya's St. John Baptist.
6. marijuana.
7. See discussion of Neras on pp. 14–15.

[13]

Singer: Tinkoṛi Dās

gōlōk hote gōlōker nāth elen dēkho dharāte
sahoje keō pāy ni tāre pele hay re kā̦dite

nando ýasōdā rānī pūrbe janme chilen tārā brāhmon brāhmoni
tārā nām dhare dharā drōni tārā kāl kāṭāten duḥkhete

otithi rūpe elen nārāyon   brāh̃monike bale śīghro karāō bhojon
bale bhikṣāte giȳāche brāh̃mon   kichui nāi mōr gṛihete

dharā hāṭe gelen cāl dāleri kāron   mudi bale dite pāri bḁdhā dile ei ston
takhon ston kāṭiȳā bḁdhā diȳā   sebā dilen otithi

From heaven,[1] heaven's Lord has come.
No one gets him easily;
  if you get him, you must weep.

Nando and Yasoda—in a previous life,
  they were brahmans.
They took the names Dhara and Droni;
  they spent their time in sorrow.

Narayon came in the guise of a guest;
  He said to the brahman lady, "Quickly make me a meal."
She said, "My husband has gone begging;
  there is nothing in the house."

Dhara went to the market for rice and lentils;
  the grocer said, "I can let you have them,
  if you give me a look at those breasts as security."
Then cutting off her breasts and giving them as security,
  she served the guest.

This is a popular homily from the *Mahabharata.*

1. *gōlōk,* the heaven of Narayan, a form of Vishnu.

[14]

Singer: Sonāton Dās Ṭhākur

gowr prem niṣṭhā cinir ras karā
enechen nitȳānando premer bhāṇḍo   surose kṣīrer baṛā

pañco ras bhiȳān karā   sitābhōg chēnā baṛā
kheȳeche rosik ȳārā   hoȳeche mātōȳārā

khele kāmer mandā daphā ṭhāṇḍa   jiȳante mānuṣ hay marā
khāō bibek luci ār jñān kocuri   onurāg kophir tarkāri

pāro ȳodi kheȳe nāō mon   udāro puri
khāccho kebol lobher muṛi   pāntā bhāt begun pōṛā

premānando bolche ẹṭe   e sab sabe nā sabār peṭe
ȳārā guṛ bale khācche ciṭe   mon ȳe āmār hatobhāgā

Making the confection of firm faith in Gowr's[1] love.
Nityanando[2] has brought the container of love,
  kṣīr baṛā[3] in fine syrup.

Sītabhōg and *chẹnā baṛā,*[3]
  confected with five syrups—
Those *rosiks*[4] who have eaten them,
  have become intoxicated.

If you eat the sweet-meat of desire, recurrence ceases;
  a living man becomes dead.[5]
Eat the bread of discrimination and the pancake of knowledge,
  the cabbage curry of affectionate devotion.

If you are able, take it and eat it, mind,
  filling your stomach.
You are eating only the puffed rice of greed,
  rice gruel, burnt eggplant.

Premanando says confidently,
  "These things can't be borne in the stomachs of those
"Who eat blackstrap, calling it light molasses,
  O my helpless mind."

1. Caitanya.
2. Companion of Caitanya.
3. Types of milk-based sweets.
4. See discussion of this word on p. 11.
5. *jiȳante marā*, "dead while alive," the state in which a yogi, while alive, attains release from phenomenal existence, including the cycle of death and rebirth.

[15]

Singers: Prem Dāsi and Ẏotin Dās

guru bhajo re ō re sōnār cā̦d
dil doriāy uṭhle tuphān   ke dibe āsān

guru bhajo guru ceno   guru karo sār
guru bine e duniȳāy   bandhu nei re ār

āite habe ẏāite habe   pār koribe ke
dehiȳā tui dāruṇ jvālā   mone koriȳā ne

ei ẏe deher madhȳe   ke koreche khēlā
pichu pāne cāiȳā dekho   ḍube gelo bēlā

bhāi balo bandhu balo   keō tō kāreri nay
diner piṭhe dēkhā śōnā   pather poricay

Worship the guru, O Golden Moon!
If a storm should rise on the mind-river,
  who will give refuge?

Worship the guru, know the guru;
  depend utterly on the guru.

In this world, other than the guru
there is no other friend.

You must come, you must go;
who will take you across?
Seeing all this, remember
the terrible torment.

In this very body,
who has played?
Take a look behind you;
time has run out.

Call him brother, call him friend—
no one looks after another.
At the end of the day,
the path's signs become familiar.

[16]

Singer: Bimal Dās; text transcribed from script of Lakṣm̃aṇ Dās (of Bardhoman).

hori tōmāy ḍākbo ḍākār samay dile koi
gēlo kāje kāje rātri dibā hori
hori tōmāke ḍākkār samay kay

mone kori bharer bēlā karbo tōmār stab
ghumer āge khōkā jege karche kalorab
ābār ṭhik suẏōge ginni jege cā̦d badone phuṭāno khoi

mone kori snāner ghāṭe ḍākbo he tōmāy
jhā̦ke jhā̦ke kalosi kā̦khe ramoni dāṛāy
here rūp mādhuri bā̦śidhāri āpnā āpni hārā hay

khete bose pañco grāse ḍākbo he tōmāy
pāōnādārer sārā peẏe sabi bhule ẏāi
takhon konṭā thuẏe konṭā khābo suktonite ḍhāli doi

dupur bēlā ẏakhon tōmār stab karte bosi
dirgho bājār pharddā loẏe uday preẏosī
bale lakṣmīkāntu cāl bāṛāntu amni mālā poṛi jhōlā soi

krome krome rātri holo ditiẏo prohor
khudār caṭe udor phāṭe tumi dāmodār
ẏodi pāi abosor he pitāmbor tobe tōmā chāṛā kārō nay

Where have you given me time to call you, Hari?
Day and night have gone in worthless work.

I think I will worship you at dawn—
before I wake, the child awakes and makes a racket.
And just at the right moment, the wife awakes;
the sweetheart prattles away.

I think I will call you at the bathing ghat—
flock upon flock of lovely maidens stand with their
water jugs upon their hips;
Seeing them, I naturally lose sight of
the sweetly formed flute player.[1]

Having sat to eat, in five mouthfuls, I will call you;
but hearing the approach of my creditors, I forget everything.
Then thinking what to eat, what to put aside,
I pour the yogurt into the *suktoni.*[2]

In the afternoon when I sit to perform your worship,
my beloved appears with a long shopping list.
She says, "My dear, the rice is finished."
So, my friend, I drop the rosary and put on the shopping bag.

At last it has become the second watch of the night;
my stomach bursts with pangs of hunger, thou Damodar.[1]
If I get the opportunity, o Pitambor,[1]
then, there will be no one besides you!

1. Krishna.
2. *suktoni* is a dish of vegetables with a mildly bitter flavor; it is taken first at a meal; the yogurt is taken last.

[17]

Singer: Śaśāṅko Dās

hori nām prem dite nitāi elo jiber bujhi sudin holo
āmār gowr ýe nām enechilo śune jībe phire gelo

probhu bollen trisandhȳā snān korbe ēk sandhȳā bhōjon
sālȳo (?) *anno nebe sabe tel matsȳo bāroṇ*
korbe ēkādośī upobāsī preȳosir bāroṇ chilo

elen abodhowto rāi probhui āmār baṛo dayāmay
ke nibe ke nibe bole ḍākchen ōre āi
nitāi āmār pūrṇo brah̄mo jñāni brah̄momay jagot dekhilo

bollen māgur mācher jhōl ār bhōr ýubotir̄ kōl
jīber bale ebār bolbo hori bol
gọ̄sāi gowr balen e kathāke e ýe gōlemāle rohilo

Nitai came to give the Hari-name-love;
I guess the best day of my life has happened.
That name which my Gowr took, hearing it, life returned.

The Lord said, "You will bathe once, eat once a day,
and everyone shall take plain food, no fish and oil.
"You will observe the eleventh-day fast; lovers are forbidden."

Abodhowto Rai came—my Lord is greatly merciful—
saying, "Who will take, who will take?" he called out, "Come all ye!"
My Nitai has full knowledge of Brahma; he has seen the universe filled with Brahma.

He said, "Cat-fish curry and the lap of a maiden,"
this time, dying, I will say Hari with all my strength.
Gosai Gowr says this: "He remained in chaos."

[18]

Singer: Lakṣm̃aṇ Dās (of Mallarpur)

version a

hṛidayo piñjore bose ō pākhi   rādhā kṛiṣṇer nām balo nā
tumi balo nām āmi śuno nā   āmi boli nām tumi śono nā

ṣōlo nām battriś akṣore   āṭāś akṣor dāō nā cheṛe
tobe ei rādhā kṛiṣṇo cār akṣore   sādhu jape nām jibe jāne nā

ō nām japo karo jōre   pośu janom ẏābe gō dūre
e mānob ātm̃ā bosbe ghoṭe   svabhāb ẏābe kichui abhāb rabe nā

khēpā kahe moner duḥkhe   ōi nām bale bā ke śone bā ke
ajapā nām pābi re kise   bole mon mele moner mānūṣ mele nā

The above text is transcribed from song; what follows was transcribed from dictation of the text by the same singer.

version b

hṛidaẏo piñjore bose   rādhākṛiṣṇo nām balo nā
e nām tumi balo āmi śuni   āmi boli nām tumi śono nām

nām japo karo pute   pośu janom ẏābe keṭe
tōmār paromātm̃ā bosbe ghoṭe   svabhāb gele kichu abhāb rabe nā

ṣōlo nām battriś akṣore   āṭāś akṣar dāō nā cheṛe
ajapā nām cār akṣare   sādhu jape nām jibe jāne nā

khēpā bale moner duḥkhe   ei kathā bolbo kāke
sadāy thāki moner duḥkhe   mon mele moner mānūṣ mele nā

a)

Sitting within the cage of the heart, o bird,
say the names of Radha and Krishna.
You say the names, let me listen;
let me say the names, you listen.

Sixteen names in thirty-two syllables;
give out the twenty-eight syllables.
Then in these four syllables—Radha Krishna—
the sadhu recites the names; the creatures don't know.

Recite that name loudly,
your animal birth will go away.
This human soul will be established;
your innate character will go, and no want will remain.

Khepa says with a sorrowful heart,
"Who says that name, and who listens to that name?"
"How will you obtain the unrecited name;
the heart is open, but the Man of the Heart is not gained."

b)

Sitting in the cage of the heart,
say the names of Radha Krishna.
Let me hear you say this name;
Let me say the names; you listen.

When you have sown the name-prayer
your animal birth will disappear.
You will acquire the supreme soul;
if your innate character goes, no want will remain.

Sixteen names in thirty-two syllables;
give out the twenty-eight syllables.
The unrecited name in four syllables;
the sadhu recites the names, but the creatures don't know.

Khepa says with a sorrowful heart,
"To whom shall I speak these words?"
"I always remain with a sorrowful heart;
the heart is open, but the Man of the Heart is not gained."

The bird is frequently used as a symbol for the human soul which flies into and out of the human body. Teaching a bird to recite the names of God as in the formula Hare Krishna Hare Krishna Krishna Krishna Hare Hare Hare Rama Hare Rama Rama Rama Hare Hare (sixteen names in thirty-two syllables) is compared to instruction of the soul.

[19]

Singer: Lakṣm̃aṇ Dās (of Bardhoman)

kẽno kul hārāli gowr rūpe nayon kẽno dili gōdhoni
tui gowr bhōgi e jagat mājhi   kalaṅkini holi gōdhoni

kuler kulobodhugon   tōrāy āmār kathā śon   premer pathe koris nā gamon
tōr nanodini kāl śāpini   diben karotāli gōdhoni

tōrā thāk dhoiryo dhori   ýās nā gharer bāhire   gowr pāne cās nā gō phiri
ō se hāl se behāl diner kāṅāl   pāy se caroṇ dhuli gōdhoni

se ýe rosik rasomay   gowr hori raser hāṭe ray   gowr hori raser kathā kay
se raser kathāy hoỹe srōtā   lājer māthā khāli gōdhoni

Why have you lost your dignity?
    Why have you given your eyes to that fair form, my dear?
You are the enjoyer of Gowr in this world,
    You have become stained, my dear.

O wives of good family, listen to my words;
    don't go out on the path of love.
Your sister-in-law is a deadly snake;
    she will applaud [your downfall], my dear.

Remain patiently at home; don't go outside.
    Don't look in Gowr's direction.
Kangal is the rudder to the rudderless wretches;
    they get the dust of his feet, my dear.

That *ras*-ful *rosik*,[1] Gowr Hari stays in the *ras* market;
    Gowr Hari speaks of matters concerning *ras*.
He has floated on the flood of speech about *ras;*
    you have lost all face, my dear.

This song, like number 10, concerns Radha's scandalous passion for Krishna.

1. See discussion of this word on p. 11.

[20]

Singer: Gaṅgādhar Dās

ki āścaryo majār kathā   sandeho tō gelo nā
āmār kathā bujhbe rosik bhakto   paṇḍit jonṭā bōjhe nā

cheler garbhe mātār janmo   ke bujhbe e kathār marmo
pitār garbhe mātār janmo   bed purāṇ tār niśānā

āmi śune elām ār ēk kathā   āche chayjonāri ēkṭi māthā
se ýe māthā tule kay nā kathā   kārur bhay se rākhe nā

āmār kathā holo kebol sriṣṭichāṛā   āche chayjonāi nodī pārā
premete diỹeche chāṛā   ēkhon keō to tāke māne nā

What an amazingly funny thing!
    My doubts have not left me.
The *rosik*[1] devotee will understand my words;
    the pandits do not understand.

The father's birth—from the son's womb;
  who will understand the secret of this fact?
The mother's birth—from the father's womb!
  the Vedas and Puranas are its token.

I have heard tell of another fact—
  there are six persons[2] with one head.
Raising his head, he does not speak;
  he fears no one.

My story has been outlandish;
  there are six persons[3] in the town Nodia;
They spread love about everywhere—
  now no one follows them.

The peculiar births described in this song are a common feature of *hẹy̆āli* (riddle) songs and may be compared with nos. 6 and 20.

1. See discussion of this word on p. 11.
2. These six persons are probably the "six enemies," i.e., passions, which inhabit each man: lust, anger, greed, infatuation, pride, and envy.
3. These six persons are the six Brahmin converts of Caitanya, and Gosais, among whom Rup and Sonaton receive prominent mention in these songs.

[21]

Singer: Y̆otin Dās

lolite kālo biṛāl ke puṣeche gaylā pāṛāte
biṛāl dharte gele y̆āy nā dharā   lāph dey uṭhe gāchete

ār y̆odi dharte pāri   pāy lāgābo premer doṛi
biṛāl bẹdhe niy̆e cole y̆ābo   ōi mathurār ṭhānāte

tōr biṛāler āsparda bhāri   sakāl sandhā dui bēlāy y̆āy āmār bāṛi
biṛāl bẹdhe niy̆e cālān dibo   ōi rādhārānir kāchete

śuno boli bonomālir mā   tōr biṛāler svabhāb bhālo nā
biṛāl ghar ḍhukeche bhāṛ bheṅeche doi khey̆eche   mukh muceche kẹṭhāte

O Lolita, who has raised a black cat in the cowherd's quarter?
If you go to catch the cat, it won't be caught.
  It jumps right up into a tree.

And if I am able to catch the cat,
  I shall put Love's rope about his feet.
Having bound the cat,
  I'll take him off to that jail in Mathura.

Your cat's impudence is immense;
  morning and evening, at both times he goes to my house.

Having bound the cat,
  I'll send him for trial to Radharani.

Listen, I say, O mother of Banamali,
  your cat's disposition is not good.
The cat has entered the house and broken the jug;
  he ate the yogurt and wiped his face on the quilt.

One of the more familiar sports (*līlā*) of Lord Krishna is his stealing of butter and curds from the housewives of Mathura.

[22]

Singer: Nārāyon Dās Odhikāri

mānob deho mōṭōr gāṛi cālāō sādhon rāstāte
tōr mon ḍrāibherke niȳo ṭhik kore sad gururo bākȳete

gāṛir sāmne duṭi ālō ray dibāniśi jvolche ālō nibhe nāhi ẏāy
sapto tālār mōṭōr gāṛi huṣ́ rekho mon cālāte

gāṛir madhȳe dujon koṇḍākṭār khālāsi tār ray ṣōlojon gāṛiro madhye
tārā nijo karme rato ẏōgāẏōg nāi kār sāthe

hirāmon kay gurur caroṇ sm̐ori tumi ese ebār āmār karo ḍrāibheri
āmi pārbo nāi ār tōmār gāṛi bisay rajȳe cālāte

Drive the human-body-motor-car upon the road of *sādhonā.*[1]
Be informed of who is your mind-driver
  by the word of a true guru.

Two lights are at the front of the car;
  they are lit day and night; they don't go out.
A car with seven locks;[2]
  keep alert, o mind, while driving.

Within the car are two conductors;[3]
  there are also sixteen acquitted men[4] within.
Each is absorbed in his own work
  and has no connection with anyone.

Hiramon says, "I remember the feet of the guru;
  come and drive for me, now.
"I cannot drive your car any longer
  in this material kingdom."

1. Religious discipline.
2. Perhaps yogic plexuses.
3. Perhaps a reference to the yogic nerves (*iḍā, piṅgolā*) which twine around the spine.
4. See discussion of song no. 6.

[23]

Singer: Sonāton Dās Ṭhākur

mon āmār ēkbār hori balo   din phurālo ōi ṭikiṭer ghanṭā holo
cale nāi ḍ̄kā bḍ̄kā duṭo cāka   kaylā bine acal haylo

isṭeṣoṇ māsṭār ŷārā   bose bhābce tārā kato ṭikiṭer sel holo
pŷāsenjār bābu ŷārā bolche tārā   ōi bāroṭār gāṛi elo

gọ̄sāi kubir cḍ̄der bāṇi   chālāi pūrā raylo cini
jādubindu din rajoni   balod hoŷe (bayhe?) marlo

O my mind, say Hari once; the day has run out,
  and that ticket's time has come.
The two wheels don't go round;
  they've become stationary without the coal.

Those station masters are sitting and thinking about
  how many tickets have been sold.
The passengers are saying,
  "That twelve o'clock train has come."

Gosai Kubir Cad's message:
  "The sack was full of sugar."
Jadubindu, day and night, having become an ox,
  has nearly died.

This song concerns remorse for a misspent life. Kubir Cad's message is that the body (sack) contained within it the refined substance (sugar) for which Jadubindu sought but was too unintelligent to recognize.

[24]

Singer: Ŷotin Dās

naylā bandhu re kato dine pābo tōmār dēkhā
māṭhe thako ghuriŷā bēṛāō   bandek māro hurā re
kato dine pābo re tōmār dēkhā

ō re . . . piṭhe boisā re   bājāō sārindā dōtārā re
kato dine pābō tōmār dēkhā

āmār bāṛi ŷāiŷō re bandhu   boste dibo (phira?)
ābār prem jale bhijāiŷā dibo   mōṭā dhāner ciṛā re
kato dine pābo re tōmār dēkhā

āmār bāṛi ŷāiŷō bandhu   e nā bārābar
ḍalim gāichā bāṛi āmār   pūb duŷāri ghar ō re
kato dine pābo re tōmār dēkhā

The use of the term *ghuriȳā* (for *ghure*), *gāichā* (for *gāch*), etc., reveal the East Bengal origin of this text; the tune (*bhāōȳāiȳā*) suggests northern East Bengal.

O my friend, how long before I get to see you?
Stay, roam about in the fields and shoot the rifle, bang!
  How long before I get to see you?

Come and sit down; play the sarinda and dotara.
  How long before I get to see you?

Go to my house friend! I'll sit you upon (a stool?).
And with tears of love I'll sprinkle the puffed rice.
  How long before I get to see you?

[25]

Singer: Rādhārāni Dāsi

nitāi āmār nāker bēśor   gowr galār mālā
ār cal gō pāṛār protibāsi   cal gowrāṅger hoi gō dāsi
mākhābo candan tulosi   koris nā keō abohelā

nitāike nālāte thōbo   tiloke jhalok dēkhābo
duḥkhitāpe mon bhulābo   gowr noȳe korbo khēlā
hṛiday mājhe dulche ẏēmon   ẏēmon pūrṇimār candrer ālā

Nitai[1] is my nose ornament; Gowr[2] is my necklace.
Let's go, girls of the neighborhood, let's go become Gowr's maids.
We will apply sandal and basil; don't anyone be negligent.

I will place Nitai on my forehead; I will display the splendor
  of the *tilok*.[3]
I will make my mind forget burning care; I will play
  with Gowr.
He is swaying in my heart, swaying like the light of the full moon.

1. Nityananda, Caitanya's chief companion.
2. Caitanya.
3. Mark on forehead.

[26]

Singer: Nārāyoṇ Dās Odhikāri

nitāi ẏodi e deśe elo   jīber sab jvālā dūre gelo
ēto dine jiber bhāgȳe   kṛiṣṇo prem uday holo

deśe elo re nitāi   tār nāmāboli gāy
hori nāmer mālā nitāiȳer dulteche galāy
mukhe jay rādhā śrī rādhā bole   nayon jale bhāsilo

gowr nitāi tārā duṭi bhāi emon dayāl dekhi nāi
parom dayāl nitāi āmār jāter bicār nāi
kiṭpatoṅgo sthābor jangom sabke horinām dilo
bhebe tāi kirit condro kay tumi śuno dayāmay
antim kāle diẏo āmāy caroṇe āśray
āmi sādhon bhajonhin muroti biphale janom gelo

If Nitai[1] came to this country,
all life's trouble would disappear.
The luck of so many days—
the love of Krishna has dawned.

Nitai came to this land with a *nāmāboli*[2] on his shoulders;
the necklace of Hari's names dangles round Nitai's neck.
Saying, "Praise to Radha, Sri Radha,"
his eyes were awash with tears.

Gowr,[3] Nitai are two brothers; I've not seen such kindness.
My greatly kind Nitai makes no caste distinctions.
Man and beast, to everyone alike,
he has given the Hari-name.

1. Nityanando, chief companion of Caitanya.
2. A scarf with the names of Vishnu printed on it, worn as an upper garment.
3. Caitanya.

[27]

Singer: Subol Candro Dās

nodī bharā ḍheu bōjho nā ẏe keō kēno torī nije bāō bāō re
bharosā kori e bhabo kāṇḍārī hālke chāṛiẏā tāre dāō dāō re
bāite jāno nā kēno dharo hāl tāi mon mājhi ōi holo re mātāl
bujhi e baṛo tāre ẏete habe pare abēlār bēlā pane cāō cāō re
nije bāitechilo pāglabhabā bhāṅā torīte jale ḍubā ḍubā
cubāno kheẏe dhareche pāy ō he kāṇḍāri āmāy bạcāō bạcāō re

Verb forms such as *chāṛiẏā* and *bāitechilo* (for *cheṛe* and *bāichilo*) indicate an East Bengal origin for this text.

The river is full of waves; no one understands that.
Why do you row the boat yourself?
I rely upon this universal helmsman;
Leave the rudder and give it to him.

You don't know how to row; why do you hold the rudder then?
Your mind-boatman has become intoxicated.

I guess we must cross to the other side in this great crossing;
take care for the untimely times.

Paglabhaba was himself rowing;
the broken boat was about to be submerged.
On the verge of sinking, he grasped the feet—
"O helmsman save me, save me."

This song preaches the need for reliance on the guru.

[28]

Singer: Sonāton Dās Ṭhākur

ō mon mayrā re kēno bhiẏān śikhli nā
sujon gurur saṅgo dhare kēno kājer marmo jānli nā

mon āguner śokti nāi bhālo ẏācchilo tōr bhokti bātās tāō kome gelo
niṣṭhā karāy chēḍā holo kono kājer lāglo nā

ghare thākte re cini tōr nāi re cenā cini andho hoy korle ciṭeguṛer āmdāni
ciṭeguṛer pāk lāgāle tāte hay ki re michuri dānā

boirāgẏo bhābete ẏodi bhiẏān korite guru datto tattvo bale ẏodi nāmāte
hayto nām rasete rasogollā hoto re bēcā kenā

bhebe madan nāg bhaṇe āge guru nā cine korte geli mayrār kāj bhiẏān nā jene
holo sabi naṣṭo moner kaṣṭo hārāli ṣōlo ānā

O mind-confectioner, why haven't you learned sweet-making?
Having got the company of a good guru,
why don't you know the secret?

The strength of your mind-fire is not good,
the wind of your devotion was blowing, but that, too,
has declined.
Now your piety-pot has gotten perforated;
no work has been accomplished.

Though there is sugar in the house,
you don't know what sugar is.
Being blind, you had cheap molasses brought—
when the molasses condenses, will sugar candy be made from it?

If you had placed your confectioning on the feeling of indifference,
if you had taken it down with the strength of the guru's
given message,
Perhaps there would have been trade in name-syrup rasagollas.

Keeping this in mind, Madan Nag says,
"Before knowing the guru, why have you gone to do the
confectioner's work?

"All that happened was the ruin of everything and grief of mind—you lost one hundred per cent."

In this song, the sexual *sādhonā* of the Bauls is compared to the process of refining syrup into candy. The necessity for instruction from the guru is pointed up by the fact that the confectioner in the song has ruined everything through ignorance of his craft. He is so unaware that he fails to see the things he seeks (metaphorically compared to sugar) within the house of his own body.

[29]

Singer: Gōṣṭho Gōpāl Dās

prem karā soi āmār holo nā
ýato prem pelo ōi phacke chōṛā dhrubo prohlād duijonā

ēk premete nimāi sanýāsi ār ēk premete ratnākor holo bālmiki ṛiṣi
dēkho ār ēk preme mirā dāsi saṅsāre mon majlo nā

ýōgāi mādhāi korechilo bhul kolsir khānā māthāv mere pelo premer kūl
adhom jīboner ki bhāṅbe nā bhul āmār jībone ghaṭlo nā

se ýe emni ēk chele bhōge bhōge janmo bole tāre bhogirath bale
tāre gaṅgāmā ýe nilo kole ei to khāti premer niśānā

To love, my friend, has not been my lot.
So much love as those two naughty boys had, both Dhruva and Prahlad.[1]

For one love, Nimai[2] became a sanyasi;
for another love Ratnakar became Valmiki Rishi.[3]
Look, for yet another love, Mira[4] could not
keep her mind on worldly matters.

Jogai and Madhai[5] made a mistake—having thrown
a water jug at the head of Caitanya they reached the shore of love.
Will not the errors of a mean life be broken?
It hasn't happened in my life!

There was just such a boy
. . . ; they called him Bhagirath.[6]
Mother Ganges took him upon her lap;
this is the sign of real love.

1. Two youths whose legendary devotion to Vishno is recounted in Puranas.
2. Caitanya.
3. Author of *Ramayana.*
4. Rajput princess and sanyasini famous for her songs of devotion to Krishna.
5. Two early adversaries of Caitanya who later converted.
6. He who brought the Ganges to earth.

[30]

Singer: Gaṅgādhar Dās

prem kārigāre rosik sujon garlo premer kārkhāna
bāper ẏakhon hay nāi janom nāti elo tinjonā

svāmi chilo gōlōkete mā dekhilo svaponete
kēmon kore hay gō chele ei tō ājob kārkhānā

gọsāi pūrṇānando bhaṇe tāre dekhte pābi dibẏo jñāne
tār nāi re janom nāi re maraṇ khēpā holo ājanmo kānā

Love-artisan, *rosik*[1] gentlemen,
has constructed a prodigy of love.
When the father had not yet been born,
three grandsons appeared.

The husband was in heaven;
mother saw him in a dream.
How did the child come about?
This is really a surprising event!

Gosai Purnanando says,
"You will get to see him through divine knowledge.
"He has neither birth nor death;
this madcap has been blind since birth!"

The peculiar births described in this song are a common feature of *hẹẏāli* (riddle) songs and may be compared with nos. 6 and 20.

1. See discussion of this word on p. 11.

[31]

Singer: Subol Candro Dās

prem sāgore rosikjonā raser tori bāy

se nā nodī ujān bāke madono ḍākāite thāke thāke sarbodāy
cālāō torī sābdhāne sumukhe ujān nāhi ṭāne
se nodīte tori mārā ẏāy se nodīte āmār (malkuṭār?) dhon luṭe niẏe ẏāy

se nā nodīr madhẏosthale cowmbok lōhāi sātār khēle mājhi theko se jāygāy
cālāō torī sābdhāne sumukhe ujān nāhi ṭāne
se nodīte tori mārā ẏāy se nodīte āmār (malkuṭār?) dhon luṭe niẏe ẏāy

chayjonāte kare āji guruke bānāiẏe mājhi bosāiẏe rekho he mācāy
chayjonā chay gọrāy bose premānande rase bhāse tārā anāyāse pāṛe diẏe ẏāy
arosike sukhnāy nāō ḍubāy sab torī tō bāite jāne nā

On the lake of love, the *rosik*s row the boat of *rasa*.[1]

At a bend in the river at high tide, Madan,[2]
is always committing robbery.
Carefully guide the boat; the flow tide does not pull ahead;
on that river boats are attacked.
On that river the wealth of my goods(?) is looted.

In the midst of that river, magnets are swimming.
O boatman, stay in that place.
Carefully guide the boat; the flow tide does not pull ahead;
on that river boats are attacked.
On that river the wealth of my goods is looted.

Today, all six together make the guru the boatman,
and place him on the platform.
The six, sitting in six corners, float on the *rasa* of the
bliss of love.
They easily get to shore.
The non-*rosik* runs the boat aground on a sandbar;
not everyone knows how to row a boat.

The first stanza is incomplete because the recording was begun late. The repetition in the second and third stanzas is due to the singer's having had trouble remembering the text.

1. See discussion of this word on p. 11.
2. Eros.

[32]

Singer: Lakṣm̃aṇ Dās (of Burdwan)

rādhār prem taraṅgo beṛi brajo bheṣeche
tāi nikuñjete premer banȳā   giri gōbordhone ḍheu legeche

koṭi candro ẏini ābhā   āj brajodhām koreche sabhā
bālśūrẏo kṣoṇoprobhā   rādhār rūper bālāi tāi
sei bṛindāboner toru latā   rādhār rūper kiroṇ choṛāȳe gēche

kālindi ẏamunāy miśe   sarosvotī gēche bheṣe
kathā hote gaṅgāi ese   taraṅgo uṭheche
ābār mathurār ōi . . . jānhobīte miślo giȳe
snān ghāṭer ōi (tōrāy?) theke   rādhār rūper bāri pān koreche

lolitā biśākhā sokhi   indulekha śȳā́mā sokhi

. . . .

tāi rāi rūpete jagote ālō   tāi bhuji śȳā́m gowr holo
kṛiṣṇo dās tār bhāb nā jene   diner odin . . . dāsi

The wave of Radha's love has swelled and flooded Braja.[1]
That is why the flood of love has struck a wave against
Mt. Gobordhon[2] in the copse.

She who has the splendor of so many moons
has today beautified Brajadham!
The young sun is a fleeting light, such is the young girl with
Radha's form!
She is Brindabon's[1] lovely creeper;[3]
the beams of Radha's beauty have spread everywhere.

The Kalindi,[4] having joined the Yamuna,[4] the Sarasvati[5]
has overflowed.
The Ganges having come from elsewhere, a wave has arisen.
Mathura's[1] . . . having joined the Jahnavi,[6]
has drunk the water of Radha's beauty from the (shore?) of
that bathing ghat.

The companions[7] Lalita, Bisakha, the dark companion Indulekha
. . . .
That is why there is light in the world in the form of Radha;
that is why, I suppose, that Syam[8] became Gowr.[9]
Krishna Das, not knowing the significance of this (remains?)
the humblest servant of the lowly.

1. Places associated with events in Krishna's life.
2. A mountain Krishna lifted on the tip of a finger to shelter the inhabitants of Mathura against a flood of rain sent by Indra.
3. A conventional metaphor for a beautiful woman.
4. The Kalindi and Yamuna are the same river.
5. A mythological underground river which joins the Yamuna and Ganges at Allahabad.
6. A name for the Ganges.
7. Of Radha.
8. The Dark One; i.e., Krishna.
9. The Fair One; i.e., Caitanya.

[33]

Singer: Lakṣm̃aṇ Dās (of Mallarpur)

sukher dhān bhānā ēmon mon bēbośā cheṛo nā
karo kṛiṣṇo premer bhānā kuṭā kono kaṣṭo rabe nā

onurāger ḍhẹki basāle bhajon sādhon duiṭi pōȳā dui dhāre dile
niṣṭhā āslāi jere calbe ḍhẹki calbe nā

rāg boidhik duijon bhānūnī tāder nām kṛiṣṇo mōhinī
ēkjon tārā gōper meȳe ēkjon telenī
tārā dhān bhāneō bhālo jāneō bhālo gāȳe tāder upāsonār gahonā

gharer bṛiddhā ýe ginni se hay seke deōýānī
siddho roti siddho moti se hay kūlo cālunī
ghure sakām more jhere ginni mā tuṣ guṛo cele nile nā

ḍhẹkir maslā ghāṭe bāsonā tōr ýābe chuṭe pār dite dite
cāl uṭhbe cheṭe mayla keṭe ṭhik ýēno michuri dānā

ei ýe gurur mahājoner dhān tāthe habe re sābdhān
lābhe lōbhe kāl kāṭābi puji bhānete habe nā

gọsāi ananto dhān bhānte pārli nā tōder āj ghoṭbe ýantronā
pāp ḍhẹkite māthā laṛāi ḍhẹki tōr gaṛe paṛe nā

This text is transcribed from the written text of Lakṣm̃aṇ Dās rather than from his singing. As a translation would be riddled with gaps, a précis of the poem is given here.

In this song Ananto (Lakṣm̃aṇ's paternal grandfather's name) compares the religious discipline of the Bauls, which is concerned with separating the eternal substance in men from the chaff of its material manifestation, with the process of husking rice. As usual, the author laments his own inexpertness, saying that the pestle of his husker (*ḍhẹki*) does not fall squarely into the pit where the paddy is thrown. Unlike the grain of the expert housewife, his does not come out clean and looking like bits of rock candy.

[34]

Singer: Ýotin Dās

ýasode ō tōr kṛiṣṇo dhon de gōṣṭhe loiȳā ýāi
sab rākhāle sājiȳāche bhāi boliȳāche brajer kānāi balāi

paṛāiȳe de pito dharā bādhiȳā de mōhancuṛā ār tō deri nāi
o dik hoiȳāche bēlā mā boli de mā bide loȳe ýāi

gagone uday bhālo eso re bhāi prāner kānhu calo goṣṭhe ýāi
rākhāl gō dāṛāiye āche bhāi boli ār tō deri nāi

Yasoda,[1] give me your dear Krishna; let us go to the pasture.
All the cowherds have dressed up, brother,
  said Balaram[2] to Braja's Krishna.

Put the yellow dhoti on him;
  tie up the bun on his head—it's getting late.
Over there the dawn is breaking;
  give him to me, I say; let us depart.

Listen dear Nandorani,[3] dress up your sapphire;[4]
  it's getting late.
The cows are mooing;
  give him to me, I say; let us depart.

The sun is well risen in the sky; come brother, my soul's Kanhu,[5]
let's go to the pasture.
The cowherds are waiting, brother;
it's getting late.

1. Krishna's foster mother.
2. Elder brother to Krishna.
3. Krishna's foster mother—i.e., wife of Nanda.
4. Krishna—i.e., the blue jewel.
5. Krishna.

APPENDIX B

jīber bujhi sudin holo

Singer: Śaśaṅko Dās Mohant
Original Tonic: f#

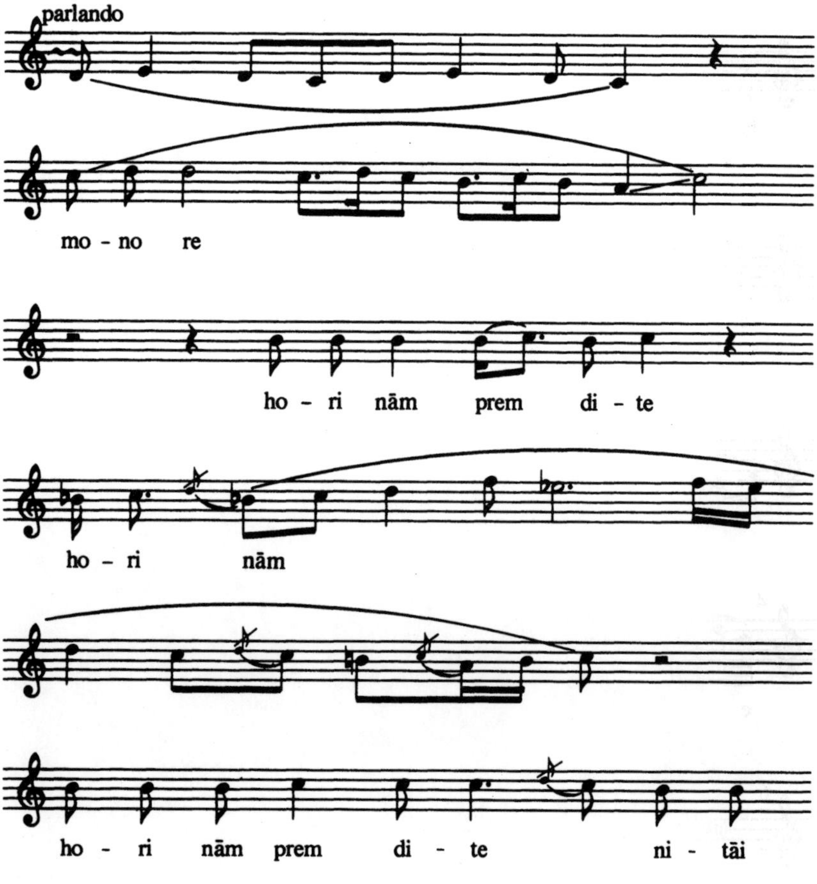

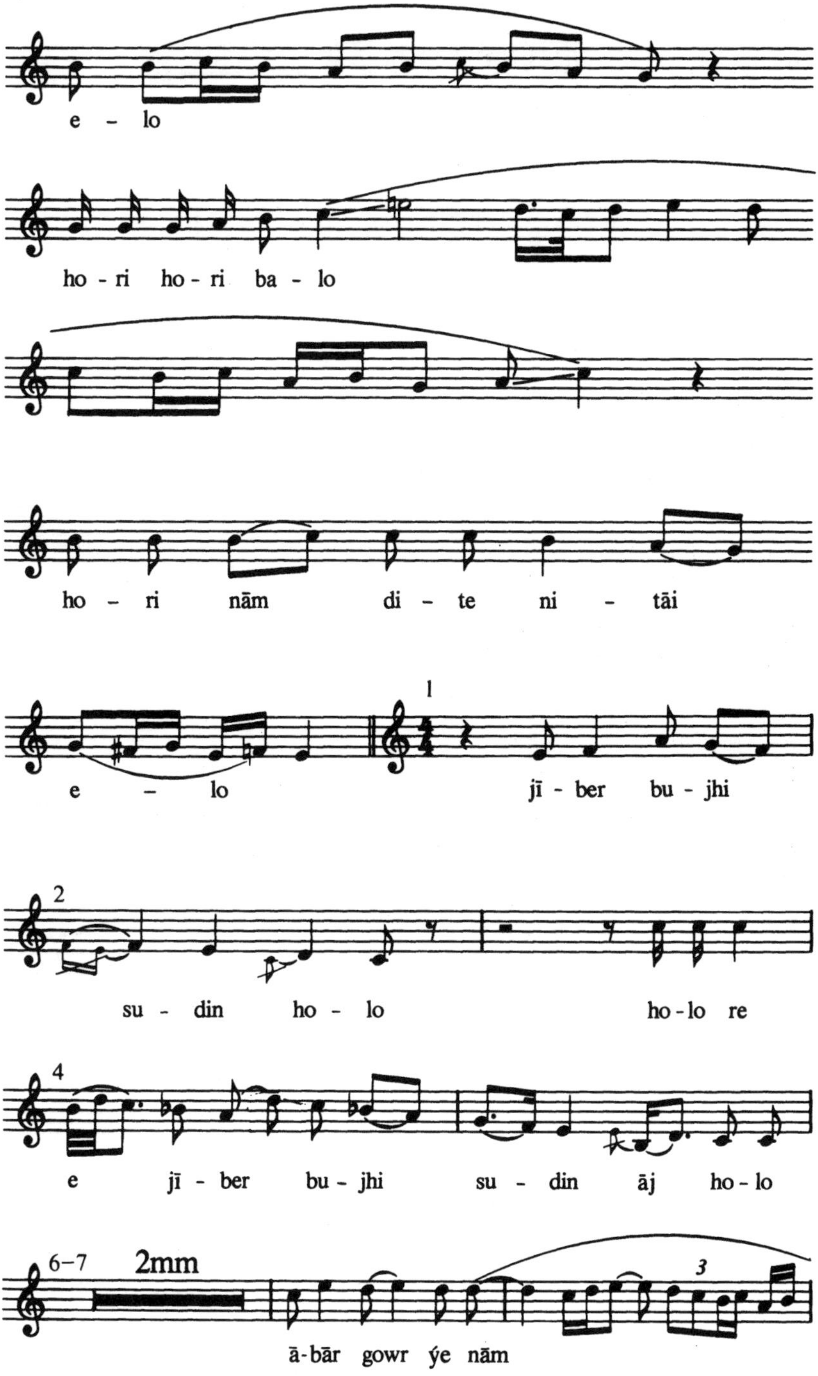
e - lo
ho - ri ho - ri ba - lo
ho - ri nām di - te ni - tāi
e - lo
1
jī - ber bu - jhi
2
su - din ho - lo ho - lo re
4
e jī - ber bu - jhi su - din āj ho - lo
6–7
2mm
3
ā - bār gowr ýe nām

10
e - ne - chi - lo
bo - li gowr ýe nām
3
12
e - ne - chi - lo
śu - ne jī - be phi -
14
2mm
- re ge - lo ā - mār gowr
18
gowr bol ho - ri bol ho - ri bol
20
ho - ri bol bo - le
śu - ne jī - be phi -
22
- re ge - lo
jī - ber bu - jhi
24
su - din āi - lo
ho - lo re
26
2mm
jī - ber bu-jhi su - din āi - lo

30
pro-bhu bol - len
32
tri-san - dhyā śnān
34
kor-be ēk san - dhyā bhō - jon
37
sāl - yo an - no ne - be sa - be
39
tel mat-syo bā - roṇ sāl - yo an - no
41
ne-be sa-be tel mat-syo bā - roṇ kor -
44
- be ēk - ā - do - śī kor -
47
-be ēk - ā - do - śī thā - k - be u - po - bā - śī ō bhāi

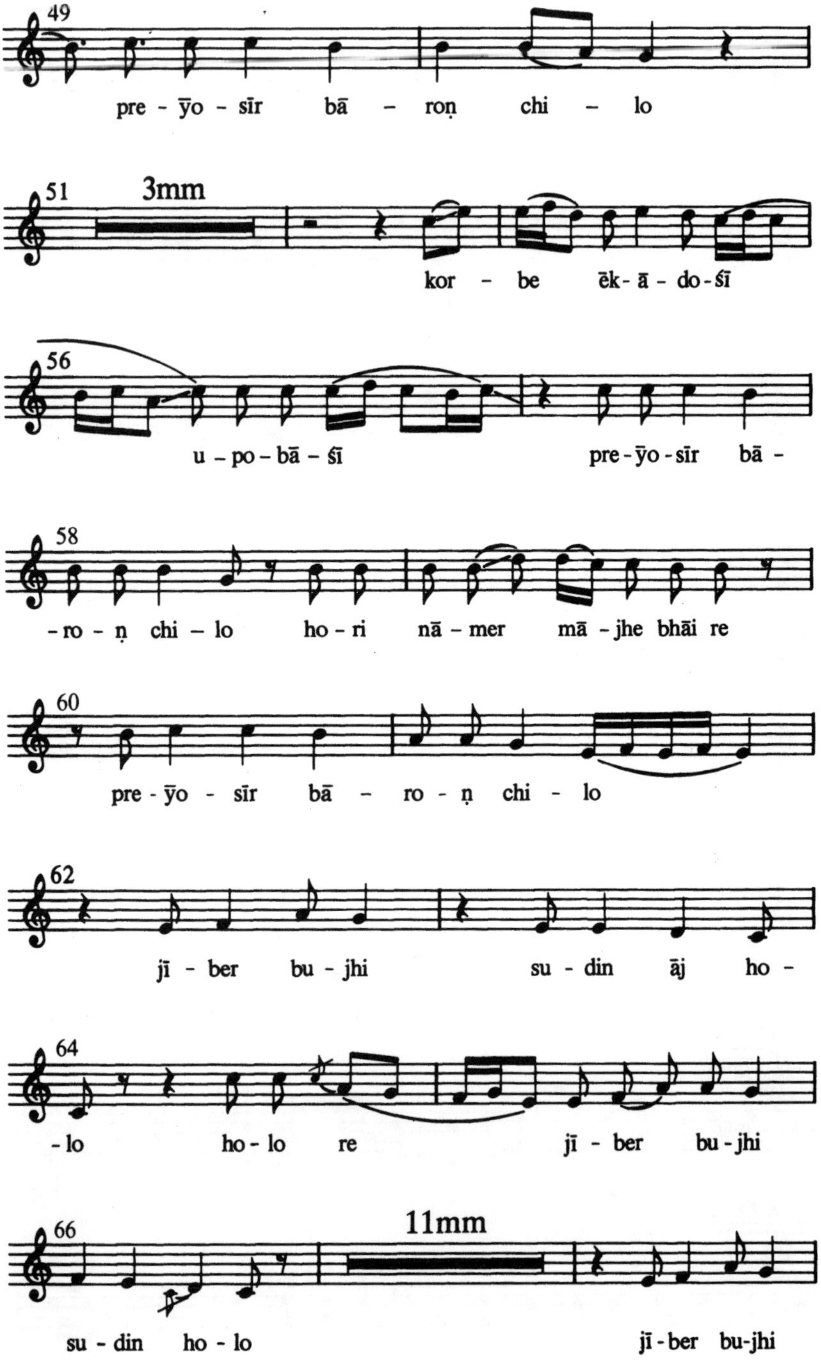
49
pre - ȳo - sīr bā - roṇ chi - lo
51
3mm
kor - be ēk- ā - do- śī
56
u - po - bā - śī pre - ȳo - sīr bā -
58
- ro - ṇ chi - lo ho - ri nā - mer mā - jhe bhāi re
60
pre - ȳo - sīr bā - ro - ṇ chi - lo
62
jī - ber bu - jhi su - din āj ho -
64
- lo ho - lo re jī - ber bu - jhi
66
11mm
su - din ho - lo jī - ber bu-jhi

79
su - din āj ho - lo
81
ār - ō bol - len pro - bhu - i ā - mār
83
ei ka - thā
85
śu - ne jīb phi - re ge - lo e - len
87
a - bo - dhow - to rāi gō e -
89
3
a - bo - dhow - to rāi pro-bhui ā -
91
- mār ba - ṛo da - yā - may
93
pro-bhu-i ā - mār ba - ṛo da - yā -

95
- may
ke ni - be ke
97
ni - be bo - le
ḍāk-chen ō re
3 3
99
āi bol-len
bol-len āi āi ho - ri
101
nām ni - se - ri ā - mi ko - re
lā - gi
103
nā - me bo - li ēk - bār muk - he
105
ho - ri bo - le ko - re lā - gi nā - me bo - li
108
.... ho - ri........ ho - ri .... ā - mi
110
ko - re lā - gi nā - mer

112
ēk – bār mu – khe ho – ri
114
e - len a - bo - dhow – to rāi
116
pro - bhui ā - mār
119
ba – ṛo day – ā – may
121
ke ni - be ke ni - be bo – le
123
ḍāk – chen ō re āi ōi ā – mār
125
ni – tāi pūr – ṇo brah - m̃o - jñā́ – ni
127
ā - mār ni – tāi pūr – ṇo brah - m̃o - jñā́ – ni

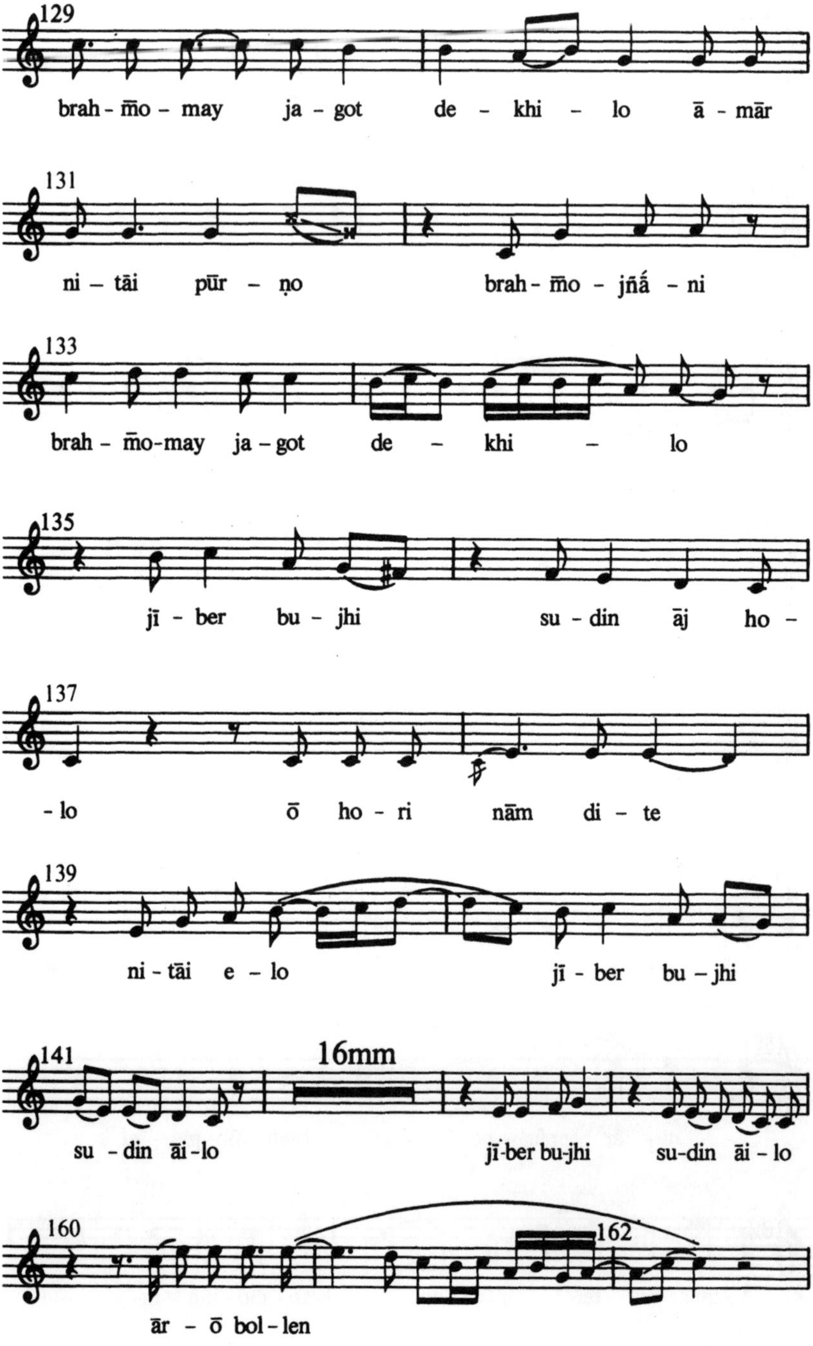
129
brah - m̄o - may ja - got de - khi - lo ā - mār
131
ni – tāi pūr – ṇo brah - m̄o - jñā́ - ni
133
brah - m̄o-may ja – got de - khi – lo
135
jī - ber bu - jhi su - din āj ho –
137
- lo ō ho - ri nām di – te
139
ni - tāi e – lo jī - ber bu – jhi
141
16mm
su - din āi -lo jī-ber bu-jhi su-din āi – lo
160
162
ār – ō bol – len

163
bol- len mā - gur mā-cher jhōl bol – len
165
mā-gur mā-cher jhōl mā – gur mā –
168
- cher mā-gur mā - cher
170
jhōl ār bhōr ýu-bo- tir kōl
173
jī – ber ba – le e – bār ma – rā
175
3mm
bol - bo ho-ri ....jī -ber ba-le
180
e – bār ma - rā bol - bo ho – ri
182
2mm
bol gō - sāi

186
gowr ba – len e ka-thā ke
188
ō re gō – sāi ā – mār gowr ba – len
190
e ka-thā e ýe gō – le – mā – le
192
3
ro – hi – lo an – dho jīb – ṭā
194
bujh – be kē – no – i e – te (ṅ) - gō – le – mā – le
196
ro – hi – lo jī – ber bu – jhi
198
su – din āj ho – lo ho-ri nām di-te ni-
201
- tāi e – lo tāi jī – ber bu – jhi

203
su – din ā - mār ni - tāi ẏe nām
205
e – ne - chi - lo śu – ne jī - be phi - re
207
ge – lo ā - mār ni - tāi e - ne - chi - lo
210
śu - ne jī - be phi – re ge – ba – lo
212
e nām
214
śu - ne jī - be phi – re ge – lo
216
jī – ber bu - jhi su – din āj ho –
218
lo ō ho - ri di - te ni – tāi e - lo

221
jī - ber bu-jhi su - din ho–lo

Notes

1. Statistics from *The Far East and Australasia* (London: Europa Publications, 1982–83), pp. 249, 455.

2. For an account of the political attitudes of this new class see J. H. Broomfield, *Elite Conflict in a Plural Society: Twentieth-Century Bengal* (Berkeley: Univ. of California Press, 1968).

3. Edward C. Dimock and Ronald Inden, "Problems in Transliteration in Bengali Studies," in *Bengal: East and West,* ed. Alexander Lipski, Michigan State University Asian Studies Center Occasional Papers, South Asian Studies, no. 13 (East Lansing, 1970), pp. 11–17.

4. The Brahman boy referred to in the second song is Candidas, a poet of uncertain date, about fifteenth to sixteenth century.

5. See Anwarul Karim, *The Bauls of Bangladesh* (Kushtia: Bangladesh Lalan Academy, 1980).

6. Spellings vary; transcribed here as heard. In the tenth edition of the *calantikā* of Rāj-śekhor Bosu (Calcutta, 1373 [1966–67]), the spelling is *gudhoṛi.*

7. Ritual necrophagy is attributed to the Bauls by some writers, for example Spratt ("baul," passim), but there appears to be no factual evidence to support such a charge.

8. The treatise dates from about the end of the eighth century (Snellgrove 1959, 14).

9. Perhaps Tagore may have adapted this character from that of the *bibek* in *ẏātrā,* popular theatricals described by S. Ray (1973, 62) as: "(conscience symbolised) dressed in *Sannyasin*-way [like a holy-man], suitably singing significant songs through more or less trained and expert voice."

10. Tagore states this explicitly (1922, 75): "the best part of a song is missed when the tune is absent; for thereby its movement and its colour are lost, and it becomes like a butterfly whose wings have been plucked."

11. "Tantrik" refers to the many sects that rely on empirical means of realization rather than on discursive reasoning or total asceticism. Most employ meditation or ritual based on a sexual principle.

12. A friend once reported hearing them sing an advertisement for Car Minar cigarettes at a tea stall!

13. R. Montgomery Martin reported a similar name as referring to a group of Muslims in Assam (1838, 517): "In Assam the followers of Muhammed have departed so far from all appearance of the faith, that they are considered, by even those of this district, as totally unworthy of the name of Moslem, and at Goyalpara, where some of them have settled, are called Baudiyas."

14. Several photos of Baul dance may be seen in M. Bardhon's book on Bengali folk dance (1969).

15. John M. Ward directed my attention to the use of this phrase by David Johnson, *Music and Society in Lowland Scotland in the Eighteenth Century* (London, 1972); see chapter 1, "Two Species of Music: Folk and Classical," and "Professionalism in Folk Music," pp. 3–19, 125–29.

16. *Khēpā* is a kind of title conferred on Bauls of special merit. Literally it means "mad," as *bāul* itself once did. *Khēpā* is often used colloquially as an affectionate address. Another favorite epithet used by Bauls to indicate exceptional spiritual quality is *pāgol,* also meaning "mad." For a learned and fascinating account of the etymology and relatives of this latter word see R. Gordon Wasson (n.d.).

17. In the passages quoted later from this article, the English is unidiomatic; rather than clutter the quotes with *sic* and offer reconstructions in more stylistic English, I have left the quotes as they are, because even in their peculiar English their significance is plain enough.

18. Recorded on *Indian Street Music: The Bauls of Bengal,* Nonesuch H-72035.

19. Carol Salomon, who did work among the Bauls in the mid-seventies, has informed me that Cakrodhar now dresses like a Baul and sings also.

20. Recorded by Pūrṇo Dās on *The Bengal Minstrel: Music of the Bauls,* Nonesuch H-72068. Another version of the song was used for the film *Natun Fasal* and was sung by the playback singer Pratima Banerjee (recorded on *Hits from Bengali Films,* Odeon MOCE 1074); in this performance, the *bhoṇitā* ascription has been changed. The tune is credited to Nirmalendu Chowdhury but appears to be the same as the tune notated by Surendro Cakroborttī (1368 [1962], 1:65).

21. The usual method described in yogic texts is to draw up the secretions through the urethra; the technique is practiced first with water, then milk, and finally mercury (U. Bhaṭṭācārŷo 1364 [1957–58], 411–12).

22. *Ṭhākur,* of which Rabindranath used the English version Tagore, is, besides being the family name of a group of polluted Brahmans, a title of respect for a guru. What significance Sonāton's use of the title has, I do not know.

23. Though even here, it should be pointed out, there is a hint of Baul philosophy in the *bhoṇitā* (signature verse).

24. As the husband is the lord (*svāmī*) of the wife, the wife normally eats her husband's leftovers in the same spirit as the devotee of a deity eats the leftovers of food offerings distributed by the priests. Leftovers are considered to have become the bodily substance of the person who touched them. As in many circumstances—even indirect contact with another's body may cause pollution—leftover food (*eṭō*) is generally considered polluting. But when accepted from an intimate superior, like a husband, a guru, or a deity, leftover food (*prosād*) sacramentally incorporates the receiver with the giver.

25. It is customary among Vaisnavas to replace their surnames with Dās (servant) to indicate their devotion to the deity as well as to obscure caste. Some Bauls keep their surnames as Biśvonāth, for example, has done.

26. See U. Bhaṭṭācārŷo (1364 [1957–58], 398): "The copulation of three successive days the Bauls call *raser bhiŷān* (confecting the syrup). Just as the confectioner puts the syrup into a pot and gradually by the heat of the fire and while skillfully stirring he makes the syrup thicken and produces sugar candy, just as churning milk creates butter, in just such a manner is a thick substance produced from a watery one. He who knows the proper syrup-condensation is mentioned in many songs as *rosik mayrā* (*rosik* confectioner)"; see the discussion of the word *ras* (as in *rosik*) on p. 11.

27. For an account of an extended chante fable by Sonāton and of the interpretation he provides for it based on sexual yoga, see Carol Salomon (1979).

28. Dating the songs is an arduous task based on fixing approximate dates for their composers, the so-called Siddhas. This is a matter of considerable controversy, and I have settled for a contraction of the dates arrived at by the Bengali linguist, S. K. Chatterji (1970, 1:123): "The period 950-1200 A.D. would seem to be a reasonable date to give to these poems." More detailed information about the Siddhas may be found in R. C. Majumdar (1963). The manuscript containing the poems was discovered by M. M. Haraprasad Sastri in the Nepal Court Library at the beginning of the twentieth century, and he thought it dated from the twelfth century, a date long thought to be too early. Using necessarily limited palaeographic resources, Tārāpado Mukhōpādhyāy, on the basis of a comparison of orthographic styles, has concurred with the original estimate of Haraprasad (1965, 96): "my estimate is that the date of writing down the manuscript of the *caryās* [the poems in question] is the end of the twelfth century. One must remember, however, that this estimate is based on the cursory examination of a few manuscripts."

29. For a discussion of the relations among Sauraseni, Avahattha, and Bengali in the *caryās*, see S. K. Chatterji (1970, 1:90–116).

30. For an elaborate account of the followers of Goraksanath, see G. W. Briggs (1938). A bibliography of the many editions of the Bengali song texts in English or Bengali, as well as some other languages of Hindustan, may be found in S. Das Gupta (1969, 367–82).

31. A distinction in name is sometimes made on the basis of whether the resonator is of gourd or wood. Both Monsur Uddīn (1942) and S. K. Bose (1967) connect the name *lāuyā* (*lāu*, gourd) with the gourd resonator and state that it is more common in East than in West Bengal.

32. If the Baul uses *mehdi*, he is apt also to outline his eyes with *kājol* (mascara) to add to the feminine look. By adopting these cosmetics, the Baul is attempting to express in a symbolic way the Vaisnava belief that all mankind is female in its relation to Krishna, who is considered the only male. The symbolism also implies that the Baul is striving to realize the feminineness within himself and to pass beyond the stage of sexual *sādhonā* in which the union of the sexes is only temporary.

33. On p. 227 the captions for figs. 61 and 62 should be reversed; photos of these instruments may be seen in Sachs (1923, 120, abb. 82 [*sārindā*], 121, abb. 83 [*sāraṅgi*]).

34. Bhakto Dās Baul in *Laxman Das Baul's Movie*, produced by Sally Grossman for Warner Brothers and Bearsville Records. (See www.baularchive.com)

35. Good photographs of these, with the names *kartāl* and *mañjirā*, may be seen in Nikhil Ghosh (1968, 33).

36. *Bāyā*, were once also made of wood and probably had a conical shape (see Sachs 1923, 69). The information he gives is confused. Abb. 48 on p. 70 shows a *dāhinā* which is labelled *bāyā*; abb. 47 on the same page illustrates a drum which appears to be something like a *khurdak* or *dukkar* used to accompany *sānāi*—but it is labelled "tabla, Bengali kettledrum."

37. Hear, for example, the cuts on *Folk Music of Uttar Pradesh*, rec. Laxmi Tewari, Lyrichord LLST 7271, side 2, band 3, "dhapali solo," and on *North Indian Folk Music*, Musical Atlas, UNESCO, rec. M. Junius, EMI Italiana (Odeon) 3 CO64-17859, side 2, band 4, "khanjri solo."

38. Hear, for example, the playing of V. Nagarajan on *Kaccheri*, Nonesuch H-72040 and *Ramnad Krishnan: Vidwan*, Nonesuch HB-72023.

39. This information on the role of the *ḍhāk* in *pujās* I obtained in personal communication with Dr. Eva Friedlander.

40. In this study, "tonic" refers to the first of seven degrees of the scale, and it is always transcribed as c′. The tonic is the degree which is almost always the final, has the greatest stability, and is generally reinforced with a drone. A "tonality" is a system of pitches, heard as particular degrees of a scale, which relate to the tonic as the first and chief pitch.

41. "Roughly equidistant" does not imply that Bauls strive to sing according to a theoretically realized system of intonation but that the twelve pitch positions have a certain latitude. With the help of electronic analysis it might be possible to determine the average positions for pitches in Baul performance, but such information would be useless as Bauls do not sing average pitches. As N. Jairazbhoy and A. W. Stone have shown (1963, 119–32), even though Hindustani theorists (and performers) often describe the difference between one *rāg* and another as being based upon minute intonational distinctions, the intonation of performed pitches depends on their contexts and the habits of the performers, not on theory. Although theory lists twenty-two positions for the degrees of the scale, there are only twelve in practice. As there is no theory for the tuning system of Baul-*gān*, the question of a discrepancy between theory and practice need not arise.

42. In this chapter, terms which may modify names of intervals as well as names of pitches and degrees are always used only to modify pitches and degrees.

43. A *tihāi*, in Hindustani music, is a rhythmic figure that is played three times and that concludes either on *sam* (the first beat of the measure) or on the beat before the *mukhṛā* (that portion of the *gat*, a refrain-like melody, that leads to and concludes on *sam*). By the soloist, the *tihāi* is used to mark the end of a passage of melodic improvisation and to signal a return to the relatively fixed melody, the *gat*, during which the accompanist performs rhythmic improvisation. The accompanist marks the end of his improvisation by playing a *tihāi* that also signals a return to a relatively fixed rhythmic pattern, the *ṭhekā*, a mnemonic peculiar to the *tāl* or meter being performed and during which the soloist will improvise.

44. The performances of Sonāton Dās Ṭhākur, who uses some *rāg*-like material in his songs, are an exception to this rule and do occasionally include augmented seconds. Judging from the reaction of other Bauls to a performance of such a song, I doubt that the innovation will find much favor among them (see pp. 58–59). While this book was in press, I attended the 1985 Smithsonian Folklife Festival in Washington, D.C., where Śyām Sundor Dās Baul sang the *pūrbī*-like tune described on p. 58. He also plays flute, but only to accompany others, and was accompanied by *ḍhōl*, a drum similar in sound and usage to the *ḍhāk* (see p. 114). This latter circumstance was no doubt due to the exceptional context.

45. This *behāg* is the old style with *śuddh madhyam* (natural fourth degree) only, and not the contemporary version which has both *śuddh* and *tībro* (sharped) *madhyam*.

46. *Chāyā* is a technical term of Hindustani theory and refers to a melodic turn which strongly characterizes a particular *rāg* and which, therefore, casts a "shadow" of that *rāg* upon any other *rāg* that incorporates it.

47. The unusual sequence, typified in a song like *āre ō jīban*, is one in which A does not achieve a conclusive cadence and must always be followed by B; as a result, the full refrain must recur after every stanza (CB, AB, . . .), and no musical rounding of the refrain is possible (AB [A̸]), although there is usually some textual recurrence. Instead, the overall structure is created by simple alternation of the refrain with the stanzas (AB, CB, . . . AB). The song *guru bhajo re*, the only one of its type I recorded, has this pattern of refrain / stanza alternation but departs still more radically from the usual pattern by having no music common to both refrain and stanzas; the resulting musical form is AB, CD, . . . AB.

48. The term "cultural performance" is used here in the sense that Milton Singer gives it in his *When a Great Tradition Modernizes* (New York: Praeger, 1972), pp. 70–75.

References

EUROPEAN LANGUAGES

Avalon, Arthur (Sir John Woodroffe)

1953 *The Great Liberation* (*Mahānirvāna Tantra*). 3d ed. Madras: Ganesh.

Aziz, Ahmad

1964 *Studies in Islamic Culture in the Indian Environment.* Oxford: Clarendon Press.

Bagchi, Prabodh Chandra

1930 "The Sandhābhāsā and Sandhāvacana." *Indian Historical Quarterly* 6(2): 389–96.

1933a "A Note on the Word Parāvṛtti." *Calcutta Oriental Journal* 1(1): 34–39.

1933b "Some Technical Terms of the Tantras." *Calcutta Oriental Journal* 1(2): 75–88.

1933c "Some Aspects of Buddhist Mysticism in the Caryapadas." *Calcutta Oriental Journal* 1(5): 201–14.

1938 *Materials for a Critical Edition of the Old Bengali Caryapadas.* Reprint of Calcutta University *Journal of the Department of Letters* 30. Calcutta.

1939 *Studies In The Tantras.* Part 1. Calcutta: University of Calcutta.

1950 *India and China: A Thousand Years of Sino-Indian Cultural Relations.* 2d ed. Bombay: Hind Kitabs.

1956a "The Cult of the Buddhist Siddhacaryas." In *Cultural Heritage of India*, vol. 4, edited by Haridas Bhattacarya, 273–79. Calcutta: Ramakrishna Mission Institute of Culture.

1956b "Evolution of the Tantras." In *Cultural Heritage of India*, vol. 4, edited by Haridas Bhattacarya, 211–26. Calcutta: Ramakrishna Mission Institute of Culture.

Bake, Arnold

1931 "Rabindranath Tagore's Music." In *The Golden Book of Tagore*, edited by Ramananda Chatterjee. Calcutta: Golden Book Committee.

1934a "Different Aspects of Indian Music." *Indian Arts and Letters*, n.s., 8:60–74.

1934b "Indian Music and Rabindranath Tagore." *Indian Arts and Letters* 5:81–102.

1948 "Çri Caitanya Mahaprabhu." *Medelingen der koninklijke Nederlandsche Akademie van Wettenschappen*, Abd. Letterkunde N. R. 11:279–305.

1953 "The Impact of Western Music on the Indian Musical System." *Journal of the International Folk Music Council* 5:57–60.

1961 "Abbasuddin Ahmed." *Journal of the International Folk Music Council* 13:93.

Banerjee, B. N.

1894 *Siva-Samhita.* Calcutta.

Basham, A. L.

1966 *Aspects of Ancient Indian Culture.* Bombay: Asia Publishing House.

Bharati, Agehananda

1965 *The Tantric Tradition.* London: Rider.

Bhattacarya, Deben

1967 *Love Songs of Chandidas.* London: Allen and Unwin.

1969 *The Mirror of the Sky.* London: Allen and Unwin.

Bhattacarya, Jogendra Nath

1968 *Hindu Castes and Sects.* Reprint of 1896 edition. Calcutta: Firma K. L. Mukhopadhyay.

Bhattacarya, Sudhibhusan

1968 *Ethno-musicology and India.* Reprints from *Folklore,* Jan.-June 1968. Indian Publications Folklore Series No. 14. Calcutta: Indian Publications.

Bhattacaryya, Benoytosh

1956 "Tāntrika Culture among the Buddhists." In *Cultural Heritage of India*, vol. 4, edited by Haridas Bhattacarya, 260–72. Calcutta: Ramakrishna Mission Institute of Culture.

1964 *An Introduction to Buddhist Esoterism.* Chowkhamba Sanskrit Series 46. Varanasi.

1971 *Gem Therapy.* 2d ed. Calcutta: Firma K. L. Mukhopadhyay.

Biswas, Hemango

1967 "A Golden Heritage." In *Folkmusic and Folklore: An Anthology*, vol. 1, edited by Hemango Biswas et al., 164–76. Calcutta: Folkmusic and Folklore Research Institute.

Bose, Manindra Mohan

1927 *An Introduction to the Study of the Post Caitanya Sahajiya Cult.* Reprinted from Calcutta University *Journal of the Department of Letters* 16. Calcutta.

Bose, Narendra Kumar

1960 *Melodic Types of Hindustan.* Bombay: Jaico Publishers.

Bose, Sanat Kumar

1967 "Baul Songs of Bengal." In *Folkmusic and Folklore: An Anthology*, vol.

1, edited by Hemango Biswas et al., 45–56. Calcutta: Folkmusic and Folklore Research Institute.

Briggs, George Weston
1938 *Gorakhnāth and the Kānphata Yogīs.* Mysore: Wesley.

Capwell, Charles
1974 "The Esoteric Belief of the Bauls of Bengal." *Journal of Asian Studies* 32 (2): 255–64.
in press "The Changing Role of the Bauls in Modern Bengal." In *Anthropology and Music: Essays in Honor of David P. McAllester.* Detroit Monographs in Musicology 9. Detroit: Detroit Information Coordinators.

Carstairs, G. Morris
1958 *The Twice-Born: A Study of a Community of High Caste Hindus.* Bloomington: Indiana Univ. Press.

Chakravarti, Surath Chandra.
1980 *Bauls: The Spiritual Vikings.* Calcutta: Firma K. L. Mukhopadhyay.

Chakravarty, Chintaharan
1963 *Tantras: Studies on their Religion and Literature.* Calcutta: Punthi Pustak.

Chatterjee, Amiya (editor)
n.d. *Introducing Purna Chandra Das, a Baul of Bengal.* Calcutta.

Chatterjee (Basu), Anjali
1967 *Bengal in the Reign of Aurangzib 1658-1707.* Calcutta: Progressive Publishers.

Chatterji, Suniti Kumar
1945 "Buddhist Survivals in Bengal." In *B. C. Law Volume*, Part 1, edited by D. R. Bhandarkar et al., 75–87. Calcutta.
1946 "Islamic Mysticism in Iran and India." *Indo-Iranica* 1(2): 9-35.
1970 *The Origin and Development of the Bengali Language.* 2 vols. Reprint of 1926 edition. London: Allen and Unwin.

Chopra, Hira Lall
1956 "Sufism I." In *Cultural Heritage of India,* vol. 4, edited by Haridas Bhattacarya, 593–600. Calcutta: Ramakrishna Mission Institute of Culture.

Coomaraswamy, Ananda
1917 "Indian Music." *Musical Quarterly* 3(2): 163-72.

Das Baul, Purna
n.d. "Baul: An Enchanting Inheritance." In *Introducing Purna Chandra Das, a Baul of Bengal*, edited by Amiya Chatterjee. Calcutta.

Das Gupta, J. N.
1914 *Bengal in the Sixteenth Century.* Calcutta: University of Calcutta.

Das Gupta, Shashi Bhusan
1956 "Some Later Yogic Schools." In *Cultural Heritage of India*, vol. 4, edited by Haridas Bhattacarya, 291–99. Calcutta: Ramakrishna Mission Institute of Culture.

Das Gupta, Shashibhusan
1969 *Obscure Religious Cults.* 3d ed. Calcutta: Firma K. L. Mukhopadhyay.

Dasgupta, Shashibhusan
1957 *Aspects of Indian Religious Thought*. Calcutta: A. Mukherjee.
1958 *An Introduction to Tāntric Buddhism*. Calcutta: University of Calcutta.
Datta, Phulrenu
1938 *La Société Bengalie au xvie Siècle*. Paris: Éditions littéraires de France.
Dimock, Edward C., Jr.
1959 "Rabindranath Tagore—The Greatest of the Bauls of Bengal." *Journal of Asian Studies* 19:33–51.
1966 *The Place of The Hidden Moon: Erotic Mysticism in the Vaisnava-Sahajiyā Cult of Bengal*. Chicago: Univ. of Chicago Press.
Dimock, Edward C., Jr. (editor)
1967 *Bengal Literature and History*. Occasional Paper South Asia series 6. East Lansing: Michigan State University.
Dimock, Edward C., Jr., and Denise Levertov, trans.
1967 *In Praise of Krishna*. Garden City: Anchor Books.
Douglas, Nik
1971 *Tantra Yoga*. New Delhi: Munshiram Manoharlal.
Dutt, G. S.
1932 "The Folk-Dances and Folk-Songs of Bengal." *The Music Review*, July, 44-52.
Eliade, Mircea
1958 *Yoga, Immortality and Freedom*. New York: Pantheon.
1968 *The Two and the One*. New York: Harper and Row.
1971 *The Forge and the Crucible: The Origins and Structures of Alchemy*. New York: Harper and Row.
Fox-Strangways, A. H.
1967 *The Music of Hindostan*. Reprint of 1914 edition. Oxford: Clarendon Press.
Gangoly, O. C.
1948 *Rāgas and Rāginīs: A Pictorial & Iconographic Study of Indian Musical Modes based on Original Sources*. Vol. 1. Bombay: Nalanda.
Garrison, Omar V.
1964 *Tantra: The Yoga of Sex*. New York: Julian Press.
Ghosh, Nikhil
1968 *Fundamentals of Raga and Tala with a New System of Notation*. Bombay: Popular Prakashan.
Guenther, Herbert V.
1969 *The Royal Song of Saraha*. Seattle: Univ. of Washington Press.
1972 *Buddhist Philosophy: In Theory and Practice*. Baltimore: Penguin Books.
Gulik, Robert Hans van
1951 *Erotic Colour Prints of the Ming*. 3 vols. Tokyo: Privately published.
1961 *Sexual Life in Ancient China: A Preliminary Survey of Chinese Sex and Society from ca. 1500 b. c. till 1644 a. d.* Leiden: E. J. Brill.

Hay, Stephen N.
1970 *Asian Ideas of East and West: Tagore and his Critics in Japan, China, and India.* Harvard East Asian Studies 40. Cambridge: Harvard University.
Henry, Edward O.
1976a "The Variety of Music in a North Indian Village: Reassessing Cantometrics." *Ethnomusicology* 20(1): 49–66.
1976b Paper read before National Meeting of the Society for Ethnomusicology in Philadelphia, November.
1977 "Music in the Thinking of North Indian Villagers." *Asian Music* 9(1): 1–12.
1980 "Non-participatory Music in a North Indian Village." In *The Ethnography of Musical Performance*, edited by Norma McLeod and Marcia Herndon, 43-72. Norwood, Pa.: Norwood editions.
Husain, Yusuf
1929 *L'Inde mystique au moyen âge.* Paris: A. Maisonneuve.
Jairazbhoy, Nazir A.
1971 *The Rags of North Indian Music: Their Structure and Evolution.* Middletown, Conn. Wesleyan Univ. Press.
Jairazbhoy, Nazir A., and A. W. Stone
1963 "Intonation in present day North Indian Classical Music." *Bulletin of the School of Oriental and African Studies* 26: 119–32.
Jaiswal, Suvira
1967 *The Origin and Development of Vaisnavism.* Delhi.
Jasimuddin
1951 "Folk Music of East Pakistan." *Journal of the International Folk Music Council* 3:41–44.
1967 "The Decline of Folk Songs." In *Folkmusic and Folklore: An Anthology*, vol. 1, edited by Hemango Biswas et al., 151–55. Calcutta: Folkmusic and Folklore Research Institute.
Kabir, Humayun
1956 "Islam in India." In *Cultural Heritage of India*, vol. 4, edited by Haridas Bhattacarya. Calcutta: Ramakrishna Mission Institute of Culture.
1967 *Rabindranath Tagore.* London: University of London, School of Oriental and African Studies.
Karim, Anwarul
n.d. "Baul Music: Its Origin and Development." Manuscript.
Kennedy, Melville T.
1925 *The Chaitanya Movement: A Study of the Vaisnavism of Bengal.* Calcutta: Associated Press (YMCA).
Kothari, K. S.
1968 *Indian Folk Music Instruments.* New Delhi: Sangeet Natak Akademi.
Kripalani, Krishna
1962 *Rabindranath Tagore: A Biography.* New York: Grove Press.

Krishnaswamy, S.
1965 *Musical Instruments of India*. Delhi: Publications Division, Ministry of Information and Broadcasting.

Kuckertz, Josef
1975 "Origin and Construction of the Melodies in Baul songs of Bengal." *Yearbook of the International Folk Music Council* 7:85–91.

Kulasrestha, Mahendra
1961 "Tagore the Musician." In *Tagore Centenary Volume*. Wollner Indological Series 2, 120–24. Hoshiarpur.

Lévi, Sylvain
1936 "On a Tantrik fragment from Kucha (Central Asia)." *Indian Historical Quarterly* 12(2): 197–214.

Mahillon, Victor-Charles
1978 *Catalogue Descriptif et Analytique du Musée Instrumental du Conservatoire Royal de Bruxelles: précédé d'un essai de classification méthodique de tous les instruments anciens et modernes.* Enlarged re-edition of 2d edition of vols. 1 and 2, first edition of vols. 3-5. Bruxelles: Les amis de la musique.

Majumdar, R. C. (editor)
1963 *The History of Bengal*. Dacca: University of Dacca.

Mansooruddin, M.
1953 "Folk Songs in Pakistan." *Journal of the International Folk Music Council* 5:51.

Marcel-Dubois, Claudie
1941 *Les instruments de musique de l'Inde ancienne*. Paris: Presses universitaires de France.

Martin, R. Montgomery
1838 *The History, Antiquities, Topography, and Statistics of Eastern India.* Vol. 3. London: W. H. Allen and Company.

Maspero, Henri
1937 "Les procédés de 'nourir le principe vital' dans la religion Taoïste ancienne." *Journal Asiatique* 229:177–252, 353–430.
1950 *Le Taoisme. Mélanges posthumes sur les religions et l'histoire de la Chine.* Vol. 2 Publications du Musée Guimet 58. Paris: Civilisations du Sud, S.A.E.P.

Mitra, Ashok
1953 *Fairs and Festivals in West Bengal*. Alipore: Superintendent, Government Printing, West Bengal Government.

Mookerjee, Ajit
1966 *Tantra Art: Its Philosophy and Physics*. Delhi: Ravi Kumar.
1971 *Tantra Asana: A Way to Self-Realization*. New Delhi: Ravi Kumar.

Mujeeb, Mohammud
1967 *The Indian Muslims*. London: Allen and Unwin.

Mukerji, Dhurjati Prasad
1931 "Tagore, the Supreme Composer." In *The Golden Book of Tagore: A*

Homage to Rabindranath Tagore from India and the World in Celebration of His Seventieth Birthday, edited by Ramananda Chatterjee, 175–78. Calcutta.

1944 *Tagore—A Study*. Bombay: Padma Publications.

1961 "Tagore's Music." In *A Centenary Volume: Rabindranath Tagore 1861–1961*, 180-86. New Delhi.

Mukherjea, Charulal

1962 *The Santals*. 2d ed. A. Mukherjee.

Mukherji, Shyam Chand

1966 *A Study of Vaiṣṇavism in Ancient and Medieval Bengal—up to the Advent of Caitanya*. Calcutta: Punthi Pustak.

Needham, Joseph

1954 *Introductory Orientations*. Vol. 1 of *Science and Civilization in China*. Cambridge: Cambridge Univ. Press.

1956 *History of Scientific Thought*. Vol. 2 of *Science and Civilization in China*. Cambridge: Cambridge Univ. Press.

O'Malley, L. S. S.

1913 "Report." In *The Census of India*, Part 1, 239–41. Calcutta: Bengal Secretariat Book Depot.

1917 *Bengal, Bihar, Orissa, and Sikkim*. Cambridge: Cambridge Univ. Press.

Nijenhuis, E. Wiersma-te

1970 Dattilam: A Compendium of Ancient Indian Music. Orientalia Rheno-Traiectina 11, edited by J. Gonda and H. W. Obbink. Leiden: E. J. Brill.

Prajnananda

1963 *A History of Indian Music*. Calcutta: Anandadhara Prakashan.

1965 *A Historical Study of Indian Music*. Calcutta: Ramakrishna Vedanta Math.

Ray, Sukumar

1973 *Music of Eastern India: Vocal Music in Bengali, Oriya, Assamese, and Manipuri with Special Emphasis on Bengali*. Calcutta: Firma K. L. Mukhopadhyay.

Sachs, Curt

1923 *Die Musikinstrumente Indiens und Indonesiens*. Handbücher der Staatlichen Museen zu Berlin 15. Berlin: Vereinigung wissentschaftlicher Verleger.

1940 *The History of Musical Instruments*. New York: W. W. Norton.

Salomon, Carol

1979 "A Contemporary Sahajiyā Interpretation of the Bilvamañgal-Cintāmani Legend as Sung by Sonatan Dās Bāul." In *Patterns of Change in Modern Bengal*, edited by Richard L. Park, 97–110. East Lansing: Michigan State University, Asian Languages Center.

Sanyal, Nishikanta

n.d. *The Erotic Principle Unalloyed Devotion*. Calcutta: Gaudiya Mission.

Sastri, V. V. Ramana

1956 "The Doctrinal Culture and Tradition of the Siddhas." In *Cultural Her-*

itage of India, vol. 4, edited by Haridas Bhattacarya, 300–308. Calcutta: Ramakrishna Mission Institute of Culture.

Sen, Dinesh Chandra
1911 *History of Bengali Language and Literature.* Calcutta: University of Calcutta.
1917 *The Vaisnava Literature of Medieval Bengal.* Calcutta: University of Calcutta.

Sen, Kshitimohan
n.d. *The Bauls of Bengal.* Translated by Lila Ray. Calcutta: Viswabharati.
1931 "The Baül Singers of Bengal." Appendix to *The Religion of Man* by Rabindranath Tagore, 209-21. London: Macmillan.
1956 "The Medieval Mystics of North India." In *Cultural Heritage of India*, vol. 4, edited by Haridas Bhattacarya, 377-94. Calcutta: Ramakrishna Mission Institute of Culture.

Sen, Sukumar
1935 *A History of Brajabuli Literature; being a Study of the Vaisnava Lyric Poetry and Poets of Bengal.* Calcutta: University of Calcutta.
1956 "The Nātha Cult." In *Cultural Heritage of India*, vol. 4, edited by Haridas Bhattacarya, 280-90. Calcutta: Ramakrishna Mission Institute of Culture.
1960 *History of Bengali Literature.* New Delhi: Sahitya Akademi.
1965 "Old Bengali texts: Caryāgīti-Vajragīti-Prahelika." Reprinted in *Indian Linguistics: Journal of the Linguistic Society of India* 3.

Shahidullah, M.
1928 *Les chants mystiques de Kanha et de Saraha / Les dohā-koṣa et les caryā.* Paris: Adrien Maisonneuve.

Sinha, Maniklal
1967 "Folk-Songs of the South Radh." In *Folkmusic and Folklore: An Anthology,* vol. 1, edited by Hemango Biswas et al., 33–38. Calcutta: Folkmusic and Folklore Research Institute.

Sinha, Surajit
1971 "Vaisnava Influence on Tribal Culture." In *Krishna: Myths, Rites, and Attitudes,* edited by Milton Singer, 2d impression of 1969 edition, 64–89. Chicago: Univ. of Chicago Press.

Snellgrove, David L.
1954 "Third Part: The Tantras." In *Buddhist Texts through the Ages*, edited by Edward Conze, 221–68. Oxford: B. Cassirer.
1959 *The Hevajra-Tantra: A Critical Study.* Part 1, Introduction and Translation. London Oriental Series 6. London: Oxford Univ. Press.

Spratt, Philip
1966 *Hindu Personality and Culture.* Bombay: Manaktalas.

Stern, Philippe
1961 "The Real Rabindranath and his Music." In *A Centenary Volume: Rabindranath Tagore 1861–1961,* 293–96. New Delhi.

Strickland-Anderson, Lily
1924 "Rabindranath Tagore—Poet-Composer." *Musical Quarterly* 10:463–74.
Subhan, John
1970 *Sufism, Its Saints and Shrines: An Introduction to the Study of Sufism with Special Reference to India.* Reprint of 1938 edition. New York: S. Weiser.
Tagore, Rabindranath
1922 *Creative Unity.* New York: Macmillan.
1931 *The Religion of Man.* New York: Macmillan.
1935 *Chansons de Rabindranath Tagore.* Bibliothèque Musicale du Musée Guimet, directed by Philippe Stern, vol. 2. Paris: P. Geuthner.
1961 *Svaralipi: An Anthology of One Hundred Songs of Rabindranath Tagore in Staff Notation.* Vol. 1. New Delhi: Sangeet Natak Akademi.
Tagore, Saurindramohan
1896 *Universal History of Music Compiled from Divers Sources.* Calcutta: N. G. Goswamy.
Tucci, Giusseppe
1949 *Tibetan Painted Scrolls.* Vol. 1. Rome: Libreria dello Stato.
1971a "The Sea and Land Travels of a Buddhist Sādhu in the Sixteenth Century." In *Opera Minora,* vol. 2, 305–19. Università di Roma Studi Orientali Pubblicati a cura della Scuola Orientale 6. Roma: G. Bardi.
1971b "Some Glosses upon the *Guhyasamāja.*" In *Opera Minora,* vol. 2, 337–38. Università di Roma Studi Orientali Pubblicati a cura della Scuola Orientale 6. Roma: G. Bardi.
Vasu, Nagendra Nath
1911 *The Modern Buddhism and Its Followers in Orissa.* Calcutta: the author.
Waddell, L. Austine
1972 *Tibetan Buddhism.* Reprint of 1895 edition. New York: Dover.
Ward, William
1817 *A View of the History, Literature, and Religion of the Hindus.* Vol. 1. Birmingham.
Wasson, R. Gordon
1971 "A Far-Reaching Siberian Word Cluster." In *Soma: Divine Mushroom of Immortality,* part 3, chapter 2, 164–81. Ethnomycological Studies 1. New York: Harcourt Brace Jovanovich.
Wilson, Colin
1971 *The Occult: A History.* New York: Random House.
Woodroffe, John
1918 *Shakti and Shakta: Essays and Addresses on the Shākta Tantrashastra.* London: Luzac and Company.
1956 *Introduction to Tantra Sastra.* Madras: Ganesh.
Zaehner, R. C.
1969 *Mysticism: Sacred and Profane.* New York.

Bengali

Bandyōpādhyāy, Sōmendronāth
1964 *bānlār bāul: kābyo ō darśon.* Calcutta: Bookland.
Bardhon, Moṇi
1969 *bāṅlār lōknṛityo ō gītiboicitro.* Calcutta: West Bengal Ministry of Information and Broadcasting.
Bhaṭṭācāryo, Āśutōṣ
1962a *bāṅlār lōk-sāhityo.* Vol. 1. Calcutta: Calcutta Book House.
1962b "*bāul.*" In *bāṅlār lōk soṅgīt,* vol. 1, by Sūrendro Candro Cakroborttī, pp. *k-th.* Calcutta: Bengal Music College (Research Division).
1963 "*bhāṭiyāli.*" In *bāṅlār lōk soṅgīt,* vol. 2, by Sūrendro Candro Cakroborttī, 14–19. Calcutta: Bengal Music College (Research Division).
Bosu, Monīndromohan
n.d. *caryāpad.* Calcutta.
Cākī, Jyōtibhūṣan
n.d. "*bāul Nabonidās.*" In *Introducing Purna Chandra Das, a Baul of Bengal,* edited by Amiya Chatterjee, 14–19. Calcutta.
Cakrobortī, Sureś
1962 "*bāṅlā lōk gītir sur-bicār.*" Appendix A in *bāṅlār lōk-sāhityo,* vol. 1, by Āśutōṣ Bhaṭṭācāryo. Calcutta: Calcutta Book House.
Cakroborttī, Sūrendro Candro
1962 *bāṅlār lōk soṅgīt.* Vol. 1. Calcutta: Bengal Music College (Research Division).
1963 *bāṅlār lōk soṅgīt.* Vol. 2. Calcutta: Bengal Music College (Research Division).
Dāś, Motilāl, and Pīyūṣkānti Mohāpātro
1958 *lālon-gītikā: lālon śāh phokirer gān.* Calcutta: University of Calcutta with the aid of Viswabharati University.
Datto, Akṣay Kumār
1870–1871 *bhārotīyo upāsok-samprodāy.* Part 1. Calcutta.
1907–8 *bhārotīyo upāsok-samprodāy.* Part 2. Calcutta.
Deb, Cittorañjan
1966 *bāṅlār palligīti.* Calcutta: National Book Agency.
Ghōṣ, Śāntideb
1962 *robīndrosoṅgīt.* Enlarged 3d ed. *Robīndroporicay granthomālā.* Calcutta. Viswabharati.
Jōyārddār, Rājkumār (editor)
1947–48 *gōpāl gītābolī.* 2d ed. Silaidaho.
Kumār, Madanmōhan
1966 *bāṅlā sāhityer ālōcanā.* Calcutta: Dasgupta and Company.
Mitro, Rājyeśvor
1959 "*Caryāgīti.*" *biśvobhārotī patrikā,* issue of *śrāboṇ-āśvin,* 1881 *śak* era, pp. 4ff.

Monsur Uddīn, Muhammad (editor)
1942 *hārāmoṇi: lōk soṅgīt soṅgraho*. Calcutta: Calcutta University.
Mukhōpādhȳāy, Amūlȳodhon
1962 *bāṅlā chander mūlsūtro*. 6th ed. Calcutta: Calcutta University.
Mukhōpādhȳāy, Dilīp
1970 *uttor rāṛher lōk soṅgīt*. Calcutta: *kalȳāṇī*. Mukhōpādhȳāy, Tārāpado
1965 *carẏāgīti*. *biśvobidȳāsoṅgraho* 131. Calcutta: Viswabharati.
Śāstri, Haroprosād
1899–
1900 *bowddhodharmo*. Calcutta.
1959 *hājār bacharer purāṇo bāṅgālā bhāṣāy bowddhogān ō dōhā*. Revised ed. *sāhitȳo-poriṣad granthomālā* 55. Calcutta: Bengali Literature Association.
1963 *prācīn bāṅlār gowrab*. *biśvobidȳāsoṅgraho* 54. Calcutta: Viswabharati.
Sen, Kṣitimōhan
1929 *bhārotīȳo madhȳoẏuge sādhonār kathā*. Calcutta.
1945–
1946 *bāṅlār sādhonā*. Calcutta.
1949 *bhārote hindu-musolmāner ẏukto sādhonā*. Calcutta: Viswabharati.
1954 *bāṅlār bāul*. Calcutta: Calcutta University.
Sen, Sukumār
1956 *carẏāgīti-padābolī*. Burdwan.
Ṭhākur, Rabīndronāth
1905 *bāul*. Calcutta.
1942 "*āśirbbād*." In *hārāmoṇi: lōk soṅgīt soṅgraho*, edited by Muhammad Monsur Uddīn, ix–xii. Calcutta: Calcutta University.
1963 *prāyościtto*. Calcutta: Viswabharati.
1966a *phālgunī*. Calcutta: Viswabharati.
1966b *soṅgīt-cintā*. Calcutta: Viswabharati.
1969–
1981 *svorobitān*. 60 vols. Calcutta: Viswabharati.

Corrigendum

Bhaṭṭācārẏo, Upendronāth
1971 *bāṅlār bāul o bāul gān*. 2nd ed. Calcutta: Orient Book Company.

Index

Charles Capwell spent two and one-half years in West Bengal studying the Baul sect as part of his doctoral research at Harvard. He now teaches in the School of Music at the University of Illinois and has published several articles on Indian music and culture.

List of Tracks on CDs

The following numbers (listed by title and singer) are on the CDs:

CD 1

1. *āmār ei rudhir dhārāy*; Phokir Dās
2. *bhāṅā ghare (uri?) diẏe*; Gaṅgādhor Dās
3. *bṛindābone tin raṅete*; Ẏotin Dās
4. *ēmon cāṣā*; Phokir Dās
5. *ēmon ulṭā deś*; Ẏotin Dās
6. *ese ēk rosik pāgol*; Pūrṇo Candro Dās
7. *ese ēk rosik pāgol*; Śambhu Dās
8. *ēto lōk periẏe gelo*; Pūrṇo Candro Dās
9. *gōlōk hote gōlōker nāth*; Tinkoṛi Dās
10. *gowr prem niṣṭhā cinir ras karā*; Monorām
11. *gowr prem niṣṭhā cinir ras karā*; Sonāton Dās Ṭhākur
12. *hṛidayo piñjore bose*; Lakṣm̃aṇ Dās (Mallarpur)
13. *jiber bujhi sudin āj holo*; Śaśāṅko Dās Mohant

CD 2

14. *kēno kul hārāli*; Lakṣm̃aṇ Dās (Bardhoman)
15. *ki āścarẏo majār kathā*; Tinkoṛi Dās
16. *nirma korle*; Śaśāṅko Dās Mohant
17. *mon ēkbāre hori balo*; Sonāton Dās Ṭhākur
18. *mon mayrā*; Sonāton Dās Ṭhākur (from All India Radio Calcutta)
19. *nitāi āmār nāker bēśor*; Brajobālā Dāsī
20. *nitāi āmār nāker bēśor*; Ẏotin Dās
21. *nitāi ẏodi e deśe elo*; Nārāyoṇ Dās Odhikāri
22. *rādhār prem taraṅgo beri*; Lakṣm̃aṇ Dās (Bardhoman)
23. *sab lōke kay*; Śẏām Sundor Dās
24. *tumi se nā deśer kathā*; Ẏotin Dās